RACE, SCHOOL AND COMMUNITY

A Survey of Research and Literature
on Education in Multi-racial Britain

RACE, SCHOOL AND COMMUNITY.

Francine Taylor, BA, PhD

NFER Publishing Company Ltd.

Published by the NFER Publishing Company Ltd.,
Book Division, 2 Jennings Buildings, Thames Avenue,
Windsor, Berks., SL4 1QS
Registered Office, The Mere, Upton Park, Slough, Bucks., SL1 2DQ
First Published 1974

SBN 85633 033 7

Printed in Great Britain by
Eyre & Spottiswoode Limited at Grosvenor Press, Portsmouth

Distributed in the USA by Humanities Press Inc·
450 *Park Avenue South, New York, NY* 10016, *USA*

Contents

CHAPTER ONE

Introduction to the General Background of the Racial Situation in Britain

I. History of Commonwealth Immigration

A. *Introduction: Demography of Main Ethnic Groups*

The situation of coloured immigrant and English children in our schools today can only be fully understood against the background of the total immigration situation and the way it has changed in recent years. This introduction, therefore, outlines the general situation and the studies stemming from it.

Commonwealth coloured immigration has been a controversial issue in Britain for over a decade. Commonwealth citizens began to emigrate to Britain shortly after World War II. There was an acute shortage of unskilled labour which the Government attempted to fill by encouraging European migrant workers, refugees and Irish workers. Certain industries actively recruited workers from the West Indies.

The main reasons behind the immigration to the United Kingdom appear to have been poverty, lack of economic and educational opportunity in the home country, the availability of jobs in Britain, the experience of Commonwealth workers and military personnel who had been encouraged to help Britain during the war, and the active recruitment of foreign workers by the Government and some industries in this country.

The main arrival of Commonwealth citizens, particularly from the West Indies, began in the early 1950s and rose from an estimated annual entry of 42,000 in 1955 to 136,000 in 1961 (Home Office: Cmd. 2739, 1965; Institute of Race Relations Facts Paper, *Colour and Immigration in the UK*, 1969). This included immigration from India and Pakistan which, though initially less, began to rise in the late 1950s as loss of land holdings through the partition of India affected families' fortunes. The British Nationality Act 1948 gave them the right to free entry and civil rights when in England.

The coloured Commonwealth immigrants are drawn mainly from three ethnic groups from three areas whose totals in mid-1966 were estimated by the Institute of Race Relations Survey of Race Relations in Britain by Rose *et al.* (1969) as:

Caribbean	454,100
India	223,600
Pakistan	119,700

There are also smaller numbers of other ethnic minorities from Ceylon: 16,000; Cyprus: 60,000; Malta: 38,000; British West Africa: 50,400; and The Far East: 60,000 (Hoopers, 1965, based on the 1961 Census report).

The approximate total of overseas-born coloured Commonwealth population in England and Wales, derived from the 1966, 10 per cent sample census, was 942,310 out of a total population of 52,300,000. (IRR Facts Paper, 1969). There were in addition 837,150 foreign-born people living in England and 698,600 people born in Eire.

These figures for Commonwealth immigrants had to be modified, however, since the General Register Office believes that the total national figures were underestimated by 1·8 per cent and that this under-enumeration was higher in the conurbations, where two-thirds of the immigrants live. This total also did not take into account children of immigrant parents who were born in this country; nor did it exclude white immigrants from India and Pakistan or African students and dependants who will return to their own countries.

A study by Eversley and Sukdeo (1969) took all these figures into consideration, and stated that the figure of 1,183,000, although probably an over-estimate, was the most accurate.[1]

Over 80 per cent of the coloured immigrants were, according to the 1961 Census, concentrated in the urban areas (towns of 50,000 or more) with half in Britain's 10 largest cities. They had gone to areas of expanding industry, areas which, in spite of demand for labour, have not been able to attract population from other parts of the country. Thus, in some towns and cities, though the overall total may be eight per cent, in particular neighbourhoods there may be 50 per cent or more (Peach, 1965). Since that time, studies based on the 1966 sample Census have indicated that, while concentration of West Indians, for example, in some of the smaller districts has increased (Peach, 1968), dispersal to secondary areas is also occuring, and Eversley and Sukdeo (1969) found that the proportions of Jamaicans and Pakistanis who lived in the six conurbations in 1961,

[1] This figure is close to that of 1,113,000 persons up to mid-1968 arrived at by the Survey of Race Relations (Rose, 1969) after estimating births and new arrivals since 1966.

had declined by 10·8 per cent and 8·4 per cent respectively.

The 1971 Greater London Census, in comparison with the 1966 sample Census, reveals dispersal of immigrant[1] population from some inner London boroughs—Camden, Kensington and Chelsea, Islington and Westminster—to the outer boroughs, the highest being Brent, Barnet and Haringey. Most London boroughs are also losing great numbers of their general population. However, eight other inner London boroughs gained immigrant population. These trends in boroughs which have gained in immigrant populations and are losing white population are causing greater 'ghetto-ization'. Abstracts of the figures for all the Greater London boroughs are in the *CRC Journal*, April 1973.

Runnymede Trust Bulletin (May 1973) also lists these figures and points out that the West Indians tend to congregate in a smaller number of areas (42 per cent of all West Indians in four boroughs) than do the Pakistanis or Indians. Fifteen per cent of the Indian-born live in Ealing but the rest are relatively dispersed.

An advance analysis of the 1971 Census states that the total New Commonwealth-born population in Great Britain is 1,157,170 on the Census date (2·15 per cent of the total population) (Kohler, 1973a).

Their distribution in the main conurbations, and as percentages of total population in those conurbations, is as follows:

Table I.1: *New Commonwealth-born Population in Main Conurbations*

Conurbations	*Total*	*Percentage of Total Population*
Greater London	476,535	6·5
West Midlands	120,725	5·1
West Yorkshire	55,485	3·2
South East Lancashire	46,690	2
Merseyside	9,040	0·7
Tyneside	5,041	0·62
Central Clydeside	10,345	0·6

Runnymede Trust Bulletin (December, 1972).

'Census 1971, Advance Analysis'.

Kohler (1973b) points out that the figure of 1,157,170 does not give us a true picture of the number of coloured people in Britain. Firstly because it includes white people who were born in the Common-

[1] Immigrant population refers to people born in the new Commonwealth countries of West Indies, India and Pakistan. Its estimate of the coloured population (CRC Journal, April 1973) indicates that one must multiply the figures by one-and-a-half.

wealth (estimated to be approximately 100,000) and it does not include coloured people born in this country, of whom it is thought there are 500,000. On this basis the total number of coloured people in this country is:

Total Population of Coloured People in Great Britain	
Number born in the New Commonwealth	1,160,000
Less white born in the New Commonwealth	— 100,000
	1,060,000
Plus coloured people born in Britain	+ 500,000
	1,560,000

This figure fits in well, he points out, with previous Registrar-General estimates.

However, when the first newcomers landed, their immediate need on arrival was to find accommodation in areas which already desperately required additional housing for their normal population. The schools in these areas were frequently overcrowded and had inadequate buildings. Any population influx into these areas accentuated these difficulties. Because the Commonwealth immigrants are identifiable easily by colour they are accused by some of the host population as the cause of these difficulties. It may be noted that in many areas the influx of Irish had been greater than that of the coloured immigrants.

B. *Reception by Host Community*

The social conflict, hostility and antagonisms engendered by the newcomers' arrival in Great Britain was not recognized initially as colour prejudice by British Sociologists, who insisted that the British situation was not strictly comparable with the American or South African situation where the colour bar had operated for generations in law, customs and individual attitudes.

Although it is true that the non-white population in Britain were 'tacitly equal in terms of their rights or citizenship',[1] compared to the American negro, who had a position of inferiority institutionalized in society since the days of slavery, unofficial discrimination and colour prejudice is now recognized to exist in British society.

In the early 1950s, when there were relatively few non-white Commonwealth immigrants, British sociologists and anthropologists interpreted the apparent hostility of the host community in terms of

[1] British Nationality Act, 1948.

non-racial theories which steadfastly refused to admit the existence of colour prejudice. While they admitted that their studies indicated that discriminatory behaviour was widespread, they did not believe that it was based on colour prejudice as such.

Richmond (1955), who had made a survey of British attitudes towards coloured colonials in a 1951 survey, divided the population into three groups, one-third extremely prejudiced, one-third mildly prejudiced, one-third tolerant. Banton (1957), who did a survey of British racial attitudes, found that only 10 per cent of those interviewed thought that coloured people were inferior to white, and this was so often qualified that he believed only two per cent endorsed it. Glass and Pollins' (1960) attitude-survey concluded that 10 per cent were severely prejudiced and 15 per cent extremely tolerant, with the remaining 75 per cent expressing some degree of prejudice.

Collins (1957), who made a comparative study of three ethnic and religious groups (Negroes, Moslems and Chinese) in three regions of Britain, found great regional variation in racial attitudes. The reasons for these differences in attitude appeared to be complex and were related to such variables as the background of the immigrant group, the time span of one immigrant settlement, the size and pattern of the immigrant group and the type of host community.

The hypotheses advanced by theorists to explain the motivations behind discriminatory behaviour prevalent in Britain in the 1950s in varying situations were:

1. *The Immigrant-Host Relationship* defined by Patterson (1963) in which 'colour is only one, albeit an important one of many factors influencing and complicating a particular immigrant host relationship'.

2. *The Colour Class Hypothesis* set out by Little (1947, 1972[1] ed.) which was developed from the stable situation he found in the Cardiff dock area in 1946, when British society was thought, partly due to its colonial past, to identify coloured people with the lowest social class. People feel that they will lose or jeopardize their social status by associating with a coloured person.

3. *The Stranger Hypothesis* supported by Banton (1959) in which he feels that the coloured immigrants are seen as the archetype strangers both in appearance and behaviour in a society where, as Gorer (1955) points out, mild xenophobia is the norm. However, he indicates that, because coloured men no longer accept the custom that they should have different rights and obligations from white men, acceptance on a new basis has to be agreed upon in the host community, 'integration' on terms of equality.

[1] Dr Bloom brings the study up to date by describing his recent study of the same area.

N. Dem (1953), a Nigerian who studied white and coloured relationships in Manchester, did not agree with the hypothesis put forward by Patterson, Little and Banton above.

He found that the factor of skin colour permeated the entire range of social relationships and that the coloured person feels that all whites are basically prejudiced against coloured people.

Colour prejudice and discrimination are, he claimed, facts in Britain and the sooner they are recognized or accepted, the easier it will be to achieve justice and fair play.

Though the attitudes quoted by Banton and Little may have been representative when there were relatively few non-white Commonwealth immigrants, they are no longer applicable. Yet successive Governments did not evolve any overall immigration scheme as did some countries in Europe who, when they invited a greater number of foreign workers, initially took responsibility for their fares, accommodation and welfare and encouraged those whose skills would match their existing job vacancies (Taylor, 1969). Neither did the central Government look into means of promoting both the integration of the coloured Commonwealth immigrants and their children by encouraging understanding and acceptance by the host community.

The increasing flow of immigrants from Commonwealth countries and their concentration in inner city areas led to growing problems of inter-group relationships. The Notting Hill and the Nottingham riots in 1958 (Jephcott, 1964) were dramatic indications that coloured immigrants were becoming the scapegoats for long-standing problems of the inner urban areas. It led MPs and others to press for some action on the part of the central Government since local authorities and voluntary organizations could not deal with these effectively in isolation.

The Government had been making plans for a negative response, namely that of control of immigration rather than seeing what could be done to improve inter-group relations.

C. *Government Legislation*

In 1962, the Conservative Government passed the Commonwealth Immigration Act (Home Office, 1962) which regulated the entry of those who wished to work by determining the number of Ministry of Labour Vouchers allowed per year. Under this Act, approximately 20,000 Vouchers were issued a year. 'A' type Vouchers to those with specific jobs to come to; 'B' type Vouchers to people with special qualifications and skills; and 'C' type Vouchers to other workers. Although this restricted immigration to some degree, it was counterbalanced by an increase in women and children joining the head of the family, first among the West Indians and then later among the Asians.

Government policy of limiting work vouchers had the effect of increasing Commonwealth immigration into the country, particularly among Asians who had planned to work for a period and then to return home to their families (Oakley, 1968).

Immigration and race became major issues for the electorate in a number of constituencies in the 1964 election. It was increasingly realized and officially made explicit that, in the words of Sir Edward Boyle, MP, (1968) 'Britain has to face the problem not of immigration, but of race relations and cannot avoid the reference to colour.' The political issues were discussed by Deakin (1965), who showed the change of opinion on control measures during the ensuing three years. Quoting from Gallup polls, he also showed the change in attitudes towards the immigrants.

Opinion on Commonwealth Immigration	*January 1961*	*July 1964*
Favour free entry	21	10
Favour restrictions	67	68
Total ban	6	20

The Commonwealth Immigration Act of 1962 was renewed in 1963/1964 by the Labour Government. The issue of 'C' Vouchers was ended. In 1965 the *White Paper on Immigration from the Commonwealth*, (Home Office, 1965) was recognized to be a concession to increasing hostility to coloured immigrants and the lack of a positive policy towards promoting good race relations. A principle point of criticism is that it instituted a quota of 8,500 Commonwealth immigrants per year who must hold work permits, whereas aliens had no fixed ceiling limit on the number of workers who are issued permits. It restricted entry to children between 16–18 years except in cases of hardship.

Although it had been possible for the Government in power to argue that the immigration legislations of 1962, 1964 and 1965 were not discriminatory, it was nevertheless true that the percentage of new Commonwealth immigrants per year was always less than those coming in from other foreign countries, even excluding the Irish. (Hill, 1970).

When in February 1968 the Commonwealth Immigrants Act (Home Office, 1968) was passed, designed to regulate the entry into Britain of Kenyan Asians who had decided to retain United Kingdom citizenship, when Kenya became independent, it was no longer possible to claim that there was not a racial basis to their policy. Due

Table 1.2: *Immigration from the New Commonwealth as percentage of the immigration into the United Kingdom*

Year	%
1964	40
1965	37
1966	34
1967	31
1968	40

to the increasing number of Kenyan Asians who had begun to come to Britain since mid-1967, the Bill limited the right of free entry to the United Kingdom to holders of United Kingdom passports who had parents or grandparents who had been born in the United Kingdom. This permitted free entry to white colonials, while the others, Asian UK passport holders, were restricted to 1,500 employment vouchers a year and subjected to other negative legislation.

II. Initiatives in Promoting Integration and Tolerance for Coloured Immigrants

A. *Integration*

Throughout the centuries Britain has always prided itself on offering asylum to foreigners fleeing from religious and political persecution; their acceptance has never been without opposition, prejudice and discrimination from some sections of the native population. The majority of these immigrants have been European whose children (if not always their parents), because they physically resemble the host community, have eventually, as they learned the language and customs, become assimilated or integrated into the community. *Integration* is defined here as the adaptation of an incoming group to temporary or permanent membership of our society in areas such as education, employment, legal and political traditions and institutions and is accepted by the host society as a group differing in religion, culture and family patterns.

Rose (1969) mentions that this is often called 'cultural pluralism' since it may involve the existence and mutual tolerance of several cultures in one society, as a permanent state for the minority group. However, 'integration' may be one phase in the process of adaptation of the host society and the minority group to one another. It may be a final phase or it may lead on to 'assimilation'. *Assimilation* as a concept implies that the minority group accepts so completely the culture and patterns of living of the host community, that it merges into the whole and loses any separate identity. 'Assimilation' implies that the host society accepts the individual or group completely in spite of any cultural, religious or racial difference.

Britain has also had coloured immigrants and visitors from Africa and her former colonies. Many from Africa were first brought over as slaves but these obtained their freedom in the 18th century. Many of the seamen from the colonies have married English women and made their home port in Britain. Members of the upper classes in overseas countries, including the former colonies, have had a tradition of sending their children to Britain to be educated here, whether at boarding schools, university or military institutions.

In the 17th and 18th centuries, prejudice against coloured people was fostered by those who wished to justify slavery. However, not many settled in England, and it was not until the 20th century that coloured seamen started to work on British ships and used England as their home port. There were some disturbances during periods of economic depression between white and coloured seamen. Little settlement occurred during this period. Those who had served and worked for England during the Second World War returned after finding inadequate work opportunities in their own countries.

As colonies achieved independence and with the founding of the multi-racial Commonwealth, racial equality was legally accepted and embodied in the British Nationality Act 1948, which gave its members status as citizens of the United Kingdom and Colonies and Commonwealth and unrestricted entry into the United Kingdom and rights of citizenship.

In spite of the increasing numbers of Commonwealth immigrants, successive Governments, however, refused to recognize that a large influx of people visibly different from the rest of the population might, as in other countries, lead to racial antagonism, rejection and discrimination, without positive measures being taken to combat this tendency and prevent discrimination.

B. *Voluntary Organizations and Governmental Committees*

The initiative in welcoming and helping the new Commonwealth immigrants thus to adapt was first commenced by voluntary organizations such as Churches, Clubs, and individuals or groups who had catered for the social activities of refugees, foreigners and Commonwealth and overseas students in the past. Some local authorities established voluntary liaison committees with representatives from the immigrant community and from as many clubs and churches in the community as possible. Their aims were briefly to promote harmonious integration of immigrant groups through activities. After the Notting Hill incidents, they tended to concentrate more on the education of the host community and less on the welfare of immigrants. Some, such as the Sparkbrook Association in Birmingham (Rex and Moore, 1967) developed a community approach, which concentrated on improving conditions in a poor urban area, which tended to channel grievances into action for improvement rather against particular ethnic groups.

These voluntary organizations did much valuable work, but by the 1960s it was clear that without some support from the statutory local authorities and positive action on the part of the Government, the activities of these groups, who had little money and a limited number of volunteers, were not sufficient to combat the growing amount of prejudice and discrimination.

The 1962 Commonwealth Immigration Act set up an Advisory Council to advise the Home Secretary on matters affecting immigrants and to examine the arrangements and powers of the local authorities to deal with the welfare of immigrants. It published four reports on housing, education and immigrant school leavers (Home Office, 1963–1965) which pointed out the problems of the immigrants in these and other areas. This Council established a National Committee for Commonwealth Immigrants in 1964 with a paid advisory officer whose duties were to collect and circulate information to local authorities on how best to improve relations between immigrants and the community.

This, though a step in the right direction, was hardly adequate to deal with the evidence of racial tension in many areas: by this time there were major settlements in 42 industrial towns in Britain.

The White Paper, *Immigration from the Commonwealth,* (Home Office, 1965), although it continued the negative policy of reducing the numbers of Commonwealth immigration, also outlined a positive governmental policy to promote better race relations in Britain through the establishment of a permanent body, the National Committee of Commonwealth Immigrants (NCCI), an independent committee, with a full-time liaison officer to promote and co-ordinate efforts towards the integration of Commonwealth immigrants.

This committee encouraged the formation of local liaison committees and met half the salary of a Community Relations Officer when the remainder was supported by the local authority, set up multi-racial/national panels of experts on such topics as housing, education and social work to investigate particular problems and promote knowledge of these through conferences of workers in particular fields (NCCI, 1966). It was soon realized that legislative action was necessary to prevent discrimination. To convince the Government and the public that this was necessary it sponsored several nationwide surveys and studies which proved unequivocally that colour discrimination did exist in employment, housing and credit facilities, irrespective of the immigrant's educational background. (PEP, 1967; summarized by Daniel, 1968.)

C. *Legislation against Racial and Ethnic Discrimination*

The NCCI sponsored a study of the effectiveness of anti-discrimination legislation in other countries and also suggested how British law might be amended (Street *et al.*, 1967). As a result of these reports the Government has passed two Race Relations Bills covering all possible instances in which racial or ethnic discrimination could occur and set up a Race Relations Board to deal with complaints, attempt conciliation or institute civil proceedings under the Race Relations Act of 1965 and 1968. Hill (1970) outlines their details, and for provisions and House of Commons debate one must consult Keesings (1968).

The Race Relations Bill 1968 extended the scope of the 1965 Bill in that it banned racial discrimination[1] in housing, employment and services such as insurance and credit facilities. The membership of the Board was increased from three to 12. The emphasis was still on attempted settlement of complaints by area conciliation committees, and only if these failed would cases go to the Board. Only when it failed would the Board have recourse to County Courts, which would have power to grant injunctions restraining further discrimination and to award damages.

The Bill also set up a new Community Relations Commission to replace the National Committee for Commonwealth Immigrants to the Government. The new Community Relations Commission was expected to co-ordinate on a national basis the Government's official policy on race relations and to advise the Home Secretary in this field. Its emphasis is to encourage the establishment of harmonious community relations between Commonwealth immigrants and the host population.

The legislation on immigration and race passed during the last decade has been both negative and creative; negative in laying down restrictive conditions of entry and creative in promoting policies which would make 'illegal' discriminatory behaviour through the Race Relations Act and encourage mutual tolerance in the host community through the Community Relations Commission.

That the effects of this legislation have not as yet been entirely effective or satisfactory in leading to these ends is obvious.

Individuals who believe that they have suffered racial discrimination (as defined by the Race Relations Act) may have their claim investigated by the Race Relations Board. Their Annual Reports

[1] Keesings's Contemporary Archives, V.1967–68, pp.23067–9. Discrimination was defined for the purpose of the Bill, as when 'a person discriminates against another if on the ground of colour, race or ethnic or national origins, he treats the other less favourably than he treats or would treat other persons' in the specific areas set out in the Bill.

(Race Relations Board, 1969–70) indicated that a minority of the cases reported were found to be genuine cases of discrimination (Runnymede Trust, 1971a). However, the Race Relations Board is beginning to use its powers under Section 7 to investigate organizations or areas where there is reason to suspect discrimination, even though individuals do not instigate complaints, since it is realized that many coloured persons in the field of employment avoid applying to firms known to discourage coloured workers. Section 7 of the Act gives the Board power to investigate in the absence of complaint where they have reason to believe that unlawful discrimination has taken place. It also puts great stress on its educational role (Runnymede Trust, July, 1972).

The legislation to limit Kenyan Asians' entry into Great Britain and the passing of the Race Relations Bill in 1968 produced fierce debate in both Labour and Opposition spokesmen. One of Enoch Powell's (MP) speeches made in Birmingham (April 20th, 1968), demanding an immediate reduction of coloured immigration to negligible proportions and financial aid to encourage such immigrants to return, roused widespread controversy.

His emotive phrases, saying 'Britons were made to feel strangers in their own country' and 'as I look ahead I am filled with foreboding, like the Roman I seem to see the River Tiber foaming with much blood', were condemned by Mr Heath, Leader of the Opposition, as 'racialist in tone and liable to exacerbate racial tensions'. He also informed Mr Powell he was no longer a member of the Shadow Cabinet (Keesings, 1968, p.22782).

There were strikes in his support by London dockers and Smithfield market porters and a letter by some immigration officers.

A number of organizations and individuals called for a prosecution of Mr Powell under the 1965 Race Relations Act, which made it an offence for anyone 'with intent to stir up hatred against any section of the public in Great Britain distinguished by colour, race or ethnic or national origins', to use in a public place 'words which are threatening, abusive or insulting' and likely to stir up hatred against that section.

However, on May 2nd it was stated by the Office of the Attorney General that Mr Enoch Powell would not be prosecuted for this speech.

Even though he was dismissed from the Shadow Cabinet, his speeches had the effect of hardening attitudes on both sides of the colour line and not along party lines. The uncommitted and moderates have tended to move towards one of the two extremes, as Gallup Poll surveys of peoples' reactions have indicated. When asked if they agreed with Powell's Birmingham speech, 74 per cent did so, 15 per cent disagreed and 11 per cent did not know (Hill, 1970, p.170–3).

The voicing of such views openly with limited rebuttal from those in power in either party appeared to sanction the fears, hostility and violence by people in urban areas towards coloured minority groups, particularly where the latter in turn had reacted with increasing militancy. There has been a rapid growth of politically orientated associations among racial groups. John (1970) describes such an explosive situation in Handsworth between immigrants, police and authority where long-standing problems of the area are expressed in racial terms. Annual Police Reports (Runnymede, July 1972) and House of Commons Select Committee[1] Reports, those on Coloured School Leavers (1969) and Police/Immigrant Relations (1972) discussed in other sections, also bring out a continuing feeling of rejection on the part of many coloured minority groups.

III. **Governmental Aid to Urban Areas**

A. *Priority Areas*

The Government began to respond to the local authorities' need for financial assistance in inner urban areas by providing substantial aid through the Local Government Act of 1966.[2] These funds were to improve housing amenities and welfare services in areas where long-standing deficiencies had been exacerbated by the large influx of overseas newcomers. This led to the designation of housing priority areas. There was considerable variation between authorities as to how they spent their funds and this aid was recognized as far from adequate.

The publication of the Plowden Report (1967), which described how children in many of these areas were educationally retarded because of deficient social conditions and inadequate school facilities, established the concept of the Educational Priority Areas (EPAs). It listed factors by which these areas could be identified, among them areas which had over two per cent of non-English-speaking children. It recommended that policy should discriminate positively in favour of schools in these areas, starting with the two per cent most deprived, working up to 10 per cent of these in five years' time. This concept, doctrine and their recommendations were accepted for these schools by the Government with some modifications. The DES suggested indices for Local Authorities to use in designating EPA

[1] Select Committee on Race Relations and Immigration.

[2] The Local Government Act of 1966 provided for a 50 per cent rate support grant in respect of special staff or extra effort by normal staff due to the presence of immigrants having a different language or culture.

schools and areas and promised to authorize special assistance. The extra assistance took the following forms:

(1) the teacher ratio was increased;
(2) teachers in these schools were given an increase in salary for their extra responsibilities;
(3) extra spending was authorised for improvement projects and for extra books and equipment;
(4) more nursery education was provided.

Although this help was chiefly for the socially deprived child who, as the National Association of Schoolmasters (1968) stated, had greater problems than that of the immigrant child, the latter, many of whom share some of these handicaps as well as those of language and cultural adjustment, were to benefit also.

It was recognized that positive discrimination had implications beyond education and areas for urban renewal and town planning have been designated by the Minister of Housing with plans for a more heterogeneous community in these areas. Corbett (1968) discusses some of the political problems involved in designating priority areas as well as providing a map of official priority areas of different types.

The increasing recognition in a number of studies by educational psychologists and sociologists of the factors contributing to social disadvantage led Plowden to recommend research as to which compensatory techniques would be most effective for children at schools in these areas.

B. *Compensatory Education Research*

The Social Science Research Council and DES gave grants in 1967 for a three-year programme of action research, directed by Dr A. H. Halsey of the University of Oxford for some schools or geographical areas in five of the EPA areas[1] in the country. Each area had its own project director who worked with a team, the school's staff and linked College of Education students, to plan DES strategies and initiate and implement projects to attain their objectives. Their overall aim was to identify skills and strategies which teachers, schools and parents can use to enrich the children's cultural and linguistic experience, as well as to encourage parent involvement.

The Schools Council has also several curriculum development projects on compensatory educational techniques at the Universities of Swansea and Manchester, as well as the two specialized language

[1] These EPA areas were in Liverpool 8, West Riding of Yorkshire, Deptford, London, Birmingham and Dundee.

curriculum development projects for West Indian and other immigrant children.

The strategies and results of EPA and Schools Council projects will be discussed in the relevant chapter.

One of Plowden's recommendations, the use of aides on a massive scale for teachers with children who required a great deal of individual help in language dialogue and encouragement, was not implemented. However, the development of summer holiday schools for children, both native and immigrant, in deprived areas in the mid-1960s for holiday activities and language programmes, has used student volunteers in this capacity with great success. (Hawkins, 1971). These summer programmes, EPA strategies and Schools Council projects will be discussed in the chapter on compensatory education projects.

C. *Urban Aid*

The Urban Aid Programme was initiated in May 1968 by the Labour Government when Mr Wilson announced that the Government would authorize the expenditure of £20 to £25 million over a period of four years, to areas of social need, which would be assessed by three criteria; those areas which had strains on their educational and housing facilities and which had a large number of immigrants. The Urban Programme grant paid 75 per cent of Local Authority expenditure on approved projects. This was conditional on the LEA providing 25 per cent of the funds. This included money for the first year's running costs. In Phase One only 23 Local Authorities qualified under all three heads and expenditure was sanctioned chiefly for nursery schools and classes, day nurseries and children's homes. Phase Two covered all Local Authorities for any social scheme meeting social needs (Rose, 1969). Phase Three was announced in June 1970 when £40 million was allocated to the programme, which was extended for four years (*Guardian,* 1970).

The Conservative party government in January 1971 committed itself to continue the urban aid programme[1] as announced, allowing £4 million on captial projects for the next two financial years. Five hundred and thirty projects were approved by the Home Secretary. The projects ranged from community centres, playgroup and day nursery centres, adventure playgrounds, reception and language training centres and housing advisory centres (Runnymede Trust, 1971b).

In Phase Four a clear attempt was made to help voluntary organizations, particularly local unofficial efforts. Most of the funds went to very 'safe' areas—nursery provision, housing aid centres and

[1] Guardian, January 1971.

family planning centres. Few non-established groups were helped (Holman, 1971).

Phase Five aimed amongst other efforts to help community projects but did not give money for running costs, which are hardest for voluntary organizations to manage.

Each phase tends to give priority to certain types of projects, but often the voluntary organizations and Local Authorities do not know of these until they have already allocated funds for their annual budgets, though this situation is being remedied.

IV. Governmental Legislation on Immigration

The policy of successive governments of combining discriminatory immigrant control and integration policies under the control of the same department, the Home Office, has not given confidence to Commonwealth immigrants that these latter policies have equal priority. The deployment of staff, as Stephens (1970) points out, is much smaller for the Community Relations Department in the Home Office than that dealing with Immigration and Nationality questions, and the funds allocated to the Commission for its work are little more than the year's salary received by a top civil servant (Bonham Carter, 9th April 1973, BBC TV 'Nationwide').

A. *Consequences of Previous Legislation*

The number of Commonwealth immigrants fell by one-third in 1969 compared to 1968. In the first five months of 1970 it fell by 44 per cent. The significant figure is a 42 per cent drop in dependants. This is partially due to a provision in the Immigration Appeals Act 1969 (IRR Facts Paper, 1970), which made entry certificates issued in the country of origin compulsory for Commonwealth immigrants,

Table I.3: *New Commonwealth Immigration Figures*

	New Commonwealth Citizens	*UK East Africa Passport Holders*
1969	33,942*	6,249*
1970	26,562*	6,839*
1971[1]	23,615†	11,564†
1972	25,069†	34,781†

* Institute of Race Relations Facts and Figures, 1972
† Runnymede Bulletin, May 1973.

[1] During the 1971 period it is interesting to note that 57,131 permits were allowed to foreign workers who wished to work in Great Britain, 10,566 of which were to foreigners already here for other purposes. (Industrial Supplement, RR Bulletin, April 1972.) The issue of 1972 yearly figures by the Immigration and Nationality Department has been delayed because of the office move to Croydon.

as well as its main purpose of giving rights to appeal against decisions affecting admission.

The total number of Commonwealth citizens entering Britain for settlement has been steadily declining, with the exception of UK passport holders from East Africa.

The annual quota of vouchers for UK passport holders from East Africa was increased from 1,500 a year to 3,000 as of 1st June 1971, and an additional 1,500 vouchers were made available for issue from 1st June 1972 to assist those in special need (Runnymede Bulletin, June, 1971). Naturally, with Ugandan Asian airlift, numbers will be considerably higher among the UK East African passport holders.

The publication of the annual immigration figures of Commonwealth immigrants subject to entry under the Act control, indicates that immigration from the new Commonwealth has been severely curtailed.

Employment voucher holders in 1972[1]

	Men	*Women*
Australia	208	59
Bangladesh	23	2
Barbados	2	2
Canada	70	20
India	160	65
Jamaica	2	13
Pakistan	55	7
Trindad & Tobago	3	5
UK Passport from East Africa and India	73	12

The International Social Service of Great Britain (1973), responsible under the 1971 Immigration Act for repatriation operations of eligible and suitable immigrants who apply to them, report their methods of seeing whether this is in the family's best interests, from the proportion who do emigrate conclude: 'The notion that very large numbers of immigrants are anxious to return home is mistaken.' Runnymede Trust Bulletin (May 1973) abstracts relevant sections of the Annual Report.

As the *Sunday Times* (1973) says, coloured immigration has been restricted, and without discussing the ethics of this policy at this time, the leader points out that now a realistic social policy must be

[1] Home Office (1973). *Commonwealth Immigrants Acts* 1962 *and* 1968; *Statistics,* 1972 Cmd. 5285. London: HMSO. Table 4. Last year the numbers of adult Commonwealth immigrants leaving Britain was greater than those coming in. Home Office (1973) *ibid.*, Table 2.

implemented to give equal social and economic opportunity to coloured British citizens, as well as to our EEC nationals.

Figures for Commonwealth immigrants and foreigners granted either work or residence permits or admitted for settlement were issued for the first quarter of 1973. These indicate that a greater number of aliens and EEC workers have been given work permits than Commonwealth workers (*The Guardian,* 9th June 1973). Work permits were given to 282 Commonwealth citizens, 4,003 foreign nationals,[1] while 1,012 EEC workers were given residence permits. A further 4,762 foreign and EEC nationals were admitted for settlement, and 6,734 Commonwealth citizen dependants entered.

At the time of the passing of the Immigration Bill in 1971 it was pointed out that people already in Britain would not be affected by the Bill. However the Bill has been interpreted by the Court of Appeal decision in May 1973 and upheld by the House of Lords in June as allowing detention and removal from the United Kingdom of any person who entered in breach of immigration laws in force *since* 1968, despite the fact that these laws had exempted 'illegal' immigrants from prosecution and deportation after a period of six months, unless convicted of a crime (*Runnymede Trust Bulletin,* June 1973).

There have been appeals for amnesty for such citizens by the International Jurists Association, the Community Relations Council and other bodies, chiefly because:

1. it is a reversal of government policy without warning to those concerned;
2. it exposes those who are liable to search by the police, to be exploited by employers, and to be subject to blackmail by those who know their history, particularly traffickers.

Such appeals have not been accepted by the Home Secretary or government although the former has said that his Department will review compassionately all cases coming to their notice. He has asked the police to halt illegal immigration but not to harass individuals.

Many Commonwealth citizens from Pakistan shall have had their status altered, due to the departure of Pakistan from the Commonwealth on 30th January, 1972 by the Pakistan Bill before Parliament. They are asking for alterations to the bill to give them more time to apply for UK citizenship and in some instances to prevent some Pakistanis from being considered aliens retrospectively (HMSO, 1973, Pakistan Bill and Runnymede Trust Bulletin, July 1973).

Such objections to both bills must be considered humanely and fairly or they will lower the level of trust which brown and black

[1] 1,059 dependants.

minorities have towards official statements of goodwill towards them.

B. *Ugandan Asian Emergency*

In August 1972 when President Amin made his announcement that he intended to expel all Asians with British passports by November 7th, and to review the status of Ugandan Asians, the British Government set up a Resettlement Board to receive them, and other Commonwealth countries and nations were approached to accept a proportion of the estimated total. The UN were allowed to organize emergency travel documents to Asians whose citzenship status was undetermined. The British passport-holding wives and dependants of non-British men were allowed entry.

The air lift began by the end of September and all Asians had left by the deadline. In September 1972, six per cent of a national sample poll believed that British passport holders should be admitted. However in October, 54 per cent approved of the way the government had handled the situation—the public's response to the government's unequivocal lead (CRC 1973 AR).

Of the 26,000 who had come to England, 10,000 settled in transit camps, 6,000 went to relatives or friends and the Resettlement Board placed 7,000 in accommodation. About 21,500 refugees passed through the camps but by the end of March only 3,626 were still in residence and, of the refugees seeking work, 75 per cent had found it or were not registered as unemployed (Runnymede R.R. Bulletin, Sept., Nov., 1972, April 1973).

O'Brian (1972) and Tilbe (1972) both describe the background to the Ugandan Asian crisis and the issues involved. International Voluntary Service Survey in December 1972 in four London Boroughs pointed out that, of the 1,039 Asians who had by-passed the camps to go to relatives and friends, 76 per cent were unsettled in accommodation and in great need. IVS suggested that the Resettlement Board should take continuing responsibility for Asians in need, whether in or out of camps (Runnymede R.R. Bulletin, January, 1973).

Nevertheless, the integration of this group into the community from the camps has been relatively rapid. Local authorities have assigned houses to a small quota of families, though some have given mortgages to those who are solvent, and individuals have offered privately rented accommodation. The government finally succumbed to pressures of public opinion to admit 300 stateless heads of families whose wives and families were already in the country, though at the same time Mr Carr, the Home Secretary, announced that 'immigration will be kept to an inescapable minimum' and that 'while we shall continue to accept our responsibility to UK passport holders by admitting them in a controlled and orderly manner through the special voucher scheme, we shall not be able to accept any further sudden mass expulsions' (Runnymede, 22nd Feb, 1973). The majority of Ugandan Asians are refugees, having been forced to flee without funds. A report on the conditions of Ugandan Asians (CRC 1973) found that in one area 25 per cent were unemployed, 75 per cent were living in overcrowded conditions, paying exorbitant rents and not receiving adequate benefits. Among those working with Ugandan Asians this report is considered typical of other areas and all stress that the Resettlement Board should take close responsibility for the 25,000 living out of camps (McCart, CRC Journal, Sept 1973).

Although there appeared to be sympathy for the plight of the Asians, a probability sample commissioned by the Community Relations Commission showed an almost equal polarization between those for accepting the expelled Asians, 41 per cent and those against, 51 per cent. The majority of the middle class were for admission and the majority of the working class against. In the South East 47 per cent were for admission and 43 per cent were against, whereas only one-third in the Midlands and North favoured admission (CRC, 1973).

C. *The New Immigration Bill and Effect of British Entry into the EEC, January, 1973.*

Both political parties in 1970 were committed to a review of immigration policy, not only to rationalize the laws governing aliens and immigrants, outlined in Stephens' (1970) pamphlet, but also to fit in with the Common Market regulations on free movement of labour of member workers within member countries (IRR Facts Paper, 1970).

The Immigration Bill, published in February 1971, which attempted to rationalize previous immigrant control for both aliens and Commonwealth immigrants in one Bill aroused criticism from many sources.

Its provisions briefly were to impose a single system of control for aliens and most Commonwealth citizens, dividing the latter into 'patrials' and 'non-patrials'.

Patrials, who have right of abode in the UK free from controls, must have direct connections with the UK in any of the following ways: (1) UK passport holders who were born, adopted, naturalized or registered here; (2) or whose parents or grandparents were UK passport holders who have lived here for five years and are permanent residents; (3) Commonwealth citizens who have a parent born in the UK.

Non-Patrials, who do not have right of abode, may be Commonwealth citizens or aliens. The former will, like aliens, need a work permit issued for a specific job for a fixed initial period, and must get permission from the Department of Employment to change jobs. At the end of four years they may apply to register as a UK citizen. Unlike aliens, they register with an employment exchange rather than the police and they may vote (British Council of Churches RRU and IRR, 1972).

The Bill was criticized by the Community Relations Commission. Mr Bonham-Carter, the Chairman of the Commission 'has advised the Secretary of State that the present Bill will adversely affect the establishment of harmonious community relations and acutely increase the insecurity which coloured people already living here feel' (CRC Annual Report, 1971). Some of the provisions to which the Commission objected are outlined:

1. The establishment of absolute right of entry to those with 'patrial' status confers unregulated rights of settlement upon an unknown number of non-UK citizens of British extraction.
2. New arrivals will no longer be able to register as UK citizens after five years' residence.
3. Work permits are issued for a specific post with a specific employer for one year only, which may tend to prevent an immigrant complaining against exploitation.
4. Registration of immigrants with the police. This has been altered to registration with Department of Employment exchanges.
5. Deportation by the Home Secretary where 'in his view' the public good requires it.
6. The liability to deportation of the immediate family of anyone recommended for deportation. This has been altered.
7. Repatriation by statute which makes for more insecurity.

Suggested amendments are also cited.

A Labour Party Study Group published an Opposition Green Paper (abstracted in Runnymede RR bulletin, April 1972), which made recommendations and proposals for a government inquiry to review and rationalize UK citizenship. It suggested that *all* Commonwealth citizens should have free movement of labour in the EEC. In addition, they also suggest that the Community Relations Commission and the Urban Programme should be transferred to the Department of Health and Social Security and that the scope of the former be widened to cover community, as well as race relations.

D. *Influence of EEC Entry*

In May 1971 the British Government accepted the Treaty of Rome including its provisions regarding the free movement of labour. On the 25th January 1972 the Treaty of Accession was published, which, amongst other things, defines a 'UK National' for the purposes of free movement within the enlarged EEC.[1] This latter definition is embodied in two joint declarations appended to the Act, printed in the Race Relations Bulletin, which Nandy (in Runnymede, 1972) indicates is more restrictive than the 1971 Immigration Act and allows EEC member states to restrict free movement of labour if there are 'certain difficulties for the social situation'. Lord Windlesham, for the Government, stated that, though 'social difficulties' had not been defined, any such would be resolved in accordance with relevant Community Treaties (House of Lords, 14th March 1972).

Runnymede Trust gives a reasoned estimate based on known statistics of the limited numbers of UK nationals, who qualify under the declarations and who also have scarce skills wanted by EEC countries. Most of these, they believe, will be unlikely to wish to work in these countries due to the superior civil rights they enjoy in Britain (Runnymede Trust, May 1972). However a number of skilled workers are needed in Germany.

The Immigration Law, which was to take effect on January 1973, had in addition two statements of Immigration Rules for control for entry and control after entry (namely HC 509 and HC 510). These, because they were rules for guidance for Immigration Officers, had to be accepted or rejected. If the latter, they had to be returned to the Secretary of State for redrafting.

These rules also outline relevant obligations under the EEC Treaty for movement of labour and right of establishment of EEC workers. The EEC workers require *no* work permit *but* after six months they must apply to the Home Office for an extension and, if accepted, receive a five-year residence permit and must register with the police as well. Workers, when jobs are vacant, may not be brought from overseas until 18 days after EEC nationals have had an opportunity to apply (Runnymede R.R. Bulletin, November 1972).

The statements of control on entry were rejected by the House of Commons in November due to a newspaper campaign by proponents of the view that descendants in the white Commonwealth would have greater difficulty of entry than other categories.

The government in the second draft of the revised Immigration Rules of January 1973 added that Commonwealth men and women with grandparents born in England may come and work without restrictions, though they do not have the 'right of abode', since an

Namely Commonwealth citizens who have accepted citizenship of the UK and Colonies after five years' residence by registration—about 200,000 as of May 1972 (Runnymede, May 1972, RR Bulletin).

entry clearance must first be obtained. These new regulations came into effect on 30th January 1973. Changes were also made in arrangements for young Commonwealth visitors coming for working holidays, dependant grandparents and rules on family deportation (Runnymede Trust Bulletin, March 1973).

The Home Secretary in announcing these revisions which theoretically gave entry to another eight million white Commonwealth citizens, made a point that in the future Britain would not accept further East African passport holders as precipitiously and in such large numbers as in the case of the Ugandan Asians.

This, as Nandy (February 1973) points out, is likely to increase the cynicism of the coloured communities, as to the racialist bias in immigration policy.

The Home Secretary, in a speech on February 22nd, outlined the guiding principles of government immigration policy (*The Times,* 23rd February 1973). The 'resounding silence' of the Labour Party to the second revision of the Statement on Immigration Controls for Entry allowing patrials unlimited entry indicates their tacit acquiescence to this policy, which is:

1. that Britain must restrict permanent settlement to an inescapable minimum, since her labour force is ample for her needs
2. to reserve a large proportion of those allowed entry for UK citizens, but in a controlled way
3. to give anyone with a grandparent here the right to come and settle and work as they please.

(Runnymede Trust Bulletin, April 1973).

He also announced that 'the Government jointly with the Gulbenkian Foundation were asking Political and Economic Planning Organization to undertake a wide-ranging study of racial disadvantage in Britain'. This appears here openly to show recognition that control and limitation of numbers is *not* the only approach to solving harmonious inter-group relations, and that a much more active positive Government policy is needed than that embodied by the Community Relations Commission—with a realistic allocation of funds to attempt such a policy or policies, since any redress of unequal opportunity must be approached on all fronts and interdepartmental levels.

The Central Policy Review Staff ('The Think Tank') has been asked to undertake an inquiry into race relations.

IV. Sources of Information about Race Relations in Britain today—Selected Background Studies and Organizations who are sponsoring Research in this Field

Most studies and literature will be described under the relevant chapters in the book. The early studies and some subsequent ones which contribute to our understanding of the background and adaptation problems of the recent racial ethnic groups who have immigrated to Britain are given here.

Very few research studies or books on race relations in Britain had been written in the 50s and early 60s. Those mentioned in an article reviewing these studies were mainly by post-graduate social scientists, studies sponsored by the Institute of Race Relations or descriptive accounts written by individuals (Goldman and Taylor, 1966). Though excellent and of historical interest, these have been superseded by more recent studies.

Many of these were sponsored by the Five Year Survey of Race Relations, a research trust set up by the Institute of Race Relations in 1962, a non-political body which was studying race relations throughout the world. The Institute of Race Relations was aware of the possibility of problems facing the Commonwealth immigrants in obtaining acceptance and becoming integrated as numbers rose and incidents occurred. It hoped, as their director, Mr Mason, said, to assemble accurate information on the state of race relations in Britain, to analyse it, to suggest means to eliminate friction, and to elucidate aims to be borne in mind when framing policy (Rose, 1969). Many of these works studied the cultures and values of the receiving and sending societies and their interaction in areas of heavy immigrant centres.

As a result of these studies, which uncovered fields of friction, which were important in the adjustment process, further work was instigated on a larger range of more specialized studies in areas such as housing, crime, employment and political behaviour Rose (1968a).

Although many of these have been published as individual works, the results of these and others not yet published have been summarized by the Director of the Survey, E. J. Rose (1969), in *Colour and Citizenship*. This is a massive and fascinating report on British race relations during the post-war period based on these studies and an intimate knowledge of how governmental policy and action evolved. This is undoubtedly the most comprehensive and authoritative source on race relations in Britain. One study by Dr Abrams on a survey of British racial attitudes, conducted between 1966 and 1967, indicated that 35 per cent of the population were tolerant of immigrants, 38 per cent were tolerantly inclined, 17 per cent were prejudice inclined and only 10 per cent were prejudiced. It has been considered too limited in its choice of variables to indicate 'prejudice' and in its interpretation of an attitude of 'tolerance' by many sociologists such as Lawrence (1969)[1], Hill (1970)[2] and Deakin (1970)[3]. Bagley (1970) re-analysed the original data for the Institute using more sophisticated statistical techniques and concluded that racial feelings are much more prejudiced than Abrams implied and that a little under half of the population surveyed displayed a marked degree of prejudice. It is obviously difficult to establish exact criteria for the measurement of prejudice since, as Deakin points out in *Colour and Citizenship*, 'The evidence from other studies suggests that expressed attitudes predict behaviour only to a very limited degree and that changes in the social situation or the roles that individuals perform over-rides the predispositions which may be expressed in answers to questions about opinion.' (Rose, op. cit. 588). However, in his abridged version of Rose's study, he reinterprets Abrams' terms and labels only 35 per cent as tolerant and the remaining categories as degrees of prejudice (Deakin, 1970).

Since Abrams' study found that responses from the national survey on racial attitudes were similar to those obtained from the 500 people from each of the five boroughs of Wolverhampton, Lambeth, Ealing, Nottingham and Bradford, subsequent studies have tended to sample from these five boroughs. Marsh (1973), who compares results from these studies, points out that relationships between conventional demographic variables—proximity, contact, and numbers of immigrants (with the exception of age)—and differences in inter-borough degress of prejudice are not consistent. Thus, though he indicates that the two tolerant boroughs, Nottingham and Bradford, had fairly similar proximity and contact with a similar number of immigrants, their attitudes towards these were less negative than people in the prejudiced boroughs, Wolverhampton and Lambeth, though relationships are far from straightforward. Schafer's study (1972) based on Abrams' complete survey of these boroughs confirms that these interborough differences in race prejudice are significantly independent of other major independent variables as well. He

1 Lawrence (1969a, b) indicates why, on methodological grounds, he believes that the prejudice-tolerance scale is biased towards 'tolerance' in his paper read to the BSA study group on race relations, summarized in these articles.

2 Hill (1970) believes that the attitude survey has under-estimated the level of colour prejudice in Britain, as reflected in the PEP Report and in other studies.

3 Deakin (1970) in his abridged version of Colour and Citizenship re-interprets the terms in the attitude survey, labelling only 35 per cent as tolerant and the remaining categories as degrees of prejudice.

suggests that differences in race attitudes are more related to the citizens' sense of positive town or civic, and personal, identity, which is more likely in stable well-defined towns, and presents evidence to support his thesis. Marsh (1972) suggests that Schaefer's more sophisticated and more elaborate multi-variate analysis is likely to ensure that his figure of about 25 per cent of the population is prejudiced, is a more accurate and definitive figure than that of previous studies, 'since he has validated a new measure of tolerance/prejudice from the existing data'. In this earlier article, Marsh (1972) covers a longer historical perspective of 'Tolerance and pluralism in Britain' with more detail on methods used in particular studies. He breaks down Schaefer's data on percentages of prejudice in greater detail. He found a tolerant response in a little short of half the sample overall, a further one-fifth (20 per cent) holding a guarded reserve towards immigrants. This 'fit' with Abrams' data is, as Marsh points out, particularly good if the 20 per cent midway group are seen as an ambiguous group to be pushed one way by supporters of the tolerance theory and the other way by their opponents. His percentage of 18 who have a consistent antipathy, and the strongly prejudiced group, about 12 per cent is over the 25 per cent given, because the 'don't knows' were not included in the totals for this analysis.

Rose based his recommendations on evidence contained in Abrams' and other studies that discrimination based on colour exists and that these immigrants and their English-born children, like previous coloured immigrants, shall encounter barriers to permanent integration or assimilation. They would not, as other immigrants to Britain, become economically or geographically dispersed, he stated, unless the government intervened through administrative and legal action. Further evidence of the marginal situation of coloured adolescents was brought out by evidence given to the Select Committee on Race Relations and Immigration, and published in their report on *The Problems of Coloured School-Leavers* (1969).

Hartman and Husband (1972) criticise previous cited scales designed to measure prejudice, for their minimum reliability or complexity of application. They describe their own instrument and technique to measure white attitudes to coloured people in Britain and give examples how it appears to be an adequate and reliable measure.

Rose made far-reaching proposals which provided a realistic programme for action in urban redevelopment, housing, educational institutions, community relations, police relations, welfare and immigration legislation. Among those proposals pertaining to education, it was recommended that all educational institutions should provide courses on the cultures of minorities in Britain, on race relations and the nature of prejudice for teachers, welfare workers and the police. In addition, he suggested that teachers should have courses which would enable them to present this background to children.

Many of the recommendations are now being actively promoted by the Community Relations Commission as well as by some government departments, although the Labour Government six months later, when Lord Watson instituted a debate in the House of Lords on the report, did not announce any major change in policy (*Race Today* News Roundup, 1970).

Deakin's (1970) abridged version is a digest of Rose's study and covers events in 1969 as well. Hill's (1970) book is also a good factual introductory survey of Commonwealth immigration and settlement, clearly and succinctly written. Sheila Patterson (1969) summarizes situations and events in the field of race relations. Philip Mason (1970a, b) surveys race relations and patterns of dominance throughout the world, studying factors which are relevant when different ethnic groups live in harmony or tension. Banton (1967) also surveys race relations world-wide, with a section on Britain. Hooper's work, though not up to date, is a useful BBC (1965) handbook with basic facts about the sending society. All these books have excellent bibliographies. Another general book on the situation in Britain in the 1950s and 1960s is by Griffith *et al.* (1960). Davison (1964) gives information on housing and employment and Huxley (1964) deals with the culture-conflict between immigrants and the host community. Allen (1971) and Banton (1972) set their studies of the mutual adjustments of the new racial minorities and the British host society members to one another more firmly in a framework of sociological theory on race relations.

Banton discusses difficulties of minority integration, the attitudes and behaviour of the majority, the pressures of the urban situation. Allen sets her discussion on minorities in the fact that the structuring of intergroup relations owes much to the overall stratification system of British society, as well as in the previous historical relationships inherent in Britain's role as a colonial power.

Richmond (1972) has edited a selection of readings on race and ethnic relations which is based on sociological and physical (social) studies of a variety of aspects in many countries including Britain. Trends in recent race relations research and theory are also described.

Hiro (1971) describes the background of ethnic minorities, including the effects of colonialism, their adaptation to life in Britain and the reaction of official and liberal British to their arrival. He describes the development of ethnic organizations. Social pluralism must be explicitly accepted and positively encouraged as governmental policy for Britons of all colours to live in harmony.

Krausz (1971) covers a great many facts about Commonwealth and other minorities in Britain, and on the extent of discrimination which they face.

Abbott (1971) concentrates on racial discrimination in relation to British society and reviews legislative governmental and private measures taken to prevent it.

The Institute of Race Relations publishes a yearly pamphlet, *Facts Paper*, with basic data on immigrant numbers, employment, housing, school population, etc., which are based on Rose's work and brought up to date where annual figures and new material are available.

Some of the many studies and books which describe the cultures of the immigrants and their interaction with the English are those specific to particular ethnic groups: the West Indians by Richmond (1954), Ruck (1959), Glass and Pollins (1960), Patterson (1963, 1968), Peach (1968). Some of the Asian studies are by Desai (1963) on the Gujeratis, Aurora (1968), Bhogal (1972), and McLeod (1972) on the Sikhs, and Butterworth (1967) on the Pakistanis, and all Asian groups in Britain by Sookhdeo (1972). Other ethnic groups have not been studied so extensively, though George (1967) describes the Cypriot community in West London, Craven (1969) the West Africans in London, and Kwee Choo (1968) the Chinese in London. The background of the Asians in East Africa is described by Ghai (1965) and Tilbe (1972) and O'Brian (1972) on the Ugandan Asians. Booklets published by NCCI, now the Community Relations Commission, though less detailed, describe the cultures of the incoming immigrants, and are listed in the free bibliographies of the latter Commission, as well as works on other subjects. Hashmi (1972) deals with the Pakistani family, Hiro (1970) that of the Indian minorities. Some authors describe the immigrant groups in terms of their religious affiliation, Taylor (1972) on Islam, Hinnells and Sharpe (1972) on Hinduism, McLeod (1972) on the Sikhs and Domnitz (1972) on Judaism. General studies were sponsored by the Five Year Survey in areas of heavy immigrant settlement in Birmingham by Rex (1967) and John (1970), in Bradford by Butterworth (1967), and in Liverpool and Bristol by Richmond (1954), and Richmond and Lyon (in Rose, 1969), respectively.

These studies of the interaction of immigrants with the host community indicated the policies of local authorities in housing and education which were important in the development of race relations. Burney (1967) studied municipal housing policies, Beetham (1967) the immigrant school leavers and employment, Hawkes (1966), Power (1967) and Bowker (1968) the educational policies towards immigrant children. Immigrants' problems in industrial employment were studied by Patterson (1968) in London and Wright (1968) in the Midlands and the North of England. John Jr. (1969) covers Indian workers' associations.

The political reactions of the host community are studied by Foot (1965) and in booklets by the political parties, Fabian Society,[1] and pressure groups such as Pressure for Economic and Social Toryism, as well as by conventional research organizations.

It is impossible to mention all the existing and the increasing number of new books now being published in this field; most new ones are reviewed by journals or newsletters such as *Education and Community Relations,* Runnymede Trust Bulletin (latterly named *Race Relations Bulletin*), *The Multi-Racial School* and *New Community, Race* and *Race Today,* or are listed in the many bibliographies and book lists of multi-racial literature.

Runnymede Trust (1973), (1974)[2] has published two useful facts booklets on race relations and immigration in the form of answers to the questions frequently asked about these themes, with the latest figures available and the sources from which they have been obtained.

1 One such, Bolton and Laishley (1972) stresses the importance of the educational system in furthering 'the recognition of equal dignity, irrespective of colour, dignity or creed'. The Government is asked to lead in establishing an adequate policy to fulfil this aim.

2 The latter *Immigration and Race Relations* was intended as a reference guide for candidates in the election.

CHAPTER TWO

General Survey of the Educational Situation of 'Immigrant' Children

I. Introduction

A. *Numbers and Ethnic Composition of Immigrant Schoolchildren*

During the last two decades immigrant children have been entering schools in Greater London, the Midlands and Northern Cities in increasing numbers.

In 1971 the total number of immigrant pupils in maintained primary and secondary schools with 10 or more such pupils in England and Wales was 263,710. This was about 3·3 per cent of all school children, compared to 3·2 per cent in 1970. The total number of immigrant children in *all* maintained schools in 1972 was 279,872, 3·3 per cent of all pupils; this figure includes pupils from Europe, North America and Australasia. The number of immigrant children in these schools in January 1972 was:

Table 2.1: *Immigrant Pupils by origin in all maintained schools, January* 1972, *and percentage of total immigrants*[1]

Country	*Numbers*	%
Australia, Canada & New Zealand	2,455	0·9
Cyprus (Greek)	9,504	3·4
(Turkish)	4,461	1·6
Gibraltar, Malta	1,252	0·4
Kenya (Asian Origin)	17,340	6·2
(African Origin)	1,385	0·5
Other Commonwealth countries in Africa	14,444	5·3
India	56,193	20·1
Pakistan	30,629	10·9
Other Commonwealth countries in Asia	8,008	2·9
West Indies (including Guyana)	101,898	36·4
Non-Commonwealth Countries		
Italy	12,009	4·3
Poland	1,958	0·7
Spain	3,275	1·2
Other European Countries	5,980	2·1
Rest of World	9,081	3·2
Total	279,872	100·0

[1] Advance figures provided by Statistics Unit, Dept. of Education and Science, May 1973 and now published in DES (1973) *Statistics of Education*, 1972, Vol. I: *Schools*. London: HMSO.

The Department of Education and Science defines 'immigrant' pupils as follows:

(i) Children born outside the British Isles who have come to this country with or to join parents or guardians whose countries of origin were abroad.

(ii) Children born in the UK to parents whose countries of origin were abroad and who came to the UK up to 10 years before the date to which the figures apply.

(iii) Children of mixed immigrant and non-immigrant parentage and children from the Republic of Ireland are excluded.

Children of immigrant parents from two overseas countries have been classified according to the country of origin of the father (DES, 1972, *Department of Education and Science Statistics*, 1971, Vol. 1, London: HMSO).

It is clear that it will not always be possible for teachers to determine the relevant facts demanded by such classifications. Brown's (1970a, b) study of Bedford found that some head teachers return the number of all immigrant pupils regardless of when their parents arrived. The heads found no difference in language and cultural problems between children of immigrants who had been in England over 10 years and more recent arrivals. They claim that using the DES definition would not give an accurate picture of their educational problems, and many admitted that they did not apply the 10-year definition too strictly. Some, as Hill indicates, drop the term 'immigrant' after a child has been in the United Kingdom for five years and it is obvious, therefore, that if these practices are repeated on a national scale, the figures cannot be completely reliable. A system of classification based on ethnic group and whether standard English is the child's first language would be more likely to give an indication of the educational problems to be faced by the schools and to enable them to be allocated the extra assistance they require.

The DES (1972) statistics for 1971 indicate that, as in the past, the number of all immigrant pupils, 270,745, is unevenly distributed among LEAs, with almost one half in the Greater London region: 135,218. The remaining half of the total is grouped in the West Midlands, 42,625, the South East, 26,907, the North West, 19,479, Yorkshire, 18,326, and the East Midlands, 16,237, as well as in certain scattered cities throughout Britain which have large concentrations.

Within the authorities themselves the immigrant children are generally concentrated in a few schools. The ethnic group composition of a school, whether preponderantly West Indian or Asian, or one with a mixture of many nationalities, has an obvious influence on language teaching arrangements which must be made.

Table 2.2: *New Commonwealth Immigrant Children in London and County Boroughs with Populations of* 50,000 *or more where they exceed* 10 *per cent of all Pupils in maintained Primary and Secondary Schools*

January	1971* *Primary & Secondary*	1972† *Primary & Secondary*
Inner London Boroughs		
Hammersmith	16·0	15·7
Kensington & Chelsea	12·0	13·6
Camden	10·7	11·7
Westminster	13·2	14·0
Islington	20·1	20·7
Hackney	21·6	22·3
Tower Hamlets/ City London	9·0	10·5
Lewisham	13·5	14·0
Southwark	12·7	12·8
Lambeth	18·5	19·8
Wandsworth	15·0	16·6
Outer London Boroughs		
Brent	25·8	25·2
Ealing	20·5	21·6
Haringey	26·6	26·5
Newham	15·8	17·3
Waltham Forest	11·4	11·2
County Boroughs		
Bradford	10·5	11·4
Birmingham	9·5	9·4
Derby	6·4	6·4
Huddersfield	12·5	12·4
Leicester	13·5	14·4
Wolverhampton	13·0	12·7
Warley	10·6	10·5
Preston	9·8	11·0

* DES (1972) and Runnymede Trust Newsletter (April, 1972).
† DES (1973) *Statistics of Education*, 1972.

Since families tend to cluster in certain neighbourhoods, even in an authority with a high percentage of immigrants, it has been found that the distribution among schools is very uneven. Thus, as Hill (1970) points out, in Haringey there are 11 schools with more than 50 per cent immigrant pupils while in 15 schools there are less than five per cent.

Because the majority of the children are under 11 years of age there are higher concentrations of immigrant children in infant and junior schools than in the secondary schools at the present time. It should be pointed out that part of the decrease in the numbers of immigrant pupils as the ages rise is due to the fact that children cease to be counted as immigrants when their parents have lived here for 10 years.

Table 2.3 gives numbers of immigrant pupils according to age group in schools with 10 or more immigrant pupils.

Table 2.3: *Immigrant pupils in maintained primary and secondary schools* in* 1971 *and percentage of all pupils in such schools.*

Ages	*Numbers*	%	*Ages*	*Numbers*	%
Under 5	9,225	3·8	11	18,873	2·8
5	30,913	3·9	12	17,909	2·7
6	30,950	3·8	13	18,677	2·9
7	28,426	3·6	14	18,962	3·1
8	25,591	3·4	15	15,031	3·6
9	22,556	3·1	16+	12,890	3·8
10	20,742	2·9			

* DES (1972) Statistics of Education, V.1 p.66 and 67.

Using Haringey again as an example, 30·8 per cent of its immigrant pupils in 1968 were in infant schools, Hill (1970).

Although Commonwealth immigration began in 1948, it did not commence on a large scale until the mid-1950s. The schools were totally unprepared for the sudden influx of non-English-speaking children. In 1956 it was estimated that 8,000 pupils in London were of overseas origin. By 1964 it was estimated that the figure was 38,000. In other areas, such as Bradford, the 1,500 children in September 1969 had risen by almost one-third six months later as the fathers, fearing further restrictions, sent for their wives and children. The rate of increase and the fact that it was occurring continuously throughout the year made the teaching and integration much more difficult for the schools. Ealing (then Southall) had one teacher for immigrants in 1957, but by 1967 it had 50 teachers. These same schools in the inner urban areas were admitting 100 pupils per week.

B. *Schools' Adjustment to the Situation*

The schools to which the immigrant children came were not prepared to handle this sudden influx since they were often in old buildings which were ill-equipped and suffered from staff shortage as well as high staff turnover. The main problem at that time was how to organize language teaching for these children. The Ministry of Education (1963) issued an excellent pamphlet, *English for Immigrants* outlining some useful suggestions, listing text books and books describing the countries from which the immigrants had originated and advising the use of teachers who had some training in teaching English as a second language.

The difficulty at this time of course was that few such teachers were available in Britain. Graduates of such courses went abroad to teach and it was not until later that efforts were made to encourage those who returned, to teach non-English speaking children in Britain. There were no in-service courses for teachers involved in teaching immigrant children. Teachers, therefore, of necessity, developed and evolved their own methods of teaching the non-English speaking immigrant child, some using and adapting courses designed for use overseas, such as the *Peak Series* (1961–63), an English course written for Asian children in the English-speaking medium primary schools in Kenya.

Few books were available which were especially written for teachers of non-English speaking pupils in England and most readers were not suitable except that of Braziers *et al.* (1965) which was evolved in co-operation with the Birmingham Education Committee. Some Authorities used overseas teachers. Southall, for example, had only five English teachers out of its 20 teachers in immigrant reception classes. Many of these needed training before they could teach in English schools. Dalrymple (1966) describes Barking's experience with a 10-week course for overseas teachers. The Margaret McMillan Training College in Bradford began a 15-month course in January 1966 and other colleges followed suit.

The arrangements made by schools to organize language classes or groups for non-English speaking children varied according to their ability to obtain extra or specialist teachers, the numbers entering the school and the rooms available in the school for special classes. Eventually it became evident that schools had to pool their resources and some local education authorities evolved a co-ordinated policy to teach immigrant children in their area's schools.

Some authorities were facing pressure from native parents who feared that their children would suffer educationally through the large numbers of non-English speaking children in the classes.

The method of dealing with the latter complaint was through the policy of dispersal of immigrant children throughout schools in the borough. This policy first commenced in Southall.

Sir Edward Boyle, then Minister of Education, in a Commons speech on 27th November, 1963 promised his 'strongest support' for authorities which 'try to spread immigrant children by introducing zoning schemes'. This suggestion was also echoed in a Home Office, CIAC Report (1964, Cmnd 2266) which thought 'arrangements to send children to some alternative schools in order to preserve a reasonable balance' was a possibility.

In 1965 the DES (1965a) issued Circular 7/65, 'The Education of Immigrants' which was also later incorporated in Part III of the

White Paper on Immigration (Home Office, 1965). This recommended that once the proportion of immigrant children formed one-third of the pupils in a school, the additional ones should be dispersed to other schools in the area. By not defining its term 'immigrant' it was not made clear whether it applied to non-English-speaking children only or to all children from abroad as such. It was not based on any research evidence as to whether this was desirable on linguistic or social grounds. The circular had a very mixed reception. The NUT Report (1967) did not believe that any predetermined percentage could be applied on a national scale. The Plowden Report (1967) thought that children should be given special consideration on account of their language and other difficulties and not on account of their colour (Power, 1967).

Authorities which have adopted a dispersal policy may combine it with special reception classes where the children receive intensive language teaching before they attend normal classes.

Among the dispersing authorities who were not necessarily those with the largest number of immigrants were Bradford, Ealing and Huddersfield. The administration and application of dispersal techniques varied and often depended on parental choice (Power, 1967). Other authorities, including many who had far greater numbers of immigrant children, were against dispersal.

It was also realized that, in order for the Central Government to assist local education authorities, with immigrant children, on an equal basis in providing extra teachers and welfare assistants in schools with a high proportion of non-English speaking children, an official count would have to be made of all 'immigrant' children.

Thus, shortly after Circular 7/65 was sent out, the DES in January 1966 asked the schools to keep an 'official' count of the numbers of 'immigrant pupils' in the schools, to be submitted in Form 7i (Schools)—a supplement to the annual return of all pupils, as has been mentioned previously. Since obviously for dispersal to occur, a count of some sort had to be made in schools operating such schemes, the definition of 'immigrant' had certain limitations in relation to the educational question, i.e. the numbers of children requiring intensive teaching in English.

The DES also asked the schools to assess the children's linguistic ability by recording:

1. The numbers of pupils not requiring special tuition in English, even though their written English might be weak.
2. The pupils whose standard of English required special tuition.

Teachers were asked to apply these classifications on the basis of the attainment of local non-immigrant children in equivalent age groups.

The figures arrived at by the DES in 1966 discussed by Power (1967) were:

1. Seventy-five per cent of immigrant pupils in primary and secondary schools had adequate English even though their written work might be weak. However, schools with under 10 immigrant pupils were not included in the survey.

2. Twenty-five per cent of these required special tuition in English.

As a result of a proposal by the University of Leeds in 1965 the Schools Council, independently of the DES had commissioned Miss June Derrick to undertake a national survey to establish: the number of children from different ethnic groups who had not been brought up to speak English as a first language or who spoke a non-standard English; from which country their parents had come; and the variety of situations and methods which the Local Authority used to teach these pupils. She found that in many authorities the proportion of children with inadequate English was very high indeed. However, the criteria of inadequate English was very variable. Some authorities had high proportions of West Indians listed as having inadequate English, other authorities did not list them in this way (Schools Council WP 13, 9167). The *Education Journal* taking a sample from the Schools Council questionnaire, found that the percentage of immigrant pupils whose English had been listed as inadequate was 53 per cent.

Neither the DES nor the Schools Council percentages, as Power (1967) points out, could be completely reliable since, until there is a standardized test to estimate adequacy in English, the judgements of individuals will vary considerably. Both studies did indicate the gravity of the problem which was particularly acute in terms of the teacher shortage. The *Education Journal* Sample survey (Power, 1967) found that, excluding infants, 36 per cent of those needing special language teaching received it, and 64 per cent did not while only 27 per cent out of 216 teachers in 1966 had had some specialized training to teach non-English-speaking children.

Townsend (1971) points out that, although the DES now asks LEAs to give numbers of immigrant pupils who by reason of language difficulties are unable to follow a normal school curriculum with profit to themselves, this definition is still a very subjective one depending on the teachers' standards. The percentage of immigrant pupils who were classified as having such language difficulties for the country as a whole was 16·4 per cent in 1970 but there was great variation among the LEAs, which are all listed in an appended table, the highest having 45·7 per cent.

He points out that the head teachers indicate that the Department's definition of 'immigrant' is not meaningful educationally, since there may be linguistic and integrational problems even though a child's parents have been in Britain over 10 years, when he then ceases to be labelled as an immigrant.

In his more recent intensive study of a small national sample of schools with a high percentage of 'immigrants' from different ethnic groups, the heads, when asked to estimate the number of additional immigrants, gave answers which overall represent a total of 21 per cent over the definition sample figure (Townsend, 1972).

C. *English Language Teaching*

The Schools Council Project found that teachers of immigrant children needed more opportunity to find the best ways of teaching their pupils and wanted help in finding materials with which to do this (Schools Council WP 13, 1967).

As a result of the survey, the Schools Council in 1966 approved the proposal submitted by the Institute of Education of the University of Leeds to set up a three-year English language teaching curriculum development project to meet the needs of pupils of Asian, African and Southern European origin, initially for those aged seven to 13 years, and subsequently for older children and infants.

The Schools Council WP 13 (1967) pointed out that the task of providing help in teaching standard English to West Indian children who spoke a 'creole' English required a different approach. Accordingly, a separate project to explore this field was established in 1967 in the Department of English language and Literature and the School of Education at the University of Birmingham under the direction of James Wight (1969, 1970).

This project first conducted research into the linguistic, social and emotional problems of West Indian children between the ages of seven and nine years. The results are published in Schools Council WP 29 (Wight, 1970), which outlines the future plans for the materials development stage. The work of these two projects will be discussed in the chapter on language development.

The arrangements made by local authorities to teach English as a second language, without dispersal, varies according to staff, facilities and philosophy.

One group has made relatively few changes in class or school organization to cater for the non-English-speaking newcomers. Hill (1970) calls this a 'laissez-faire' policy. The other group has developed a variety of arrangements to teach English to children whose first language is not standard English.

Few Authorities in either group initially made special arrangements for children in infant schools, since it was assumed, as mentioned in the Plowden Report, that the young child would learn the language quickly in the informal atmosphere of the infant class. This has recently been challenged by Stoker (1970) who, as a member of the Leeds Schools Council Project, has surveyed the language teaching methods for immigrant children in Infant Schools. The results of her survey are discussed in the chapter on language. Townsend (1972), in his study on multi-racial schools, found that there was a high proportion of immigrant infants recorded as 'weak' in English.

D. *Ancillary Helpers*

It was immediately recognized by local Education Authorities in most areas where there were large numbers of either disadvantaged or immigrant children, that extra staffing was necessary, both in terms of extra teachers and ancillary staff. The Plowden Report had indicated that auxiliary helpers, particularly in the primary schools, could help the teacher in many ways both with use of audio-visual aids and in other non-professional duties.

An empirical study of the types and time duration of non-teaching activities, (mainly preparation of materials) both within and out of school hours, done by the sample of primary school teachers observed by a team of specialists is reported by Duthie *et al.* (1970). Its findings make clear that the use of an assistant, even on a limited scale, would enable the teacher to use her professional skills more effectively, particularly in infant classes or in classes where teachers use individual and group methods and where there are children who need extra teaching attention. It was found that in large infant classes, the capable teacher would have been able to delegate much of the structuring, supervision, and affective motivation to an auxiliary, whose duties were very strictly defined, so that the teacher could then concentrate for longer periods on skilled teaching. It was found that few teachers could count on long uninterrupted teaching periods when using group or individual teaching methods.

The Department of Education and Science (1971) describes authorities such as Slough, who use welfare assistants for every new immigrant class, and other authorities where infant class auxiliaries have helped to improve children's conversation as well as their social training. Some use ancillary helpers to help the children and their parents by explaining the school's requirements, so that the former may adjust more easily. There is wide variation in the extent to which auxiliaries and other staff are used by LEAs, with responsibility for aiding the education of immigrant children. There are higher proportions of such helpers in LEAs with over 5,000 pupils. Townsend (1971) provides a table of numbers of total staff involved (including teachers) per authority, according to their number of immigrant pupils. Some LEAs have one ancillary helper for each language class while others have none.

II. Schools' Organization for English Language Teaching

A. *Introduction*

Several recent publications include detailed information about educational policy of local authorities towards immigrant pupils. The Department of Education Survey 10 (1971) contains brief details about the 10 Local Education Authorities visited. *Immigrant Pupils in England* by Townsend (1971) provides the latest information on the incidence and general educational arrangements made for immigrant pupils in England, based as it is on a postal questionnaire sent to all 146 LEAs, who were asked if they made special arrangements for schools with immigrant pupils. Although 71 LEAs replied 'yes' and 75 replied 'no', 16 of the latter added a small amount of information in answer to some of the remaining questions. Ten of these latter authorities had over 500 immigrant pupils in their schools. The proportion of immigrant pupils in the authorities' schools did not give any better indication whether special arrangements were made or not. It was found that, although only 11 authorities had taken up the suggestion of dispersal, others achieved a similar effect by altering the catchment area. However, many schools felt it mitigated against integration.

Few authorities seem to realize that the English of many West Indians is not standard English and that their language difficulties are just as great as those of the Indian or Pakistani child who has only had a basic English course.

Few make special language teaching arrangements for West Indians who are considered to need remedial work, rather than to learn basic English, which is almost another language from their West Indian English. It was found that West Indian pupils were rarely dispersed even when it was the policy of the LEA concerned to spread pupils with obvious linguistic difficulties.

Detailed information of LEAs' arrangements for the teaching of English according to the number of immigrant pupils in the authority and to type of school—infant, junior or secondary—is available in Townsend's report (1971).

The Townsend (1971) study is the latest full scale survey of Local Authority arrangements but is presented in overall numerical terms.

The Select Committee on Race Relations and Immigration (1969),

Table 2.4*: *Arrangements for the teaching of English to immigrants by* 71 *LEAs out of the national total of* 146 *LEAs*

	Infant	*Junior*	*Secondary*	*Number of LEAs*	*Making a full return*
No special arrangement	12	4	0	146	71
Special arrangements do not apply to West Indian pupils	19	22	22		
Full time language centres not in ordinary schools	7	11	17		
Part time language centres not in pupil's own school	12	19	27		
Full time language centre in pupil's own school	14	19	26		
Part time language classes with pupil's own school	51	54	61		
Other arrangements	7	9	7		

* An abridged version using total figures only from Table A5, p.123: Appendix in Townsend (1971).

which visited many Local Authorities[1] and their educational institutions, heard and published evidence from a wide range of local representatives, heads, parents, administrators, leaders of organizations and citizens of both minority and indigenous origin. They print the accounts and memoranda which describe school organization and practice in these local authorities. Though the arrangements described may not be the most recent as schools' pupils' needs change, the picture of how the policies and school arrangements are determined, differently perceived, interpreted and modified by the LEA, central government policies and pressure groups in the community constitutes a fascinating document, necessary to our understanding of the 'politics' of educational arrangements. In 1973, the Select Committee commenced taking evidence on educational arrangements and problems of immigrant schoolchildren. Volume I of the Select Committee's (1973) recommendations has been published. The evidence which has been collected, and on which these are based will appear in subsequent volumes.

[1] The authorities visited are not a scientific sample of all local education authorities with multi-racial schools, but a representative cross-section of authorities throughout the country with such schools.

Townsend's second report (1972), *Organization in Multiracial Schools*, is a study of the organizational measures of a sample of multi-racial schools. It was not possible to use an objective rigorous sampling method to choose the 200 (Primary and Secondary) schools involved. These had to include certain proportions of schools with the following: West Indian, Indian, Pakistani, Kenyan, Cypriot and Italian pupils; modern and comprehensive schools; mixed and single sex schools; and schools in areas using dispersal and non-dispersal policies, and in different parts of the country. However, the technique used has enabled a fairly representative sample of schools to be chosen according to the above criteria. The main deviation was that the sample had relatively too few West Indians and too many Indians. The percentage of 'immigrant pupils' in the sample is 30 per cent in the primary schools and 22 per cent in the secondary schools, compared with the national figures of 3·6 per cent and 2·9 per cent respectively.

Townsend classifies LEAs' methods of English teaching according to the numbers of immigrant pupils in the authority, numbers with weak English, and according to type of school. Tables in the Appendix give us a good statistical picture of the situation in Britain in a completely anonymous manner.

Special arrangements are made in most LEAs with over 500 pupils and by some with less. The scale of these arrangements is very diverse, but fewer arrangements are made for infants and juniors than for secondary schoolchildren.

B. *General Survey of Organizational Structures*

Many of these structures developed on an ad hoc basis initially and were designed to fit the resources available in the LEA until the situation could be appraised and long term plans developed.

Initially, teachers catered for linguistic needs by using group methods in normal classes; other schools had withdrawal groups which received special help with language only if an extra or a remedial teacher was available. Some LEAs still use these methods. Nottingham, with more than 10 per cent of immigrant children, uses group methods.

In the early 1960s in secondary schools, where few specialized teachers were available, it was found that the immigrant children were in the lower streams of the school and in remedial, or ESN classes. This was not due to low intelligence, since few authorities had evaluated their ability levels or carried out diagnostic tests to assess their English speaking ability. Tapper and Stopes (1963) pointed out that about half the immigrants at one secondary school were placed in the 'D' stream each year. In Wolverhampton in 1969 a headmistress said most Indians and Jamaicans were in 'C' streams where teachers were teaching indigenous populations of below average ability and that it was difficult to cope with the non-English-speakers in the class as well (Select Committee 1970).

The Home Office in 1967 began to provide a 50 per cent rate support grant, under the 1966 Local Government Act towards the staffing services affected by the presence of immigrants. The Department of Education and Science also gave these areas a more generous quota allowance of teachers.

These additional resources—whether in specialist teachers or extra classrooms—the size and number of different ethnic groups as well as the philosophy of the LEA have shaped the diverse arrangements made by the authorities. In some areas the wishes of the immigrant parents, as well as those of the host community, were taken into consideration and did indeed coincide.

1. *Reception and placement of children.* Townsend (1971) finds that few local authorities make special reception arrangements, other than the two who arrange for medical inspection of new arrivals of school age. A small number interview parents and children to determine where to place the child. Two authorities have a reception centre for all immigrant pupils for an assessment and orientation period and those who need linguistic help stay on for initial language work. Other LEAs have reception centres only for non-English-speaking pupils or older secondary school pupils; these are chiefly children of Asian origin.

2. *Full-time and part-time language centres.* These (Townsend, 1971) were provided by relatively few LEAs, seven doing so for Infant pupils, 11 for Juniors and 17 for Secondary pupils. Pupils attached to these are still nominally part of a normal school. The aims of these centres varied from those who provided short intensive courses, to those who tried to include language and knowledge necessary for a full syllabus, and lengths of courses varied accordingly. Pupils are mainly Asian with few West Indians, though the latter may form a large proportion of the LEA's immigrant children. Townsend touches both on their advantages and the concentration of resources and specialized teachers and on the disadvantages of isolation from non-immigrant pupils and normal school activities. The latter disadvantages are partially overcome by part-time language centres which usually provide the same facilities, though time spent at these varies in number of weekly visits and course duration.

The research team found that some heads felt that language teaching in part-time centres might not enable the pupils to achieve 'literacy of curriculum subjects' as readily as in a full-time centre.

3. *Full-time and part-time language classes in pupils' own schools.* Local Education Authorities who provide full-time language units within the pupils' school number 14 for Infants, 19 for Juniors and 26 for Secondary pupils. This form of organization enables the children to be part of and to use the schools' facilities and may enable the language teacher to co-ordinate her work with subject language requirements of the specialist teacher.

Part-time withdrawal classes form the most popular arrangement among authorities, figures being 51 at Infant level, 54 at Junior level and 61 at Secondary level. Such withdrawal classes fit into schools' traditional practice for remedial and reading work. LEAs provide extra staff but often extra rooms and adequate aids are not available. Such classes often form follow-up periods for pupils who attend centres.

4. *West Indian children.* The survey (Townsend, 1971) also found that 10 of the LEAs with over 500 immigrant pupils did not make special arrangements for English language teaching and that of the 71 who did make special arrangements for other ethnic groups, 12 LEAs with under 1,000 West Indians and 10 with more than 1,000 West Indian pupils did not do so for these groups. This has been due chiefly to the fact that until recently it had not been realized that West Indian English is not incorrect English, but is quite a different language. Some authorities have, however, appointed peripatetic teachers of English for West Indian children and others are looking to the Schools Council Project (1970) for guidance.

C. *The organization of some LEAs and Schools*

Several studies describe in practice the variety of arrangements which specific LEAs and schools use to teach English in terms of the general pattern outlined by the above. These studies are actual examples of the organizational practices of schools and centres which, though they are likely to alter and adapt to new teaching developments and demographic changes over time, show us how they operate in real situations. Such descriptions are valuable to read about in full, both to understand the background and to realize how current procedures arose.

1. *Withdrawal groups or classes in schools and centres*[1]. Specialist teachers are employed in Birmingham. The ways in which they are deployed are: (1) teaching in 15 specialist classes pupils who are drawn from three schools, but who meet in one school for these particular lessons; (2) teaching about 60 small groups, in the children's own schools, three times a week. The children participate with the English children in the main part of the school. Bradford

[1] Select Committee (1969) Vol. II, page 643.

has been distributing its non-English-speaking Asians to full time language tuition centres since 1965 when large numbers of Asian children aged 13+ began arriving.

The Inner London Education Authority has centres where special staff members teach non-English speakers from secondary schools. One of these, in Battersea, is described by Lee (1965). Other secondary schools have their own arrangements. The primary school immigrant children are catered for in their own schools with the help of off-quota teachers. In larger centres some teachers work part-time in the centre and part-time with groups of children in their own school.

Hackney has set up seven centres for special tuition in languages, mainly for older pupils who need intensive teaching before they can join in other activities. They spend part of their time at the school and part at the centre. Dispersal is considered neither feasible nor desirable.

Wolverhampton follows a dispersal scheme to keep a 60/40 ratio of immigrants to non-immigrants in the schools. It has 60 reception classes in junior and secondary schools with 24 children per class and welfare assistants for some classes. Of the 51 immigrant teachers in the schools, 33 are in charge of classes of immigrant children.

Huddersfield, until September 1964, channelled all of its immigrant school population (2·8 per cent) into Spring Grove School, which had a special English department. Children were taught to speak English, reading and writing, and joined the main school for subjects such as PE and needlework. When sufficiently well-established they joined the appropriate primary or secondary school near their homes. Burgin and Edson (1966) described the work of this school at that period. This reception centre technique was also used by such boroughs as Bradford, Bolton and Slough. In September 1964, Huddersfield had to establish special English departments at other primary and secondary schools. Spring Grove is still a reception and distribution centre. The children stay for a period of six weeks. They have early social training for school routine, learn basic English, recover from cultural shock, if recent arrivals, and are then transferred with the teacher to an appropriate school for an intensive English course and ultimately placed in a class commensurate with their ability to follow a normal timetable. This ensures that only one school has over 30 per cent of immigrant children on the roll, six schools have over 20 per cent, 23 have over 10 per cent and the rest range from 0 to 10 per cent (Select Committee, 1969, *Problems of Coloured School Leavers,* vol III, pp 590–660).

The West Indian children are treated separately from non-English speaking children and are placed in neighbourhood schools. If their language is inadequate and social readjustment appears warranted, they receive special tuition. This has been met by a diagnostic testing unit for newly arrived children over the age of eight which helps in placement and treatment and by a team of peripatetic specialist teachers under the control of the Senior Remedial teacher. There are also tutorial classes within the schools for maladjusted children who are not ESN.

Burgin, at that time (1968) a deputy CEO with special responsibility for immigrants, has had an organizer co-ordinating all activities with those of the teachers, the School Psychological Service and Educational Welfare Services (Select Committee, 1969, vol III, p. 659).

Birmingham, in the 1960s under Chapman, set up a department for the teaching of English as a second language and used a team of peripatetic teachers for withdrawal classes in schools with small numbers of English speakers or at full-time language centres. As there was initially a shortage of teachers of English as a second language, they organized training sessions at evening classes and workshop sessions for newcomers on the specialist team. Later in 1968 these facilities were extended to the ordinary class teacher (Rose, 1969).

2. *Some secondary school arrangements.* Ealing has special reception classes in one secondary school. Children are given intensive lessons in English and introduced to other subjects or interests when they are able to understand the language. Oxford's secondary school has no adequate facilities for this category. Students are given the beginning of language teaching and at 15 transfer to Colleges of Further Education.

Wigg (1970) in the TES describes Wolverhampton arrangements at the Eastfield Language Centre which takes secondary school age children for two terms when they first arrive. The children have a full time crash course in English and are introduced to science, maths and visit the community. After two terms they go into secondary schools but are helped by peripatetic teachers.

In a secondary school in High Wycombe, Tempest-Woods (1970) reports how non-English speaking children are taught separately for the first two years. The children are taught English through the specialist subject of their year group, geography, mathematics, science and social science. There is a high staff and volunteer ratio to enable new arrivals to receive individual coaching. They study the recorder, art, PE, woodwork and house crafts with the school's specialist teachers. It is hoped that by the third year they will be able to move into the normal third year class.

3. *The older non-English-speaking adolescent.* Authorities have a variety of arrangements to cope with the older child whose English is

inadequate and for the later arrival who may have only a year at school before commencing work. There is also a tendency, regardless of ability, for a higher proportion of immigrant children than those in the host community to wish to continue to Further Education to obtain higher qualifications or skilled training, as indicated by several studies by Beetham (1969) and Tylor, J. (1971). For example, in Wolverhampton in 1968, 47 per cent of the immigrant school leavers elected to continue further education against 31 per cent of the indigenous population. (Select Committee on Immigration, 1969, 'Memo to County Borough of Wolverhampton' Vol. II).

Ealing's Pathway Centre commenced in 1966 to help the immigrants over 15 years old who present special problems to the Youth Employment Service. It is equipped with a language laboratory and a staff briefed to help students be absorbed into the work community. It gives specific vocational training with the help of the local technical colleges, who provide facilities in the form of pre-apprenticeship training and workshop practice.

It also offers day release facilities for immigrants at work who have been selected for further training but who need special help with their English first. It assists employers who wish to take advantage of a grant from the Industrial Training Board to have language classes at work. One such Pilot Project undertaken by the Pathway Further Education Centre (1970) to teach industrial English to a group of Asian women in company time is described. Redhead (1972) in the *Financial Times* and Runnymede Trust (1972) (Occ. Reprint 5) describes other such courses run by the Pathway Industrial Unit under Jupp and an evaluation of results in terms of productivity increases is given. Runnymede Trust has incorporated this in its Occ. Reprint 5.

Hackney has a centre for older immigrants who have defective educational background, as well as five Colleges of Further Education out of its 13, who have general education courses for those who cannot fit into the secondary school syllabus. These Colleges also provide pre-specialist courses and vocationally biased courses for students still in secondary school, and plan to extend it to young immigrants on day release. (Select Committee, 1969, Vol. II.)

The proposal to establish language teaching in association with Youth Clubs and Recreational Institutes is considered to act as a focus and impetus to better knowledge of the language.

The College of Further Education at Oxford has special English classes for all those over 15 who need help in language. They may take the same range of courses available for all students, but extra tuition and tutorial help is available in the subjects of their choice if this is necessary, whether in General Studies, Engineering,

Commerce or other subjects. In Wolverhampton, the College of Further Education tests for ability to follow normal courses and provides pre-entry courses in English, Mathematics, Crafts or skilled subjects if they are not up to standard (Select Committee, 1969, Vol. II).

A limited pilot study in 1969/70 of a representative section of secondary schools with different immigrant ethnic groups (though a selective sample) provides similar information and comes to similar conclusions as other studies on this topic (DES Survey 14, 1972). In its study of arrangements for adolescents it finds that, though many of the immigrants have help to overcome the initial difficulties of communication, there is a need for more efficient ways of enabling them to acquire a mastery of more complex language.

It describes specific practices of some LEAs and schools and assesses their advantages, difficulties and disadvantages. It stresses the need of total staff involvement on a systematic basis in terms of an overall school policy in relation 'to the linguistic, intellectual and social needs of second phase immigrant pupils'. Such a policy will enable English departments, where the staff have had appropriate training, to work out effective schemes for second phase pupils. This study shows how much has yet to be done to develop adequate second phase work for immigrant children to enable them to profit fully from secondary school education. The two latter studies cited have carefully studied the arrangements for second phase English teaching and believe that the difficulties for the E2L pupil or West Indian pupil are far from resolved.

A number of studies discuss the variety of arrangements from Hawkes (1966), Schools Council Working Paper 13 (1967) and Bowker's book (1969). The most recent are by the DES (1971, 1972) and Townsend (1971). The Select Committee (1973) describes English language teaching practices in schools in the areas visited, showing great variety in organization. Difficulties from the E2L pupils do not appear to be resolved at the second level English stage. Townsend (1971) and his research team point out that the pupil may have many handicaps to overcome.

1. His previous education in his home country may have been inadequate or intermittant.

2. The time spent in learning English may cause him to miss subject background for secondary school curriculum.

3. His subject teachers do not have time to teach him the language of their subject speciality.

4. He may have difficulty in understanding the variety of teachers' accents in the secondary school.

He suggests that this indicates a need for research to establish whether there is a necessity for further help to handle the backlog of subject language and subject content.

4. *Dispersal.* The Department of Education and Science (1971) pointed out that in 1970 there was no dispersal in about two-thirds of the 64 areas with significant numbers of immigrant pupils, marginal dispersal in about a quarter, and that daily dispersal was practised by only 11 areas. In only three cases was this done on a large scale, as Townsend's (1971) studies of LEA policies indicated.

The DES (1971) discusses the arguments for and against dispersal, admitting candidly that no research is available as to the advantage or disadvantages of such a policy.

The ground for dispersal in circular 7/65 was 'educational need'. There are two aspects of educational need:

1. the language education aspect;
2. the cultural education aspect.

They state that it is far more efficient in terms of scarce specially trained teachers and expensive special teaching resources for children to be taught standard English in schools or centres where these can be concentrated.

However, equally, evidence of the importance of education in the cultural background of a society, its concepts and usages, for realization of any immigrant's intellectual potential, has been brought out by psychological studies listed in Chapter 4, which show the importance of cultural factors on test performances. On these grounds it is believed by some educationists that immigrant children and those children of recent immigrants, would gain by 'learning about their new environment from their non-immigrant contemporaries'.

The difficulties of evaluating this view—a long term project—are seen in American attempts to assess the effects of school integration on black Americans.

The opportunity for children of the indigenous population to learn about the culture and common humanity[1] of children from different ethnic groups cannot, however, be overestimated, assuming the school takes advantage of their multi-racial population for multicultural education. On educational grounds, the disadvantages of dispersal, particularly for parents of primary school children is that the child is involved in long journeys and that his parents cannot readily visit the school.

The legal, administrative and financial problems of a dispersal policy are pointed out.

[1] Studies point out that such a step does occur, where children are found to recognize leadership and academic superiority, regardless of ethnic origin, even though social integration within and after school may not occur.

1. Under the Race Relations Act of 1968 dispersal on racial grounds is illegal.

2. If a percentage of children from all immigrant schools are dispersed, then shall empty places be filled by allocating these to indigenous children from other areas, or shall these schools gradually be resited in areas of mixed settlement?

3. The financial cost of busing and provision of extra accommodation in receiving schools can be very heavy.

The Department, in presenting these problems, and the following conclusions, comment that the latter modifies significantly their views on dispersal in circular 7/65 (DES, 1971).

1. 'Busing of primary school children should not be undertaken unless there is a compelling need to do so.'

2. 'That each local authority should keep its arrangements for the education of immigrant children under review in light of the changing educational needs of pupils.'

3. 'That no policy affecting groups or categories of children should be allowed to override the reasonable wishes of individual parents in the matter of choice of school.'

As they point out, many immigrant parents prefer their children to attend muti-racial schools and their wishes have been consulted by many dispersing authorities. With the exception of the latter, the Select Committee (1973) recommends that dispersal be phased out. However, neither the Department nor research evidence is as yet able to answer the question as to whether dispersal or non-dispersal will have the better influence on educational and integrational needs of immigrant or indigenous children.

Little *et al.* (1971), in a literacy study of junior and junior infant schools in all Inner London Education Authority schools concerned with children in their second year of junior schooling found that children who go to schools which have a higher percentage of immigrants do not suffer noticeably when judged by reading ability. He also found that the immigrants do not benefit much from being in schools where they are in the minority. Differences in reading quotient were related less to class size than to whether or not children came from homes where parents were interested in their educational progress.

III. The Education of Teachers for a Multi-racial Society

A. *Training of Teachers*

The study and evaluation of the best methods of teaching English as a second language to children who speak no English or who speak a dialect English—children who in addition are adapting to two cultures—and the training of teachers to help these children should preferably be two separate projects.

The Schools Council instigated two curriculum development research projects: one for all immigrant children, and a later one for West Indian children. These projects, which, together with related ones, will be discussed in the later chapters, also run courses for teachers on their methods of teaching English to particular groups.

However, owing to the necessity of coping with large numbers of children already in the classrooms, it was important to provide some training for teachers on the basis of the information available. The teachers involved with immigrant pupils by the mid-1960s had formed two organizations which acted as self-help groups who pressed for such courses for their members.

The National Association for Multi-racial Education, commenced as *The Association for Teachers of English to Pupils from Overseas* (ATEPO). ATEPO was concerned initially with helping the teacher of immigrant children with the linguistic aspects of their education reflected in the title of its journal 'English for Immigrants', though it was aware of the social factors influencing linguistic deficiencies. When the organization became a National Federation of associations, it broadened its objectives. It now aims to educate *all* pupils for life and understanding in our muti-cultural, multi-racial society. It has been influential in suggesting research to the Schools Council on provision of materials and procedures to achieve the aims they supported. (ATEPO, 1970, *English for Immigrants,* v 33. Its journal is now called *Multi-racial School.*)

The Association of Teachers of English as a Foreign Language, (ATEFL) is for teachers who are teaching English as a second language at home or abroad. Both organizations have conferences and seminars for their members, study groups, and also publish journals. ATEPO publishes booklets by members on their techniques and experiences (ATEPO 1972).

Although these organizations provide invaluable help for their members by enabling them to benefit from one another's experience in teaching immigrant children with different problems, the schemes usually deal with limited aspects of language teaching and particular age groups.

The primary need was for courses to be developed for non-specialist teachers in methods of teaching English to children in multi-racial classes. One of the first to initiate such a course was the University of London Institute of Education, which established a one-year course leading to a Diploma in the teaching of English as a foreign language. It also began an experimental one-term course for primary school teachers to teach by the direct method under the direction of Anne Blatch. Other areas set up similar courses, but often Institutes and Colleges such as Leeds and Edgehill College of Education found a shortage of applicants due to the fact that schools felt that they could not spare their teachers for a term. Many Universities' Departments of Education and/or Departments of Languages and some Colleges have courses in English as a second language for graduates and teachers. The academic courses in Universities and Colleges relevant to the teaching of English as a foreign language are listed by the English Teaching Information Centre (ETIC, 1970; published yearly) and by 1970 show that, although many courses are designed for a variety of students, including those for British and overseas students, some lead to higher degrees or to a qualification in Linguistics. There are also a limited number designed for graduates or experienced teachers, either British or foreign, intending to teach English as a second language in Britain; these may be of a year, a term or a week's duration. These are listed in Teacher's Course List No. 1 and in the Teacher's Short Course List, both published annually by the Department (DES, 1972/1973a, b). The number of short courses on the teaching of English to immigrants has increased to 14 during 1969 to 1971.

The DES has organized a series of courses for overseas teachers in Colleges throughout the country. In the six centres established between 1966 and 1969, 15 courses have been in session involving 320 students. (DES, Education Survey 13, 1971). Dakin (1971), who has conducted a survey of courses for immigrant teachers, many of whom are Asian, claims that there are not enough courses for the estimated 2,000 to 3,000 who, though qualified, need further training in language and methods before they can teach in Britain. The Committee on Research and Development in Modern Languages has a list of several ongoing research projects in their files in the area of teacher training courses. The Select Committee (1973) says that 430 teachers, mainly Asian, have been on DES courses to improve their English and knowledge of British education. However, the total number of immigrant teachers is not known.

More recently, Colleges of Education have begun to take up the challenge of providing courses for their students to teach children to live in a multi-racial society, but these are mainly on the cultural background of the immigrants, on prejudice and on race relations.

Townsend (1970) found that about one per cent of the teachers had recorded attendances at courses in 1964–67, though he found that many had not included a single lecture or course of a day's duration.

The DES (1970) made a report as well, which, in conjunction with the Townsend (1971) study, suggests that about 300 courses, from a single lecture to a year's course, will have catered for 10,000 teachers in 1969–70. These courses are provided by LEAs, DES, universities, colleges, the Schools Council and other bodies. The DES points out that LEAs provide half the total courses. The majority of these, as Townsend (1971) demonstrates in Table A21, are very brief. The majority are part-time and of less than a week's duration. During this period longer courses, provided by other bodies, consisted of one-term, full-time courses followed by 108 teachers from 23 LEAs and those of one year's duration followed by 34 teachers from 14 LEAs.

Thirty of the LEAs who make special arrangements for immigrant pupils have no in-service training. Often LEAs which provided courses found that among secondary school teachers, only English and remedial teachers were interested. The research team found that authorities which employed peripatetic teachers to staff its language centres and classes, had adequate in-service training.

The number, type, duration of in-service courses provided by LEAs and other institutions during the period of 1967–70 is indicated in several tables in Townsend's (1971) work. Other educational activities relating to the education of immigrant pupils such as working parties, book exhibitions, centre activities, are also given.

Specific examples of some of the types of in-service training schemes run by LEAs in areas of high immigrant pupil population have been described in some studies. The ILEA has a one-term course for teachers who have had some teaching experience. Truman (1970) describes the approach used, which is to train the teachers to talk within controlled limits of structure and vocabulary and to help them devise instructional material appropriate to the age and language level of the pupils.

Hackney has one research centre and 40 local teacher centres. Programmes include a variety of courses to help teachers understand and deal with problems of immigrant children, as well as those of socially deprived and handicapped children. It also trains teachers in the skills of teaching English as a second language.

Huddersfield runs in-service training courses for its own teachers. There is one major course per term. These are:

1. *Induction Courses* for newly appointed teachers, which cover talks on immigrants' social backgrounds, language teaching skills, and displays of equipment and books.

2. *Weekly Teach-ins* for overseas teachers, consisting of topics such as speech, methodology, out-of-school activities and teaching practice with groups.

3. *Experienced Teachers' Study Groups*, which study groups and production of teaching materials and have close liaison with School Council projects.

Bradford attaches its teachers without experience of teaching immigrant children to one of its language centres where she observes and helps experienced teachers, until she is trained. Each centre acts as a reference and information centre for teachers in the area. Birmingham uses its specialist teachers for in-service training of teachers in their own schools (DES, 1971). The ILEA has established centres for teachers in training directed by teachers with training in English as a second language. Teachers go from these centres, once trained, to schools in special centres (Truman, 1970).

The Department describes the work of other areas in In-service Training as well as the importance of 'the growing involvement of teachers of immigrant children in curriculum development work and in the production of teaching materials at Teachers' Centres set up by Local Education Authorities' (DES, 1971).

However, it points out that there is still a continuing and pressing need for appropriate in-service courses organized by Local Education Authorities, since there are significant numbers of teachers teaching immigrant children who have not had any training in this field.

Although the Department believes that initial training for all student teachers should have courses designed to help them promote harmonious community relations, they point out that, since only a small proportion of these will be teaching immigrant children in their first post, courses on specific techniques may not be appropriate for all. Other than those who have a vocation for this field, it is not always possible for Colleges to provide teaching practice in immigrant schools, although some have taken the initiative in exchanging students, in order to enable their own students to have this opportunity in high immigrant contact areas.

The Education Officer of the CRC has also recently compiled a register of Colleges and Institutes of Education who offer facilities for field work and teaching practice in specialized options including that of teaching English as a second language, and who are able to exchange students. (CRC Education Officer, 1971).

It also drew up a register with details of Local Authority Projected Summer Programmes who wished to use Colleges of Education Volunteers. This register was circulated to the Colleges of Education. (CRC Education Officer, 1971b).

B. *Education for a Multi-Cultural Society*

A survey conducted by the Education panel of the NCCI asked colleges to delineate between their courses relating to race relations into two categories. Those whose main emphasis was on:

1. The Education of Immigrant Children and Adults (EIC), enabling the educationist to impart the basic technique and social skills to the immigrant community.

2. Education for a Multi-Cultural Society (EMCS) through promotion of understanding and tolerance on the host community.

In 1966 under category 1, it was found that 15 per cent of the Colleges provided or intended to provide such systematic courses (IRR Newletter, January 1966). By autumn of 1968, it was found that in the 113 Colleges who replied to the second NCCI questionnaire, 53 per cent were providing courses of a systematic nature, eight per cent were proposing to institute such a course and 39 per cent did not plan to do so. The Teacher Training and Curriculum Development Group of the Community Relations Commission (CRC, 1970), under its chairman, T. Millins, has studied and published the syllabuses and course teaching practices of Colleges of Education. It distinguished between those Colleges which offered or proposed to offer courses designed for all students in a complete year group (CYG—33 per cent) and those for self-selected students (some students) who chose to specialize in the education of immigrant children (39 per cent).

The syllabuses offered cover a variety of approaches to the problems of teaching immigrant children. Those designed for a complete year group (CYG) are usually short courses of 10 hours or less and accordingly can deal only briefly with the history of immigration, analysis of cultural patterns of the main ethnic minorities in Britain, racial prejudice and discrimination, school organization in areas of immigrant settlement and the language problem.

Those designed for 'some students', who choose a specialized course, are of longer duration, more comprehensive and specialized. In these, one-third have a bias towards language studies, one-third towards sociological and psychological considerations, and the remaining one-third strike a balance between the two. The organization of these courses varies according to the number of departments involved, the nearness to schools with immigrant children and the duration of the course.

The majority of the syllabuses are thorough in their analysis of sociological, psychological and political aspects relevant to the immigrant communities' integration and adjustment. English language teaching schemes stress the structural situational approach as the best foundation for reading and written work, though techniques vary.

Education for a multi-cultural society is the second type of course given in Colleges of Education which attempts to encourage and promote mutual tolerance and acceptance between immigrant and host community.

The 1966 Report indicated that about 30 per cent of the Colleges were providing systematic courses. The latest Report shows that 31 per cent now do so.

In the two fields EIC and EMCS no colleges were providing for the complete year groups of students in both categories of courses. Eighteen per cent of the colleges were providing for CYG in one category and 'some' students in the other. Ten per cent of the colleges were providing for 'some' students in both categories.

Altogether 66 per cent of the colleges were providing systematic courses in one of the two fields. In many colleges, however, studies of immigrant children and race relations are integral elements in courses on Developmental and Social Psychology, Educational Priority Areas, Language in Society, Deprivation, Social Geography, and others, but it has not been possible to tabulate these elements.

This report shows the advances colleges of education have been making in providing more courses for their students enabling them to develop immigrant children's potential. The advance in courses to promote a favourable attitude towards a multi-racial society has been slower.

A Newsletter for Colleges and University Departments of Education was commenced by the CRC in 1973 which publishes courses and syllabuses in progress at colleges in the country. Information about resources and books teaching English as a Second Language and multi-cultural and multi-racial education as well as forthcoming conferences are features of the journal (CRC, 1973, *Teacher Training and Community Relations*).

Candlin and Derrick's (1973) study quoting results of a pilot survey of language study in colleges is discussed in Chapter III.

The Select Committee on Race Relations and Immigration (1973) *Report on Education*, Vol 1., in its chapter on teacher training, points out that:

1. it found 'in-service training is inadequate' and that LEAs should, with the cooperation of educational institutions, expand in-service courses for teachers in multi-cultural schools and arrange specialist training of teachers in those schools, perhaps by visiting groups;
2. that further training is needed for teachers and lecturers to be able to provide realistic effective courses for multi-cultural education;
3. their evidence suggests that there is a serious and continuing shortage of teachers able to teach English as a second language and teachers to train them, and that steps must be taken to meet this need;

4. 'All students on initial or post-graduate courses can and should be aware that wherever they teach, they will be doing so in a multi-cultural society';

5. that there should be more immigrant teachers employed, since their numbers are not proportionate to the immigrant population, and that their own experiences and insights will make them valuable as teachers in multi-cultural schools.

The three main problems which face those who are concerned with the education of 'immigrant' children, are still those which were considered prominent by Goldman and Taylor (1966), and discussed in detail by the Schools Council WP 13 (1967). These problems are:

1. language education;
2. problems in assessing present and potential ability levels;
3. problems of social, and cultural integration.

The greatest advances have probably been made in the field of language education. This is undoubtedly the first necessity since without adequate language the child cannot learn in the schools, realize his potential, or interact meaningfully with those from the host community.

The progress of research and descriptions of classroom practices as outlined in published material, in these three fields, will be discussed in subsequent chapters.

CHAPTER THREE

Language Education

I. Introduction

English language acquisition is the most important need for the non-English or inadequate English speaking child, whether born abroad or in this country. 'For native or immigrant children, English is the key to their future in this country, thus the teacher has to see that they acquire language for the full range of communication within the school' (Derrick, 1968). Until he can learn to speak, understand, read and write the language used in schools, a child cannot learn specific skills nor develop his potential ability.

Alleyne (1962, 1965), in his study on the effect of bi-lingualism on educational attainment, compared bi-lingual groups with a control group of matched mono-linguals. He found that on three objective tests of educational performance the mono-linguals were significantly superior to bi-linguals. Even when the experimental and control groups were matched on non-verbal ability tests it was found that bi-linguals were inferior to mono-linguals on the verbal ability tests. There was clear evidence that bi-lingual deficiency was due to the experimental group's lack of involvement in English life and culture. It was meaningful that native bi-linguals were not found to be significantly inferior to their paired mono-linguals, whereas the foreign bi-linguals showed a distinct inferiority. The greatest danger Alleyne discerned was that the child learns the language for a certain segment of the environment in which he will operate, and another language for other specific situations. Alleyne's findings emphasize the need to develop an oral approach and the necessity of learning the language in relation to real life situations, as well as reading skills.

A. *Importance of Language for Intellectual, Emotional and Social Development*

The work of Bernstein (1958, 1960) in recent years, in analysing the influence of types of language learned on ways of thinking and the development of verbal intelligence in the sub-cultures of our own society, has made us aware of the importance of an adequate language for a child to develop its intellectual potential. Through his studies of the speech of the lower working-class and middle-class boys he developed his concepts of language types, the 'restricted code' and the 'elaborated code', to describe their respective modes of speech (Bernstein, 1961). Those brought up to speak a syntactically simple, restricted language were found to think in this same uncomplicated way, even though they may genetically have been able to conceptualize at a higher level had they had the linguistic equipment. Those using the 'elaborated code' possessed a more complex structure and variety in their pattern of language which enabled them to think on a more abstract level than the first group.

Bernstein believes that modes of speech are related to differences in social and cultural environment of children—especially their family structure and child rearing practices. Lawton (1968), who extended Bernstein's work, found that children from the two codes continue to diverge through the secondary school.

Bernstein's and Lawton's work has led educationists to consider compensatory language programmes for children who are culturally and linguistically deprived. Many educationists stress the importance of pre-school education so that the very young child may have the extra social and language development which will furnish him with the linguistic tools to benefit from the infant school at five. [These children need smaller classes and individual attention to develop linguistic competence (Lawton, 1968).] Pre-school programmes will be discussed more fully at the end of the chapter.

Many of Bernstein's research findings are also relevant to the education of immigrant children, who, though born here, may not speak English or standard English nor be familiar with our social ways. Teachers of immigrant children who are teaching children English should be aware that, in so doing, they are also introducing them to our culture, whose adult/child relationships, values and attitudes may not only be different from those in their own homes but may also clash with these. In a collection of Bernstein's research (1971, 1972) over a 12-year period, he concludes that the types of social relationships and role systems in a family (whether positional or person-centred) will influence and determine the verbal and planning procedures used. Such procedures and codes influence a child's social and emotional orientation to his environment.

The child in today's situation of exposure to the school and the media is exposed, he stresses, to the 'elaborated code' but must be given the opportunity to use it and practise it, particularly in the school context. However, in so doing, it must be recognized, he stresses, that not only a person's linguistic patterns are being altered but often their patterns of social roles and social relationships and, possibly, values.

Lewis (1970) argues that a pre-school child is too young to reconcile the two cultures and to cope with the two languages before his own mother tongue is firmly established in its appropriate setting. He believes that teachers must recognize that these school children may have different patterns of cognitive and emotional development encapsulated in their first language. These differences must be adapted to and understood in teaching them English.

Although Lewis' point of view may be valid in some cases, there is as yet no research evidence in this country to support it. Krear (1969) believes that the school should not discourage the child from using his own language at school, when not learning English. The child may develop a sense of guilt or loss or identity otherwise.

Bi-lingual education: An approach which believes that the minority primary school child should be taught in his mother tongue while he learns English carries Lewis' view to a further stage. The promotion of bilingual and bi-cultural education is a relatively new type of programme founded in the United States in 1967, when the Bilingual Education Act was passed. This is the first federal legislation to promote the preservation of non-English languages spoken in the USA by supporting their use as mediums of instruction in government schools (Gaarder, 1972). Gaarder points out that the Office of Education interpretation of bilingual education, is of a well organized programme which encompasses all or part of the curriculum and includes the study of the history and culture associated with the mother tongue. Federal funds have been made available for over 134 bilingual education projects in 30 states. Gaarder, who has made a preliminary study of the first 74 bilingual projects, analyses some of their difficulties, achievements and models for teacher training. His focus is on the case of the Mexican-Americans, nevertheless the rationale of bilingual education which he outlines, is applicable to children from all ethnic groups in any country.

1. To avoid retardation in children who enter school with insufficient command of English to enable them to make normal progress through English as the school medium.
2. To facilitate a strong, mutually-reinforcing relationship between the school and the home community.
3. To avoid the destructive effect on the child's self-concept which may result when his own language and culture are ignored and scorned; conversely, to give him the strength which comes with a secure sense of his own identity and worth.
4. To give him the advantage—when he becomes an adult—of being fully literate in two languages.

5. To preserve the national resource which is our people's native knowledge of foreign languages. (Gaarder, 1972, p. 69.)

Conte (1971) points out that the child can progress academically as fast as he is able in his own tongue. Since language and culture are inseparable he will be taught bi-culturally as well, which should reinforce his self-image and cultural patterns. It is hoped the child will be better adjusted socially and academically.

Conte quotes research and bilingual English language projects in Los Angeles. In Britain we may be able to draw on our experience of bilingual education which occurs in the Gaelic highlands of Scotland and the Welsh-speaking schools in Wales, but we should also study bilingual education projects in the United States and their implications for the education of our own British ethnic minority children where relevant.

B. *Types of Linguistic Limitations*

Linguistic limitations among children from different ethnic groups may be present in varying degrees and be classified into the following categories:

1. *Total language deficiency*, where not only is a foreign language spoken, but the written script is alien.
2. *Partial language deficiency*, where some, but very little English is spoken in the home, or where the child has acquired some English from a longer residence here. The vernacular script may or may not be based upon the western alphabet.
3. *Dialect impediments*, where some children may speak English fluently, but dialect interposes, or a 'pidgin' English is spoken so that problems of listening, interpreting, and later reading and writing are present. This is a particular problem for some West Indians where Creole dialects are evident.

As has been mentioned in the previous chapter, teachers of immigrant children initially drew on courses used for pupils overseas or on methods used to teach English to children who already spoke English. However, neither of these methods was really appropriate. The Schools Council Working Paper 13 (1967) points out that overseas language courses are not often related to language as a social or educational medium and use contrasting analysis of the pupil's own language in relation to its English teaching. In Britain, few language classes are organized on the basis of one ethnic group alone.

Teaching English as a mother tongue is not language teaching, since it pre-supposes the ability to understand, speak and think in English and is really teaching the skills of reading and writing. Neither method is strictly appropriate to the immigrant child here.

Little research had been done on the language teaching needs of immigrant children of different language groups who were represented in Britain in 1966. Research projects had to decide what skills in English immigrant children needed in order to work with 'English' children and benefit from education in Britain.

As the Schools Council Working Party pointed out (1967), 'though the question can be answered educationally, it cannot be answered linguistically until an analysis is made of language used in the classroom by English speaking pupils and teachers in all subjects at different stages'. This is being done by the *Child Language Survey* (1970), commenced in 1965 and now supported by the Committee for Research and Development in Modern Languages at York University in co-operation with the Schools Council Modern Languages Project. Surveys of language patterns of children of eight to 12 years and 13 to 15 years have been made and some of the material published (*Dialogue*, 6, 1970 and *Child Language Survey*, 1970). Only then, as they point out also 'can reliable tests of English proficiency for immigrant children be constructed to facilitate their initial placement and transfer to normal classes' (Schools Council Working Paper 13, 1967, p. 26).

However, as the survey by the Schools Council (1967) found, neither teacher nor the curriculum development team could wait for such research. Many teachers of immigrant children had formed associations, such as ATEPO (The Association of Teachers of English to Pupils from Overseas), throughout the country to pool their experiences and techniques and they also organized workshop sessions. Teachers felt their most urgent need was for specially designed materials and for help in making their own schemes. A knowledge of language grading was required to develop this kind of material and most teachers did not have the necessary training nor the time to prepare the lessons. Few texts were available and Derrick's (1966) was one of the first which used the structural approach to language teaching and listed other text books and sources of audio-visual material in this country.

II. Curriculum Development and Action Research Projects

A. *Objectives of Schools Council Curriculum Development Project: English for Immigrant Children*

I shall now discuss the Schools Council Curriculum Development projects for teaching English to immigrant children; the objectives are:

1. to prepare ranges of materials and carefully graded language schemes to meet the needs of teachers of non-English speaking

children to enable them to achieve an adequate command of English for school and society;

2. to support the provision of in-service training to explain the purpose of the new material to teachers and give teachers an opportunity to use and criticize them and to offer some positive suggestions.

Although it was recognized that there were often different teaching problems for each ethnic language group—Indians, Pakistanis, West Indians and other nationalities—which should be handled distinctively, it was decided that, until research evidence became available, the first priority was to produce general teaching material for all non-English speaking children. The project team, under the project leader, June Derrick, consisted of experienced teachers, a linguist, a sociologist and an artist.

They decided to concentrate their resources on an all-purpose English Introductory Course for children between eight and 15 years, regardless of ethnic group, which would give them a good grounding in oral English and introduce them to simple reading and writing. It was planned so that teachers could adapt it to the length of time they had programmed to teach their immigrant pupils—whether for a whole day, or part of a day—and to the size of the group—a whole class or a small group.

1. *Introductory courses: juniors, Scope I; and Scope senior course*. The introductory course provides a scheme which links the language to topics of interest that seem relevant to the child's experiences. Fourteen situational themes which revolve around language necessary in such places as: The classroom, the family and home, shopping, visiting the doctor, etc. are used as a basis to teach spoken English and then to start them learning to read and write English. The teacher's book outlines the language scheme which emphasizes the structural patterns of English. Visual aid material was prepared and designed to help children talk about familiar situations. The scheme was then tested by 140 teachers of non-English speaking children after they had attended a briefing conference. Fitchett (1967) describes how he used the material in his classroom and the ways in which it could be adapted to a variety of teaching situations. During this period the teachers also met in groups to discuss their problems and sent back their comments to the team; team members visited classrooms to see their material in use. As a result of teachers' suggestions, the course was revised and re-written and was published in 1969 as *Scope I*, Schools Council: 'English for Immigrant Children' (EIC).

Teaching materials consist of magnetic board figures, wall pictures, work cards, flash cards and records, as well as picture books, work books and readers. The language of the reading scheme is based on the oral work.

Scope Senior Course (*Schools Council: EIC*, 1972) is an alternative to Scope I. The material is written for newly-arrived children aged 14 to 16, in Secondary Schools and Further Education establishments, for adults. This course is built around the interests and social needs of the recently arrived non-English speaking pupils and has books for teachers and pupils on life in England and about finding work. It uses simple, controlled speech related to basic themes such as 'At The Grocers', 'Can you tell me the way?', in Book I, *We live in England*, and progresses in Book 2, *Out and About in England*, to sections on—'Finding out about Jobs', 'At the Hospital', 'The Interview', which requires more complex language; and then to Book 3, *Ready for Work*. Tapes and work books are also available.

2. *Second stage course for multi-cultural classrooms: Scope* 2. (Schools Council EIC, 1972), *Scope* 2 is designed for children aged eight to 13 years who are at the second stage of language learning. It uses a thematic approach—building up language schemes for learning, thinking and communication, on the basis of the subjects or themes which are studied often in schools, e.g. Homes, Water and Travel. The materials consist of pupil's books, teacher's book and work cards.

The schemes may be used in multi-racial classes or in a specialist class for children who have difficulty in use of English, whether they are English or E2L speakers, or children who speak a dialect form of English.

Each theme is divided into topics and resource materials, such as stories, information and pictures, are provided. Cards are graded at different levels of difficulty and enable children to practise their language on an individual or group basis. The *Homes* book has chapters on the pupils' homes, street furniture, British architecture and land transport (*Education and Community Relations*, 9, 1972).

The Scope Handbook 2 by Rudd (1971b) deals with pronunciation difficulties for non-English speakers from India, Pakistan, Cyprus and Italy and gives methods and practice material to help.

B. *Other projects*. The National Foundation for Educational Research and the Committee for Research and Development in Modern Languages have co-operated in a Project to construct diagnostic tests for different aspects of English proficiency for junior school children, for whom standard English is not their first language. This Project is described in chapter IV (Rudd, 1971a, b). Doughty, Pearce and Thornton (1972) of the Schools Council Programme in Linguistics and English Teaching have produced material to 'make more effective the teaching of the mother tongue in schools' which is relevant both for pure English teachers as well as those in multi-racial classrooms.

In the four Educational Priority Areas curriculum development was regarded as an essential part of the programme, one of whose aims was to raise educational standards. Although most areas concentrated their language development work with the pre-school age group, some, such as Birmingham and the West Riding, aimed to improve reading and language in the primary school-age group. Halsey (1972) describes these projects. Some evaluation was possible but results were not always positive since courses and other variables could not be rigorously controlled. However, the function of these projects is seen as a pilot for future national effort and much was learned about planning programmes and the influence of uncontrolled variables on the outcome.

B. *Schools Council Project: English for West Indian Children*

1. *Studies of West Indian Creole Dialect English.* During the survey conducted by Derrick the teachers pointed out that the learning problems of the majority of West Indian children who spoke a dialect English required a different approach to that of immigrants who were completely non-English speaking. It was also found that English-born children of West Indian parents had learning problems similar to those children born in the Caribbean and that both groups formed significant proportions in urban schools. The problem of teaching standard English to those speaking West Indian dialects was recognized by educationists in the West Indies. Jones (1965) at the University of the West Indies, studied the dialect English used by many West Indians and outlined the difficulties in teaching them English as a foreign language, Jones (1966). Research to ascertain the languages at present in use in the West Indies has been undertaken by Cassidy (1961) and Cassidy and Le Page (1966). Le Page (1968) describes the range of broad Creole and other West Indian dialects.

In 1967 the Schools Council set up a project on the teaching of English to West Indian children in England. The research phase found that, although many of the handicaps suffered by children of West Indian parents, whether born there or in England, were similar to those of English children in many inner city schools, distinctive West Indian problems were related to the structure of their language and to difficulties of social and cultural adjustment. The Creole dialect, though it appears to be careless English, is an English which follows different rules of grammar, pronunciation and vocabulary. It makes it difficult for West Indian children to understand and be understood by teachers unfamiliar with this dialect. It is, as Jones

(1965) concludes, 'an immature language which is clearly inadequate for expressing the complexities of present day life . . . ', and is not, as Wight (1970) points out, adequate for the development of intellectual skills required of the school.

2. *Introductory course for juniors in multi-racial classrooms.* The initial research phase concluded that priority should be given to developing materials for the seven to nine year age range and that these should be designed for whole multi-racial classes (Wight, 1970). The materials developed (Schools Council; English for West Indian Children, 1972) in particular *Concept* 7–9, have been tested by a national sample of teachers and their classes and comprise three units and a dialect kit.

Unit one, *Listening with understanding*, aims to increase the children's skills of oral comprehension. It emphasizes memory, control, concentration and de-coding complex language, and uses pre-recorded cassettes.

Unit two, *Concept Building*, has the aim of increasing children's skill and flexibility in classifying data. Individual or group activity enables children to reinforce their learning and writing.

Unit three, *Communication*, aims to increase children's oral skills of description and inquiry. The children work in pairs or in small groups to practise their skills of description with each other.

Unit four, *The Dialect Kit*, is designed to counter the main effects of West Indian Creole dialects on the writing of standard English. It concentrates on features of standard English which present difficulty to Creole speakers.

There is a teacher's manual for each unit and adequate material for small and large group activities.

Norris (1972) discusses the use of Unit One, *Listening with Understanding* in this project to show how, through lessons on tape, it increases listening and oral skills. Exercises enable the teacher to see in which context the child does not understand: whether it is the length of the utterance, the speed of delivery, conflicts of order of real events, and order of expression within a sentence; the effects of concentration, memory and self confidence of the child—all these bear on the ability of the child to understand (Norris, 1972, page 13).

III. Infant and Pre-School Language Education

A. *Language Teaching in Multi-racial Infant School Situation*

1. *Infant school survey.* A survey of infant schools with a high proportion of immigrant children has been made by Stoker (1970) in order to ascertain the methods and problems involved in teaching English to the five- to seven-year-olds, before the project team began

developing material for this age group. Several interesting points emerged from this survey.

Although the bulk of immigrant children are in infant schools, she found that many infant teachers were unaware of sources of information and help which were available. She found the informal infant school gave the immigrant child an opportunity to work at a wide range of activities at his own pace. The teachers could not always capitalize on this situation in order to help with oral language learning and reading development of the immigrant child, since each teacher had many groups to supervise and frequently no suitable pre-reading oral comprehension apparatus to help them. Where the day was unstructured, teachers had no way of checking how good a command of English the children had. Immigrant children often found it difficult to adjust to the unstructured permissive situation in the informal class since this is often a different structure of adult-child relationship to that which they encounter at home. The variety of activity choices may be confusing and it appeared that they felt more secure in formal classes where they knew what was expected of them. They appeared to master the techniques of reading and writing very quickly. They did not, however, always have true understanding of the words or become linguistically proficient, since as she points out 'formal lessons put more stress on uniform class participation rather than on individual needs and . . . . many children conceal their lack of understanding' (Stoker, ibid.). She found that few infant teachers had had training in teaching English to immigrant children as most local authorities encouraged junior and secondary school teachers to attend these courses, which are primarily geared for children in those age groups. 'This is probably due to the fact that most Local Authorities have assumed that infant non-English speaking children do not need any special tuition.' The few language specialists found in infant schools are seldom infant trained. She believes that, contrary to current theory, teaching English to groups of infant school children, while making sure that other pupils are constructively occupied, requires systematic training in structured, controlled language for infant teachers and extra ancillary assistance in the classroom.

She suggests that the high incidence of immigrant children in junior schools who need special language help refutes the notion that infant pupils pick up English automatically. Many finish infant school with an inadequate command of language for educational purposes.

As a result of this survey, the infant section has produced two books of stories and plays, and a handbook for teachers suggesting ways in which the 'immigrant' infants may have languages encouraged and structured while they are doing their normal class activities. These appear under the Schools Council: EIC (1973) Project as *Scope Handbook* 3, *Language Work with Infant Immigrant Children* (1973). Taylor and Ingleby's (1973) collection of stories for children aged five to twelve in multi-racial classrooms: *Scope Storybook* (1973) and Manley's (1973) *Scope Supplementary Plays and Dialogues* for new readers to supplement Scope Stage 1 Readers.

2. *Playground language study.* The theory that non-English speaking infants pick up the language by playing with English children in the playground has been questioned by many educators. Lucas (1972a and 1972b) reports on the results of a research project to test this proposition though her design was structured to test several concomitant or related issues. The issues therein discussed are:

(a) To see whether immigrant or native children choose to associate with each other in a free choice play situation, and whether there is a relationship to the proportion of immigrant children to native children in the school as a whole, the 'newcomer/native school ratio'.

(b) To see what kind of language these children used in a controlled play situation—whether there were differences and whether the immigrant children had the opportunity to acquire adequate English.

Very briefly, it was found that there was more mixed play in schools which had a low immigrant intake than those with a large intake and that infant children do not play together indiscriminately. Indices taken measure the amount of speech, and the diversity of speech errors made were counted. Differences were found and were related to language situations which rested on unequal status due to the largest number of errors made by the immigrant children and consequent frustrations felt in communication failure and withdrawal behaviour. Though these findings should be replicated, the author points out the implications of this research for teachers of such infants. These are that:

(a) The period of great growth in the acquisition of English, when children first enter school, should be the time when these children are given special language teaching. Such structured language teaching would facilitate understanding and concept formation and enable them to communicate and understand native children more easily and be accepted more readily as equals.

(b) Such structured language teaching is not only likely to be more efficient from the academic point of view, but from the psychological point of view will enable the immigrant child to be a more rewarding companion to the native speaker and may foster attitudes of equality of esteem in adult life to members of other racial groups.

Lucas also touches on the importance of positive action in the area of social integration and questions whether equal relationships are being structured in the classroom. In her study, few schools had 'organized play' in play periods and she raises questions as to whether such periods might help foster positive social integration in the hands of trained helpers.

This author is aware that language learning is as important for the intellectual development of the learner as it is for the development of positive intergroup relations and suggests further research into playground behaviour.

3. *Infant language research.* The Programme Development Unit (1973) of the Schools Council Compensatory Education Project has produced a teacher's handbook *Language Development in the Infant School* as well as supplementary materials aimed at stimulating language development, particularly for disadvantaged children. It has also developed instruments to help teachers identify children in need of compensatory education, one area of which is reading and language needs (Williams, Congdon, Holder, Sims, 1971). The longitudinal Schools Council Compensatory Education Project's Studies of infant school children (1973/74) I, II and III, examine the effect of deprivation on linguistic, cognitive and emotional development. Other publications of this project will be reviewed in Chapter VI.

Another Schools Council curriculum project which has produced materials for children of five to seven years based on their spoken language and experiences, designed to teach initial literacy and reading before the child has mastered handwriting and spelling is described by Knowles (1969). The 'Breakthrough to Literacy' materials and readers produced are listed in Schools Council Index (1972).

B. *Pre-School Language Research*

1. *Introduction.* Although research is not conclusive, it is now widely believed by educationists in the United States and Britain and other counties, as Wein (1970) points out in his article, which compares pre-school compensatory programmes in different countries, that the most advantageous time to influence the child academically is in the pre-school years. Van der Eyken (1969) quotes from the US Educational Policies Commission.

'Research shows clearly that the first four or five years of a child's life is the period of most rapid growth in physical and mental characteristics and of greatest susceptibility to environmental influences. Consequently it is in the early years that deprivations are the most disastrous in their effects. They can be compensated for only with great difficulty in later years and then possibly not in full . . . . 'Finally, experience indicates that exposure to a wide variety of activities and of social and mental interactions with children and adults greatly enhance a child's ability to learn.' (p. 152)

Klein's (1965) survey of research studies describing the variations in socialization and child rearing practices in English sub-cultures, makes it clear that some children have very inadequate training in 'school readiness skills'. Their background is inadequate in language development and conversation, ego control of behaviour, achievement orientation, the lack of inculcation of a problem-solving approach and low parental aspiration for achievement.[1]

Thus it is evident that, as Yudkin (1967) points out, although 'all three- to five-year-olds should be offered opportunities in a nursery school type of environment, studies indicate that for some children in this age group this sort of care is very pressing'. These include children who are culturally deprived, who come from overcrowded homes, who have behaviour problems, whose mothers must work. Among the latter, many who have no nearby relatives must leave their children with unregistered child minders, many of whom have inadequate accommodation or toys for the children to play and develop intellectually in the normal way. The effect of such conditions on these children is described by doctors and health visitors in Yudkin's (1967) work. These children may come from both host and immigrant communities.[2]

The organization Priority Area Children (1971) recently gave a preliminary report describing the growth of unregistered child minding and is concerned with its educational consequences.

In one area Prince reports that he is seeing an increasing number of pre-school immigrant children under five who are aloof and withdrawn (ACE, 1970).

Watson (1971) reports that, with the aid of a grant from the Van Leer foundation, it intends to set up two action research projects to investigate child minding in these areas and to set up an educationally sound service in these areas.

1 Douglas (1964) and Plowden's (1967) national survey and Miller's (1970) studies indicate the importance of positive parental attitudes and support in influencing children's academic achievement.

2 Certainly Yudkin (1965) points out that there is a higher proportion of immigrant mothers of young children who work when their children are still young, than among the host population. Greve (1971) in his London survey, points out that a higher proportion of immigrant families live in overcrowded conditions, partly due to discrimination in housing.

Inadequacy of day nursery and nursery school provision means that this situation is likely to continue. It is obvious that these children will come to school ill equipped to benefit from the school environment. Douglas (1966) has shown that the gap in performance between these children and those from more favoured environments becomes progressively greater.

In the past some studies have been made to evaluate the effect of nursery education on educational performance, but since relevant variables were not always controlled, the results are not conclusive. Neff (1938) found that a disadvantaged environment led to progressive academic deterioration in children. Douglas and Ross (1964), using a sample from their national survey of 5,300 children, divided them into two groups, according to whether or not they had had nursery education. The nursery school educated group had higher scores on ability and performance tests at the age of eight years than the non-nursery school educated group. At the age of 15, the first group scored slightly less than the second group. The differences in test scores at both age levels were not statistically significant. However, since the children were not matched for socio-economic group, it was not possible to tell whether those who had come from disadvantaged backgrounds had improved. No comparisons were made according to the type of nursery school education. The type of nursery education, whether based on play or academically oriented, was not taken into consideration.

Few pre-school groups have been set up or existing ones evaluated to see if their environment might dramatically contribute to the young child's intellectual development. Van der Eyken (1969) describes three projects. Pyke set up the Malting House Schools in Cambridge to provide an environment which could encourage intellectual inquiry. Susan Isaacs, a psychologist and the Director kept detailed records of the children's development. Wann, Dorn and Liddle's (1962) study in America observed children aged from three to five in five schools in their neighbourhood and evaluated test situations the teachers gave to the children under their direction. They concluded that not enough was done in nursery schools and kindergartens to extend and clarify the understanding and range of interest the children exhibited.

However, in 1969, through the declaration of America's 'War on Poverty' by President Johnson, the ensuing legislation enabled a plethora of government programmes for compensatory education to be instigated in deprived areas. Chazan and Williams (1968) and Halsey (1972) survey some of these and mention that though pre-school education has not been as effective as expected it is accepted that some programmes produced cognitive gains. Those programmes which have used closely structured intensive programmes for such intellectual development as language skills have produced gains in children's achievement. Gray and Klaus (1965) discuss the successful Early Training Project at George Peabody College, Tennessee. Bereiter, *et al.* (1966) and Deutsch and Goldstein (1965–68) describe effects of their enriched nursery school programmes on the intelligence and achievement scores of disadvantaged children. The National Foundation for Educational Research and the Educational Priority Action Research Projects have studied these American projects and the evaluations of their achievements.

Little research has been done in Britain on the effectiveness of nursery education nor on evaluating the different practices within nurseries on children's subsequent achievements.

2. *National Foundation for Educational Research Project.* The National Foundation for Educational Research at Slough started a five-year pre-school project for disadvantaged children between three and five years in 1968, which is designed to encourage language development and to provide perceptual stimulation for the children and develop their ability to listen and to observe. Wiseman (1971) points out that it was found that a typical day for nursery school children in deprived areas had no more than 40 minutes or so of structured language teaching. The Foundation believes that the nursery school teacher has the power through compensatory programmes to bring the linguistically disadvantaged child up to par before he starts school. Quigley (1972a, b) describes the aims and methodology of the NFER project and the language development programme. Four nurseries in Slough with 200 children, both English and immigrant, are involved in the project then in its second and third year. The children's progress in infant school is being assessed in the final two years. In the fifth nursery, a special programme has been designed by an ex-Head Mistress which the NFER is evaluating.

The Language Programme has adapted the Peabody Language Development Kit (PLDK), an American language stimulation programme which aims to develop language and cognitive skills, developed by Peabody College in Tennessee. The teacher gives the children structured teaching for two hours daily in 10- and 20-minute periods. Perceptual development and auditory skills are developed with a wide range of materials in the group language sessions and informally in normal nursery activities. Parents have been involved initially through discussion groups on pre-school education, books, toys and suitable activities for this age group. Later they have been invited to participate and observe in nursery sessions.

The methods and adaptations used in the language programme are described in detail by Quigley (1972, b). Preliminary results of the short-term effects of the activities on the experimental groups show that their performance is superior to that of the control groups.

Evaluation is in three stages: (1) tests in language, intellectual and perceptual ability during their nursery period; (2) tests on entry to infant school on readiness for schooling, and (3) tests at the end of their sixth term in infant school on attainments in reading and mathematics.

Assessments are also to be made of the children's emotional adjustment and motivation.

3. *Educational Priority Area Action Research.* The Newsom and Plowden reports drew attention to the importance of pre-school education for children, particularly for those in educational priority areas, and recommended positive discrimination for children in schools in these areas and 'research to discover which of the developments in the EPA areas have the most constructive effects so as to assist in planning the longer term programme'.

As a result of the Plowden Report, the Department of Education and Science and the Social Science Research Council jointly sponsored a three-year action research programme under Professor E. H. Halsey (1972) to establish compensatory educational projects for children in four EPA areas in Britain and one in Scotland.

The activities of the different projects will be discussed in relevant sections of the review, although the reports have not all yet been published. Halsey allowed each project director to plan his own strategies for compensatory education. However, one of the overall objectives was to improve linguistic competence.

One of the main inter-project comparisons was the national pre-school experiment to explore ways to help the language development of EPA children. The instrument used by the NFER project, the adapted Peabody Language Development Kit, was chosen for several reasons. No British pre-school language programme was available and because it was to be used in difficult playgroups, many of whose leaders were unqualified, it was believed that a structured programme with lessons to achieve specific learning goals would be necessary. Teachers in nursery classes would find it useful in drawing attention to language problems of the children in a systematic way.

The kit was used on an experimental one-year basis in nursery classes and playgroups in three of the project areas. Two tests of language ability were chosen to measure the children's progress before and after the experimental period and the overall trend appeared to indicate that the PLDK assists language development, though a nursery class with good language work also had equally good improvement. Problems of children turnover in the groups and problems of matching children from other control groups and nurseries made statistical comparisons less valid.

Children following a numbers concept programme which involved individual conversation between teacher and child were compared with the PLDK groups and it was found in some tests that the latter groups progressed more. It was concluded that novelty and increased teacher-child communication formed part of the explanation of gains.

However, the projects' evaluation of the PLDK suggested that language programmes had great potential. All projects undertook to develop pre-school language programmes which were more appropriate for English children. These four programmes have indicated ways of producing material and methods suitable for their localities and acceptable to British tradition. The West Riding Scheme worked at an individual level, group level and with the parents in school and at home, thus linking new language with the child's experience outside the group. It showed that gains made in the pre-school programme could be maintained in infant schools. The Dundee Project, which concentrated on the development of language, will be published in Volume V of the Educational Priority Area Publications (1972–74).

The main emphasis of the Dundee Project under Milne, Lee and Watts is the assessment of a structured pre-school programme to cover language development, conceptual and perceptual development and social development, accompanied by parental involvement (Saunders, 1969).

The children are divided into three groups, each receiving one of the three types of enrichment mentioned for approximately half-an-hour a day. Each of the three groups will be evaluated to see the effects of the enrichment programmes on achievement.

Midwinter (1972a) also describes the Liverpool area's production of a pre-school language kit, for which, nevertheless, the team made no great academic claim. It was 'an approximate attempt to offer a realistic and structured aid to the playgroup workers' (Midwinter, 1972, p. 90).

4. *Other pre-school projects.* In 1969 the Schools Council established a Pre-School Education Project under Parry which studied in depth nursery schools in five areas of the country and play groups in three areas. The aim of the project was also to consider how current practice was meeting the needs of deprived children for intellectual stimulation and language development and to describe good practices in play and language development in guides and films (Parry, 1969, 1971). Teachers were found to be increasingly aware of the importance of language teaching.

As a result of this project a Pre-School Language Project under Tough (1971) was set up, first to see if differences in language of children from linguistically favourable and unfavourable homes could be identified at the age of three, and if so, how tests can help teachers to be aware of these. Secondly, it was to see if the language differences which exist between these children at the ages of five and seven could be reduced by nursery education. It is hoped that teachers' guides describing good existing strategies for initiating and elaborating talks through play and activity will be available (Schools Council Project Index, 1971). Didsbury College of Education has initiated a programme in an educational priority area of Manchester for nursery and follow-up infant school-children (Morton, and Goldman, 1969, and Wein, 1970b). There are experimental and control groups involved in the curriculum which will emphasize three elements: (1) development of oral language, conceptual and perceptual development; (2) improvement of the child's self image; (3) encouragement of parent and community involvement.

There will be yearly evaluations during the three years of infant school to see whether the children maintain any of their gains (Wein, 1970b). Wein points out that, since most of these experimental programmes both in Britain and abroad involve small numbers of children, it would be very useful if similar evaluative techniques were used so that cross-cultural comparisons could be made.

The children should also be re-tested at five, then again a few years after the programmes and the results should be linked with other achievements, such as level of secondary and further education and occupational group attained.

Some schools who have adequate staff facilities do intensive language work which may be very effective in teaching the child English. In a multi-racial infant class, Eavis (in McNeal and Rogers, 1971) describes the class procedure used by infant teachers for language work.

'We have used part-time teachers, students and others to help relieve the situation in one classroom by taking out small groups for specific teaching . . . Basic skills are taught in small groups.' When this has been done regularly and systematically the children have made progress. The value of small groups enabling children to form a close and more intimate relationship with an adult cannot be overestimated. In smaller groups it is possible to develop children's powers of concentration, the skill of listening and the chance to talk and to be listened to by an adult.

IV. Further Sources of Information about Language Teaching Approaches and Research

A. *Materials Developed by Teachers in Multi-racial Classrooms*

The majority of teachers who have been faced with large numbers of non-English speaking children in their classes have had to develop methods and materials and organization to cope immediately with the situation. Willes (1971) reviews a small selection of books on the principles of foreign language teaching which are authoritative and accessible. A more detailed annotated list may be obtained from CILT (1972a).

Many have described techniques which have been successful in teaching their children, but these are relevant to particular age groups, ethnic groups, the amount of classroom time available and the classroom organization used to teach the non-English speaking children. Many valuable articles are briefly reviewed in *Language Teaching Abstracts* which covers journals concerned with language teaching both in Britain and the USA. The original articles should be consulted for fuller details. Details of ongoing research are now also outlined (CILT, 1972b). A useful source of information is a CILT Report (1970) which is an abridged version of a conference held in 1970 to make expert opinion widely available to language teachers.

Articles and research in *Language Teaching Abstracts* may be grouped as follows.

1. *Ethnic group difficulties.* Candlin (1969) analyses the pronunciation difficulties of speakers of different Asian languages and suggests techniques to help them. Hanson (1969) describes methods used in withdrawal remedial classes for West Indian- and English-born pupils whose vocabularies are inadequate to achieve their potential. Jones (1969) explains teaching techniques in a West Indian dialect context at Secondary School level using dramatization of social situations followed up by oral and written work. Dimson (1971) is investigating the correlations between linguistic differences due to social factors and the ability to learn a second language.

Manley (in McNeal and Rogers, 1971) describes the successful use of dialogue and other techniques to teach secondary school girls.

2. *Practical materials and techniques.* Everton and Freakes (1968) describe schemes of work devised by a group of Haringey teachers from schools covering the five–16 age range, which include such practical aids as games, tapes and work sheets. Buckby (1968) outlines four types of games to practise listening, speaking, reading and writing. Klyhn (1969) stresses the importance to their language

development of English and non-English speaking pupils by involving the former in the preparation and use of tapes, drill and conversation to help the latter. The National Association for Multi-racial Education, formerly ATEPO (Association of Teachers of English to Pupils from Overseas) has also published booklets by teachers of non-English speaking children on developing their skills in oral work (Hester, 1972), writing skills (Levine, 1972), teaching tenses (Hanson, 1972) and making of materials by Leicestershire teachers (1972). Hester (1969) describes the use of the tape recorder for taping a language teaching story for young children. This enables the children to hear it repeated with the same words and structures, and those who need it can listen to it several times on their own.

3. *Schemes of work.* A one-term intensive English course at primary and secondary age levels is outlined by Malpas (1968). Ure (1969) described a very sophisticated but practical method of teaching students patterns of spoken language appropriate to different language behaviour situations, which she designates as 'registers'. These language registers are taped conversations organized to contain the phrases used in a particular situation, e.g. questioning situations, describing situations or explanatory ones (how to perform a practical activity).

Llewellyn (1970) is studying the language needs of non-English-speaking immigrants when they first start work, particularly in interviews, induction courses and shop floor training. A course is being devised for teachers who teach immigrants in Evening Institutes and Reception Centres.

B. *Language Research Information and Bibliographies*

The first inquiry into research concerned with language education of immigrant children, initiated by the 'Committee on Research and Development in Modern Languages' in May 1966 found 33 current and projected projects though only a few were concerned with improving English teaching. Until its demise in 1970, the Committee sponsored necessary research in this field and recommended the establishment of CILT, the Centre for Information on Language Teaching and Research to co-ordinate information about the teaching of modern languages and to maintain and publish a register of research into modern language teaching (including teaching English as a second language) which is in progress in Britain (CILT, 1968, 1972a). CILT also provides summaries of ongoing and completed research[1], which with relevant book reviews are published in the quarterly *Language-Teaching Abstracts* in

[1] These summaries of completed research are to be used as supplements to their current editions of *Language Teaching Bibliography* (CILT and ETIC, 1972b).

conjunction with the English Teaching Information Centre (ETIC) of the British Council, with whom it shares library resources and certain related projects. ETIC is mainly concerned in helping those who teach English abroad, while CILT publishes helpful information guides for teachers of immigrant children. ETIC (1968) provides annotated catalogues of texts for English as a second language, many of which are for children of particular mother-tongues or for particular examinations overseas. CILT also produces an up-to-date bibliography of textbooks on modern language teaching and English as a second language CILT (1972b), as well as bibliographies on language teaching which are listed in the bibliographies under this title. A number of these contain lists of audio-visual aids as well as textbooks, readers and literature. These have been compiled by such organizations as the Community Relations Commission (1972/73), the National Book League (1973), to name two. This latter booklet, *English for Immigrant Children*, selected and annotated by June Derrick (1973) contains not only books on language teaching and courses available for teachers, but lists of structurally graded reading schemes, stories, poems and songs, dictionaries and visual aids with helpful comments and the cost of items. It was compiled for a touring exhibition of these books, sponsored by the National Book League for teachers of multi-racial classes, and teachers of English, a very useful exhibition for busy teachers.

Another useful journal is *English Language Teaching* edited by Lee which includes a wide range of materials for English language teaching and reviews new books and new teaching materials.

Candlin and Derrick (1972), both of whom have been deeply involved in language research for teaching English as a second language, have written a monograph on the place of language study for teacher education produced by the Community Relations Commission. It summarizes many points made by other researchers and teachers of non-English speaking children and the linguistically deprived native child. Namely, that these children, to be successful in school, particularly at secondary school level, must learn the specialized language of particular disciplines (registers) and the English spoken by the teacher, since some of these language registers are often different from their language at home and in the peer group.

The authors believe that all subject teachers should study the nature and functions of language at colleges and universities so that they may be aware whether the knowledge they are communicating is understood and that they may not prejudge children who are immature in language development. The authors describe techniques of how language study could be taught.

Section three discusses the principles of language teaching to both E2L learners and West Indian children and the importance of the children's attitudes towards such learning in terms of their cultural and ethnic background.The authors point out the difficulties for colleges in providing practical experiences for student teachers in language work. Experts suggest that the opportunity for student teachers to understand individual language development and learning is best achieved by putting them in a one-to-one confrontation with a language learner. Other studies, by Wight (1970b) and accounts of Holiday Language Projects, Hawkins (1971), have also found that such a situation enables the language learner to practice his language skills more effectively as well. Some language schemes have in-built dialogues arranged to enable children to converse in a structured way with one another.

They touch briefly on the need for fair measures of pupil's language and educational progress, which shall be discussed in the next chapter. There is an excellent information section which lists relevant curriculum development projects, bibliographies, professional associations, and courses.

The major theme of the monograph, as pointed out by the authors, is 'that the teaching of English to immigrant children should best be seen as a special application of language study, the groundwork of which should be supplied in a common language course available to all students'. Although a pilot survey conducted by the English Department at Lancaster University showed that some colleges have recognized the importance of language study, it was found that its presentation was the responsibility of many different departments and that the study was not concentrated in any one year or for any one audience. It publishes six different syllabuses which colleges use. It recognizes that, since it may be some time before language study is available to all, there should be special courses in immigrant education, which may give insight into language.

This monograph ranges the whole field of language study, its application to education in a multi-cultural society, and its relevance to colleges of education. It is particularly important in stressing the training of teachers to communicate and to help their pupils to speak and to understand which is relevant not only to our non-English-speaking children but, equally and of greater long-term relevance, for children from deprived backgrounds in our own society.

C. *BBC English by Radio Series to Help West Indian Immigrants*

A radio series of 26 programmes, to help West Indians with standard English, is produced by Viola Huggins (1972) for Radio London and is also broadcast periodically by other local stations. It is called 'The University of Brixton' and consists of lively dramatized episodes about the life of a Jamaican family and their friends in Brixton. These episodes are followed by teaching commentaries which discuss particular linguistic points (*Multi-racial School*, Summer 1972).

The episodes are humorous and linguistic points are lucidly explained—the differences in Creole English and standard English and practice exercises. Huggins (1972) has edited the book text.

The book text *The University of Brixton* by Marriott and Wells (1972) who devised dialogues and linguistic points and exercises respectively, is available from the BBC, Bush House.

CHAPTER FOUR

Problems in Determining Present Ability Levels, Academic Potential, Linguistic Competence and Assessing Aural, Oral, Writing and Reading Competence

I. General Survey of Contemporary Views on the Measurement of Academic Potential

During the last two decades psychologists and sociologists in the course of their research have become aware of the close connection between language learning and social and cultural factors on the development of the child's intellectual potential.

A number of psychologists, among them Vernon (1969) and Hudson (1971), on the basis of their own research and that of others, refuse to accept that any test can predict an individual's existing or future intellectual potential, especially if his cultural background is different from that of the constructor of the test. They do not believe in the fixed potential concept of innate intelligence, which can be measured, but consider intelligence, as Pidgeon (1969) points out, 'as a set of developed skills with which the person learns to cope with any environment'. However, this group of psychologists, he continues, do not hold that one can observe and measure the effects of interaction of whatever is inherited with stimulation from the environment. The different views of intellectual potential are ably presented by Butcher (1968), Wiseman (1967) and Guilford (1967). This is not the place to discuss the arguments for or against the different views of intellectual potential, nor assuming it can be assessed, whether genetic or environmental factors have the greater influence on its development and whether programmes can provide equality of educational opportunity. This issue has been fully debated recently in the United States in the *Harvard Educational Review* (Winter 1968, Spring 1969) as well as the issue of Jensen's (1969) assertion that there is an average 15 IQ points difference between black and white Americans in the United States and that this is due mainly to genetic factors. The statistical basis for his estimates of the heritability factor on intelligence has been strongly criticized both in the United States and in England as a result of his visit to a conference at The University of Cambridge (Mason 1969).

Eysenck (1971), in his recent book, supports and relies on Jensen's data and attempts to reinstate the genetic superiority of white intelligence, as Haynes points out, 'through an unwarranted misinterpretation of the relatively poor negro response to "culture-fair IQ tests" '. He shows remarkable insensitivity in taking for granted the 'identical environments of certain white and negro groups'. She points out that 'he is extremely reticent in reporting the research findings concerning the effects of impoverished and culturally different environments' (Haynes, 1971, p. 34–5).

Both Rex (1971) and Mason (1971) and Vernon (1971) criticize Eysenck's over-simplification in comparing groups from 'similar' environmental backgrounds, and his selective use of evidence to support his points.

Vernon (1971) points out that the evidence Eysenck cites is falsely polarized into hereditary and environmental points of view and that the evidence 'is tangential or irrelevant to the issue of causes . . . Both evidence and inference are confused . . . the problem is as intriguing as it is intractable, of how to show what an individual would have been had his experience been other than what it was.' Vernon criticizes specifically his disregard of both the difficulties of extracting clear sense from the experimental studies he has quoted and the environmental explanations given for some of these.

Jensen's (1971) article on 'whether schools cheat minority children' gives a detailed analysis of tests administered and results of an elaborate experiment which compared a large controlled sample of negro, white and Mexican children from five to 19 years in *de facto* segregated schools. Although it was found that there were no appreciable differences in scholastic achievement or evidence of a cumulative deficit between minority and majority pupils, he found differences in overall levels of ability and patterns of abilities between the three ethnic groups. From the results he hypothesizes two broad hierarchical classes of ability levels—Level I, associative ability, and Level II, conceptual ability—which he hopes to prove are distributed unequally in social classes and ethnic groups and which are genotypically independent types of mental processes.

He suggests that schools should vary their instruction procedures to the level of the pupils which might improve the educational attainments of the majority.

Leading psychologists in Britain were invited by the journal *Educational Research* to comment on Jensen's article. Butcher (1972) points out that heritability does not imply immutability and that different methods of instruction would be a retrograde step. Nisbet (1972) suggests that two strategies of teaching are unfair since we wish all pupils to think conceptually whatever the level. Vernon (1972) objects to the non-verbal culture-free test used to assess IQ and indicates that no one asks how one selects children to be educated, and that expectations might be self-fulfilling.

Richardson, Spears and Richards (1972) have edited a useful review of the theories on environmental and genetic influences on intelligence and have also placed them in their historical perspective by including essays examining the basis of the conflicting theories.

Irrespective of their views on intelligence, most educational psychologists accept that these tests are useful as diagnostic aids to assess a child's abilities and difficulties and to indicate in which areas they need help (Goldman, 1968). However, none would claim that any test is free of culture bias. Children from minority groups in our own culture do badly on intelligence tests current in the dominant culture, whether they are gypsy, Irish or slum children, partly because, as Houghton (1970) claims, their different language structure and values affect their performance on these tests and furthermore because the dominant culture wants them to conform to its values, and considers them deviant if they do not do so.

Without an adequate language suitable for education and communication, the child is intellectually handicapped and is unlikely to fulfill his potential. Thus, as Bernstein (1961), Lawton (1968) and Vernon (1969) points out, such children will suffer restricted intellectual development as indicated by low scores on intelligence tests, and attainment tests, unless there are more effective methods in teaching them language. Lawton (1968), who has extended Bernstein's study of language codes on children of 12 to 15 years, found that they continue to diverge in attainment as they move through the secondary stage of school.

Recent classic studies of children in our own British culture, as well as in the United States, indicate the influence on children's intellectual performance of such social factors as child rearing practices, stable home background and parental encouragement and expectation (Douglas, 1966; Wiseman, 1967; Plowden, 1967). These studies and others are summarized by Klein (1965). Vernon's many works have also demonstrated the importance of social factors on performances in intelligence tests by children from different cultures. These are discussed in his *Intelligence and Culture* (1969). Other studies by Flowers (1966) and Rosenthal and Jacobsen (1968) suggest that the teacher's expectation of a child's performance has an influence on his achievement level, as mentioned by Pidgeon (1970), though the results are not conclusive.

II. The Influence of Cultural Factors on Test Performances of non-European Pupils on Western Type Intelligence and Achievement Tests in their Countries of Origin

It has been interesting to note that more research has been devoted to studying the validity and efficiency of instruments for measuring intellectual abilities in developing countries than for immigrant groups from these countries in Britain.

These studies illuminate problems which may influence test performances of immigrant children in Britain, particularly if they are encapsulated in their parental culture.

A. *Studies Indicating the Influence of Environmental Factors on Intelligence Test Performances*

Ferron (1965), in his survey of the results of researches on the test performance of 'coloured' children, describes the advantages and disadvantages of the different types of tests used. He finds that research indicates that, where circumstances exist which ensure that white and coloured groups have a common way of life, a common language and equal opportunity, as among the oriental groups in the western coast of the USA, the differences in IQ are small and non-existent. However, the existence of colour prejudice and other social pressures may affect intelligence test scores as a result of differences in emotional and motivational climate.

Where the difference in environmental opportunity between children in advanced civilizations and those in some underdeveloped areas are not too great, the differences in ability scores can be expected to be correspondingly smaller as the Porteus (1930) Hawaiian and American study shows. Where cultural differences, linguistic handicaps and differences in environmental opportunity are great, intelligence test scores are lower among children in non-technological societies than among those brought up in a West European or North American culture, which are industrial.

Vernon (1961) studied the intellectual development of a sample of West Indian schoolboys in the British West Indies in 1960. He compared them with a representative sample of English schoolboys in a later study (Vernon, 1965) and found that the former were retarded by environmental handicaps. Although the West Indian scores indicated only a moderate degree of retardation, the deficit of West Indian boys varied considerably with different tests and was most noticeable in practical and non-verbal 'g' tests, and much less serious for educational attainment tests which seemed to be based upon drill and rote learning. His major finding was that the factors which handicapped the children's mental development were 'low socio-economic status, poor cultural and linguistic environment, inadequate education and family instability'. The major factor apparently influencing children's performance in 'g' and verbal tests was the cultural level of the home, parental education and encouragement, reading facilities and probably speech background. Thus it seems evident that, although non-linguistic tests may be more suitable, children from non-technical cultures are seriously handicapped in picture and performance tests as well.

Although tests for non-Western peoples are available (Couch, 1963), it is highly improbable that culture-free tests or culture-fair tests can be devised, yet if such tests were possible they would be less useful for cross-cultural comparisons. Vernon argues that, since the nations and their citizens are aiming to achieve Western style technical civilizations, it is important that they should produce more individuals with Western-type mental skills.

Vernon (1965b) outlines nine major environmental handicaps to mental development, which are of importance in understanding whether we can help non-Western children achieve their potential and whether we can measure that potential. A recent study on educational development among Canadian Indians and Eskimos (Vernon, 1966) concludes that the whole pattern of a culture determines the educational and vocational potential and combines to reduce the development of effective intelligence required in contemporary technological society. Ferron (1966) infers that differences on test scores at pre-school level between two groups of nursery school children, one a class of Freetown Creole children and the other a class of English children, are due mainly to environmental differences. Ferron (1964) summarizing studies of West African children, lists cultural factors which contribute to test performances and which could be controlled.

Vernon's studies were part of a programme he instigated to explore factors that hinder the development of abilities of pupils in under-developed countries or depressed minority groups or disadvantaged children, particularly immigrants in our own culture. They are published now in one book (Vernon, 1969) which discusses factors influencing children's mental development, the application of tests in non-Western cultures as well as cross-cultural studies. Alleyne (1962), comparing intelligence and attainment of children in London, Wales and Trinidad, whose mother tongue is not English, shows that a very high percentage of bi-linguals born outside Britain are undeniably handicapped in IQ tests, especially verbal ones, and that even non-verbal intelligence tests would not be really satisfactory for comparison with English-speaking mono-linguals.

B. *Influence of Administrative Techniques, Oral vs Verbal Directions, Coaching on Children from Different Ethnic Groups*

A large number of objective tests of achievement are being produced in many developing countries for secondary school selection. Vernon (1967), as a result of comparing different methods of administering group intelligence tests to East African pupils, believes first that test items intended for pupils of a culture different from that of Western Europe and North America should preferably be formulated by psychologists who are members of that culture.

The method which was least satisfactory in instructing pupils in how to do the tests were printed instructions. Oral instructions gave better mean scores than printed ones, and when given in Swahili the results were better than when done so in English. His main finding was that the practice and coaching effects on numerical and visual media tests are never larger than three to eight standard score units. British experience suggests that effects of training on verbal materials would be less than on non-verbal tests because pupils are practised in answering these types of tests in school. Jahoda (1969), in the cross-cultural use of the perceptual maze test, found that, though it functioned satisfactorily, it was necessary to provide the subjects with ample opportunity to familiarize themselves with the test. Pidgeon (1970), using a non-verbal test for primary school children from three ethnic groups in Africa, tested the effect of coaching on their performance. It was found that the coaching effect was significantly greater for European and African children, but that the Indian children gained very little. Though various cultural reasons were postulated for the low improvement of the Indian children and high gain of the Africans, these results indicate that non-verbal tests are not necessarily 'culture-free' and that more has to be discovered about how cultural background influences children's motivation to perform in these tests. Okonji (1970) found

Table 4.1: *Gains made Between Initial and Final Tests for Groups of European, African and Indian Children*[1]

Group	*European*	*African*	*Indian*
Experimental	10·60	14·55	6·10
Control*	7·39	6·95	5·65

* Group who had no coaching.

[1] From Pidgeon, D. (1970) *Expectation and Pupil Performance*, Slough: NFER.

that there was considerable effect of special training (given to an experimental group) on their subsequent performance on a classificatory behaviour test, in comparison with the control groups.[2]

The study appears to provide evidence that some orthodox tests in abstraction may not reveal the capacity levels of individuals but reflect only the extent to which they have been exposed to experiences which promote the growth of these cognitive functions.

Irvine (1966), in an excellent review of research done in the field of cognitive measurement in Africa, points out that test content, format, school conditions and role expectations affect scores in Africa to an extent and in a manner which would prevent detailed psychological comparisons between European and African groups. A five-year follow-up of secondary school selection procedures in Central Africa provides information about the utility of tests used for selection and provides an outline of methods used. A major influence on scores was the quality of the school attended. There was little significant association of scores with father's occupation, number of siblings, or the number of languages spoken (Irvine, 1968). Bibliographies listing studies on psychological testing in African countries and studies of problems on adapting selection tests to different cultural setting are described in works by Biesheuvel (1949), Hopkins (1962) and Andor (1966). It seems likely that some of these findings will be relevant to the psychological testing of children from other cultures who attend English schools.

III. The Influence of Social and Cultural Factors on Test Performances of non-English Pupils in Britain

Psychologists who have been engaged in testing the academic potential of children from non-European cultures in their own countries with a variety of instruments tend to think that, as Vernon (1969) states, 'in attempting to assess educational potential of immigrant children verbal tests are preferable to non-verbal or performance tests—either standard tests in English if they can communicate or similar tests in their own tongue[1].

A. *Influence of Residence and Language on Test Performances*

The first major surveys of the attainment of immigrant pupils (at the age of transfer) in Britain was conducted by the Inner London Education Authority in 1966 in 52 of its primary schools which had more than 33 per cent of such pupils on their roll (Little *et al.*, 1968). The study was of all pupils transferring from primary to secondary schools. Performance ratings were based on specific tests of English,

1 The results were statistically significant for the experimental group.

verbal reasoning and mathematics ratings, as well as the school's assessment of pupils' attainment.[1]

This study found clear and consistent differences between the performances of immigrant pupils as a whole and all authority pupils. The immigrant pupils had only two per cent in the top group and approximately one-third fell into the bottom group. While half of the authorities' pupils were termed as below average in performance, approximately four-fifths of immigrants fell into this category.

However, more relevant than these figures was the finding that immigrant performance related to knowledge of English, length of stay in the United Kingdom, and country of origin. A high proportion of immigrant pupils had spent less than three years in Britain.

The small groups of immigrant children who had received most of their primary school education in Britain had a spread of ability up to average and, in some cases, above the average of all pupils. There was consistent and marked improvement in immigrant performance with increasing length of education in England.

Important in determining the level of the pupil's performance is his knowledge of English and the frequency of daily use of speech in English or standard English. It is unlikely that many of the immigrant children speak English at home. However, even in the English-speaking group only eight per cent were in the top two groups, which should account for 25 per cent of such pupils. The lower attainment of those who spoke an inadequate non-standard English was most marked. Analysis of English-speaking immigrants by country of origin was undertaken. There were only five per cent of the West Indians in the top two groups compared to between 12 per cent and 21 per cent of the rest of the immigrants placed in these groups. One might question, in the light of previous research surveyed, whether these tests are true measures of intelligence of children whose English language ability is far from adequate, and whether under these circumstances teachers' assessments are completely objective. Bagley (1968b), who analyses the report, quotes from studies here in Bagley (1968a), and in the United States on factors influencing teachers' assessments and the latter's influence on pupil performance, particularly studies by Baratz (1967) and Rosenthal and Jacobsen (1968).

Beetham (1967), although his sample was small, found that immigrant children's scholastic performance was low, but the majority had had less than four years of English schooling. Wiles

[1] Children in ILEA schools are classified in one of seven profile groups on the basis of their ratings on these tests.

(1968) found, in her study of immigrant children in a comprehensive school, that when the children had had most of their education in England their performance was as good as that of their English peers and in some cases better.

Saint (1963) attempted to assess the scholastic problems faced by 100 Punjabi boys in secondary schools. Seventy-six of these had been in England less than two years, and 49 less than one year. Of those who could attempt the tests, numbering 40, almost all lacked aural-oral skill in English and this contributed to their retardation in reading and to a lesser degree in arithmetic. Although the mean IQ of the group was 15 points below the normative sample, it cannot be regarded as evidence of inferior intellectual capacity. That cultural factors are important determinants of performance in these tests appears to be indicated by a moderate positive correlation between IQ and length of residence and schooling in the Western environment.

Houghton (1966) has published a very interesting study at infant level on relative performance on intelligence tests by two groups of matched children, West Indian and English. He found that there was little difference in mean scores; the Jamaican group's was 90 and the local English group's 92. These results are similar to, although much lower than, those found in a similar American study by Goodman (1964). Houghton advances the hypothesis that these depressed British scores might best be explained in terms of deprivation—social, linguistic and environmental. Linguistic difficulties appear to be an important factor in the development of the West Indian child, as Baker (1965) makes clear in his study of immigrant junior school children. Burgin and Pickup (1964) have also made a study of the problems of testing the abilities of non-English-speaking children at their primary school.

Payne (1969) compared samples of West Indian and British children, matched for verbal ability in tests of vocabulary, non-verbal intelligence, word reading and concept-formation. Although on the first three tests there were significant differences between the performances of both groups, there were no significant differences between the groups in the test of concept-formation based on the work by Vernon (1965) and devised to be less affected by culture milieu than the traditional test of ability.

B. *Cultural Influence on Verbal and Performance Tests*

McFie and Thompson (1970) studied the test scores of West Indian and English children on the WISC and Schonell GWRT comparing: 1. performance of the two ethnic groups; and 2. performances of West Indian children who arrived before and after the age of five years.

Significant differences were found both in vocabulary tests and on four of the five performance sub-tests, with early arrivals tending to do better than late arrivals.

Performance abilities were as culturally determined as verbal abilities since the differences between the West Indian and English groups in tests of the former were highly significant. The authors believe that high priority should be given to teaching mechanical and constructional activities as well as language teaching.

Their conclusion is that calculation of children's intelligence quotients from test results is open to question. In absence of IQ norms derived from country of origin, test scores only give an incomplete indication of ability.

C. *The Influence of Parental Aspirations on Motivation and Performance*

There are few research studies on the influence of social factors on the educational aspirations and performances of immigrant pupils. These are frequently linked with occupational aspirations and have been mainly of a descriptive nature.

Influences which appear to be strongest in order of importance are the attitude of the parents, the school, of the ethnic peer group and the immigrant group's image of the attitudes of the host society. The employment opportunities available for the young school leavers in the area also appear to be of importance in some instances in determining their school leaving age.

Beetham's (1967) study of a sample of fourth-year pupils in a sample of Birmingham Secondary Modern Schools, found that Asian and West Indian school children had higher educational and job aspirations than their English counterparts. Of those in the fourth year, 81 per cent of immigrant pupils and 36 per cent of the English children intended to stay on. Over 10 per cent of the immigrants and one per cent of the English children expected to attend further full time education. Admittedly 52 per cent of the immigrant children had had less than four years of schooling in England, and because they had high job aspirations, realized their inadequacies and the importance of further education. Beetham considered these aspirations unrealistic. Nandy (1969) queries this conclusion and states that if adequate educational provision is available over time, and the child has the motivation to make good his deficiencies, his aspirations are not necessarily inappropriate if his ability is adequate.

Beetham found that the main influence on immigrant children's career aspirations was that of their parents, who were prepared to enable them to stay on for further education. Sixty-three per cent of the Asians, 35 per cent of the West Indians and 28 per cent of the

English said their career choice was the same as that of their parents.

It is hoped to measure the effect of cultural and social factors on non-verbal intelligence test scores of Asian children and English children. Sharma (1969) is studying the home background of a sample of Asian and English children in Britain and that of a matched sample of Asian children in India before administering tests to the children. Taylor (1971) in a study of the scholastic achievement and school leaving age of English and Asian pupils in a sample of secondary schools found that Asians did better than the English on all but one of the measures used. Fifty-three per cent of the young Asians continued beyond statutory leaving age compared with only 23 per cent of the English boys.

In terms of qualifications obtained by the school-leavers, it was found that though a higher proportion of English leavers had been to selective schools, almost two-thirds of the English pupils left with no certificates, compared to only one in 10 Asians. The proportions still in full time education at the time when interviewed were 34 per cent of the Asians and seven per cent of the English sample. Both groups hoped to stay in full time education until they had achieved school 'A' levels. However, in measuring aspirations, Taylor found that the majority of the Asians wanted a professional career, the English sample were less ambitious. Thus out of five measures of aspirations, the Asian sample did better than the English sample, except on the one count,[1] even though 42 per cent had not come to England until the age of 13.

Interviewed two years afterwards, Taylor found that although performance was disappointing, the Asians were still pursuing their studies even if it meant retaking 'A' and 'O' levels, and readjusting their sights to other institutions of higher learning.

Looking for reasons for the superiority of the Asian school children, Taylor found that there was more positive support for the children to stay on at school among the immigrant parents, 35 wishing them to stay on out of 53, whereas among the English parents only 19 out of 56 wished them to do so. This superior support, coupled with the fact that 43 per cent of these children (a high proportion compared to Asians in previous studies) had arrived in England during their primary school years, contributed to their stronger motivation and tenacity.

In attempting to assess socio-economic class of the parents in his school sample, Taylor found that a higher proportion of Asian parents owned their own homes (92 per cent) and were self-employed (55 per cent) whereas 79 per cent of the English parents were tenants and 75 per cent were employees. He concludes that the Asian

[1] Namely that a higher proportion of English had attended selective schools.

parents may be more ambitious for their children. He also advances the theory that the children's strong motivation is due to two cultural traditions of the Punjabis: 1. that of respect for education in the Punjab; and 2. their distinctive character of tenacity and enterprise.

Hilton (1972), in studying the ambitions of fourth-form schoolchildren in Manchester according to ethnic group, found that the Asian and West Indian boys all have a narrow field of occupational aspirations. These appeared to be influenced more by peer group expectations than their father's occupations. The longer they had been in the country, the more the immigrant boys' expectations became distinct from and lower than their 'fantasy aspirations'.

IV. Selection and Ascertainment Procedures under the Education Act

A. *Selection for Secondary Education or Comprehensive Placement*

Local Education Authorities under the 1944 Education Act have to provide an education for pupils according to age, ability and aptitude. Their first concern for immigrant pupils was organizing language teaching facilities and initially few LEAs felt it was possible to evaluate their ability levels for secondary school selection. These children were moved on to modern schools and, as Tapper and Stopes (1963) point out, half were often, as in one secondary school, placed in a low stream. They moved up as their English improved. Many were well represented in mathematics and science prize winners.

A few authorities, such as Bolton, as Sampson (1964) points out, attempted to evaluate the ability levels of pupils whom they thought might profit from a grammar school education, by non-linguistic tests. Other means of assessment which were used included oral tests and extended interviews.

The disadvantages of selection procedures based on tests of ability and attainment standardized for non-immigrant pupils, with language difficulties and who may have an inadequate background on the subjects, for immigrant pupils are now obvious.

Among the 71 LEAs who had special arrangements for teaching immigrant pupils, 47 in 1969 had selection procedures for secondary school allocation. Only three of these LEAs mentioned that they took into consideration the language difficulties of the immigrant pupils in these procedures and only three LEAs considered those of West Indian pupils. A few LEAs give some extra consideration to immigrant pupils by allowing them to try again at 13, and in other ways.

Table 4.2: *Immigrant and non-immigrant pupils in all maintained secondary schools and in maintained grammar schools in England (January* 1970)*

	Non-immigrant	*Indian*	*Pakistani*	*West Indian*	*Other Immigrants*	*All Pupils*
Pupils in all maintained secondary schools in England (a)	2,957,167	19,437	10,202	31,320	27,848	3,045,974
Pupils in maintained grammar schools (b)	601,063	764	251	495	2,343	604,916
(b) as a percentage of (a)	20·33	3·93	2·46	1·58	8·41	19·86

* Provisional figures provided by DES in Townsend (1971) *ibid.*, Table 5.2, p. 57.

Townsend's research team only found it possible to present a limited overall picture of immigrant children in maintained grammar schools. This was due firstly to the diversity of secondary schools and their degrees of selective entry, and secondly, to the fact that only 11 LEAs in 1967–69 (out of those 38 LEAs with over 500 immigrants with selective procedures) kept records of immigrant pupils' entry to selective schools. Table 4.2 presents the results of their survey.

Despite the fact that these figures represent the minimum number of immigrant pupils following GCE Courses, it is clear that they do not represent the true academic potential of the immigrant pupils as a whole, and responsibility for such low figures is attributed to the inadequacy of language and selection procedures, discussed by psychologists and the Department in subsequent sections.

In Townsend and Brittan's (1972) more intensive survey of a sample of multi-racial schools, it was found that two-thirds of the schools in the sample with junior school age pupils transferred some pupils to selective secondary schools in 1970. A higher percentage of all pupils, including immigrant pupils of all ethnic groups, were transferred to selective schools than in the previous study.

Table 4.3: *Percentage of Pupils transferred to Selective Schools in a Selected Sample of Multi-racial Schools*

Ethnic Group	*Percentage*
West Indian	4
Indian	9
Pakistani	9
Other immigrant	7
Non-immigrant	25
Total	19

Townsend and Brittan (1972) *ibid.*, Table A 11

B. *Ascertainment Procedures for Allocation to Schools for the Educationally Sub-normal*

The lack of adequate culture-free diagnostic tests for immigrant children with severe language difficulties and who may have behaviour problems due to cultural adjustments has led many of these children to be relegated to the lowest stream in the school or to be assessed as educationally sub-normal.

Awareness of the large numbers of West Indian children in ESN schools in the Greater London region, which appeared to be out of all proportion to their numbers in the school population, began to cause concern among West Indian parents in 1967.

In 1967, an ILEA Report (1967) pointed out that 28·4 per cent of children in all Inner London ESN Schools were of immigrant origin and of these three-quarters were West Indian, although in January 1969 there were only 16·5 per cent of pupils in *all* ILEA schools of immigrant origin.

Thus in Ealing, although West Indians formed only six per cent of the school population, they represented 19 per cent of those in ESN Schools (*Race Today*, October 1969). Haringey's 1966–1967 figure of 54 per cent black children in the Borough's ESN schools was challenged by the North London West Indian Association, who reported these placements as discrimination to the Race Relations Board, although the number had dropped to 47 per cent in 1968–69 (*Race Today*, February 1970). The Board ruled (*The Guardian*, February 22nd 1971, page 7) that, although Haringey and five other authorities had classified a 'disproportionate' number of immigrant children as educationally sub-normal, this had not been a breach of the Race Relations Act. The error was due to the inadequacy of current tests to distinguish between subnormality and cultural or social deprivation.

Although there is no standard technique for classifying children as educationally sub-normal, as Houghton (1970) and others mention, a child must usually (1) be judged to be three years retarded in his school work; (2) take an intelligence test (based on American norms) which is administered by an educational psychologist, or by a school medical officer; (3) have an IQ of between 50 and 70.

The Wechsler Intelligence Scale for Children (WISC) is used widely and sometimes interpreters are available.

The overall national percentages of immigrant and non-immigrant pupils according to numbers in their respective groups in ESN schools in 1970 were as follows:

Non-Immigrant	*Indian*	*Pakistani*	*West Indian*	*Other Immigrant*	*All Pupils*
0·68	0·32	0·44	2·33	0·58	0·70

(Townsend and Brittan (1972) *ibid.*, from Table 5.1)

Coard (1971) a West Indian teacher who has taught in ESN schools and worked in youth clubs in Britain has written a book for West Indian parents about the factors in schools and society which contribute to West Indian children being often wrongfully classified as ESN.

The factors he outlines are those already mentioned in other studies, biases in assessment by teachers or tests, due to differences in culture, social class, and to cases where children are emotionally disturbed. Children's academic achievements are also influenced by low teacher expectations, lack of motivation and a negative self image due to negative social attitudes. He points out the inadequacies of ESN schools for children wrongfully placed, asks for safeguards and preventative measures to ensure that this does not occur, including that parents exercise their rights of objection and appeal. He rightly stresses the necessity of extra help in school, parental interest and involvement at home and at school, and the necessity of Black studies of history and culture for black and white British children. It is an exhortation to the West Indian community-parents and professionals on how they themselves can help their children, as well as by insisting that the LEA give them the extra educational help they require.

The number of West Indian pupils in ESN schools is two-thirds in excess of the figure that would be expected in proportion to their total numbers. Subsequent analysis by Townsend and Brittan (1972) indicates that these excess numbers of West Indians in ESN schools are mainly in 18 authorities with large numbers of West Indians. They discuss critically some of the arrangements used by LEAs for immigrant pupils' assessment, but do point out the difficulties in carrying out their duties 'when no valid instruments exist with which to measure the ability of pupils of different linguistic, cultural and educational backgrounds' both for ascertainment and selection.

C. *Assessment of Ability and Attainment Within the Schools and Types of Grouping*

Townsend's (1971) national survey does not report on the use of tests for assessment within the schools, but in his smaller sample of multi-racial schools he reviews methods used by the schools.

Over half the primary schools used objective tests of ability and only five restricted their use to non-immigrants. Almost half the secondary schools used such tests for their pupils, two using them only for non-immigrants and two for immigrants only. Those not using tests mentioned that they realized that these were not reliable for immigrants.

The research team found objective tests of attainment were used by over one half of the primary schools and over one third of the secondary schools. English, mathematics and/or verbal reasoning were used, with tests of English outnumbering the latter by 10 to 1.

Although heads said they did not make numerical allowances for immigrants, many said they added a subjective element in judging to the results. Townsend and Brittan (1972) also list other methods of assessment used by schools. The forms of assessment are tabulated by the numbers of different types of secondary schools.

The types of groupings and streaming or setting procedures used by heads in primary and secondary schools are described in broad general terms in Townsend and Brittan's survey of multi-racial schools. Less than a quarter of infant schools grouped children by ability and some others provided language or slow learner classes. In the junior schools, there tended to be an increase in schools which streamed although mixed ability schools outnumbered streamed ones. In schools which streamed, the four immigrant groups were found to be in lower streams than non-immigrant, with West Indians, 'generally more lowly placed'. The situation was found to be infinitely more complex in secondary schools but the results are similar to those in primary schools.

Over two-thirds of the secondary schools in the sample streamed by ability and the heads' views of the spread of immigrants across these streams according to ethnic group is indicated in Townsend and Brittan (1972, Table A 10). There is a clustering of immigrants in the lower streams of one school.

Although the research team found that heads link causes to linguistic deficiencies and lack of ability, it is recognized that other factors are influential, since European immigrants appear to be more highly placed in both primary and secondary school stages. Townsend and Brittan suggest further study and research into the reasons for this situation.

A recent report from the Department of Education and Science (1971a) based on the findings of a pilot survey carried out by an HM Inspectorate into current practice and opinion on the assessment of pupils from overseas, says that in the testing of immigrant children, the methods and materials are frequently inadequate and of doubtful theoretical basis.

It found that testing in infant and junior schools was often by the teacher's subjective judgement. When children were transferred to secondary school, most of the authorities had them take the standard tests, although it was recognized that these were of little relevance in assessing intellectual potential. It, nevertheless, determined a special place in the school.

Teachers recognized the problems and the need for specially devised standardized tests to assess immigrant children's potential, if such an exercise was theoretically possible. Many felt that better methods of assessment could be developed which could also identify problems and assess cultural, social and linguistic progress of non-immigrant children as well.

Most teachers recognized that the first priority was appropriate methods of assessment in the field of language development, proficiency in English and educational attainment. They wished to be able to assess when a child had sufficient language to work full-time in an ordinary class and to be able to monitor their subsequent progress (DES, 1971a).

V. Studies in Progress to Devise or Adapt Objective Tests of Academic Potential and Language Attainment

A. *Introduction*

It is clear that *some* of the difficulties faced by LEAs, their schools and the teachers, in dealing with immigrant pupils' educational development, stem from:

(1) the lack of objective tests to assess ability or potential, tests standardized for their ethnic group;

(2) the lack of such objective tests of attainment, in different subjects, with the greatest priority for tests to assess language levels and competence.

There is also not complete agreement among all psychologists as to whether such objective tests of ability can measure ultimate potential for any pupil.

Some psychologists such as Bloom (1964) feel that as situational factors affect test scores significantly, measured intelligence is not meaningful in determining a 'ceiling level' of the learning ability of the disadvantaged child. It should be accepted as measuring the operating capacity at a given moment of development, but not as an indicator of potential.

A recent experiment by Watson (1973) with slow learning West Indian and English pupils illustrates this point aptly.

The West Indian pupils who obtained less than 80 in the verbal WISC scores were retested 18 months later. The control group of non-immigrant pupils of similar ability were also reassessed. For every immigrant there was a rise in score of eight points of the 20. The control group mean rose only 0·25. The difference between the means is significant.

Previous studies have shown that retesting subnormal pupils does not lead to a significant increase in mean IQ, but it is found to be the case for a group of immigrant pupils.

It is suggested that this study be repeated on a larger scale.

Nevertheless, there appears to be agreement that such objective tests of ability are useful instruments to enable teachers or psychologists to assess a child's present level of functioning, if not of future development.

Tests of attainment should enable them to diagnose the needs of pupils, and show how to meet these in terms of the present level of functioning.

B. *A Test to Diagnose Ability to Learn for non-English Pupils*

The National Foundation for Educational Research appears to be the first organization which is attempting under Haynes (1971), to develop objective tests to assess ability to learn in school, for use with children who neither speak nor write adequate English in multi-racial schools.

Haynes believes that intelligence tests given to immigrant children are not able to measure adequately their present or future performance because of their verbal bias and cultural assumptions, which are not those of the children's culture. Their scores on such tests are unfair and may be misleading. She has devised new tests, which it is hoped are less culturally and verbally biased. They are devised to assess the learning ability of children with linguistic handicap. Some of these tests are based on ability to draw correct geometrical analogies, classify sets of objects according to perceptual attributes and to associate familiar objects with unfamiliar names. 'These new tests,' says Haynes, 'should provide a situation, where it is possible to assess a child's ability to learn on the basis of verbal learning, reasoning and concept formation.' (*The Times*, March 16th, 1971.) She describes these tests in detail, how they were administered, the ratings given for co-operation, confidence and concentration, and what additional factors scoring took into account.

The tests have been tried out with a sample of Indian and English children in the first year Junior School and at the end of two years were validated against measures of actual scholastic progress. Although the immigrant children did not do so well as the English children on all tests they did score better on Haynes' tests than on the traditional intelligence tests which they had taken. These tests were found to be more accurate in predicting children's attainment than the traditional intelligence test or teachers' assessments. It was found that they were useful for English children, although different norms will be necessary for each group.

Although this shows encouraging results, the NFER point out that they are allocating £10,000 for follow-up research on other ethnic group children from six to 13 years before the tests can be used for all groups by teachers in the classroom. They may at the moment, however, only be used by educational psychologists for certain ages.

Haynes and Townsend (1971) mention that the former's test is not one of intelligence but 'a battery of tests of learning potential involving a battery of individual tests of learning involving the teaching of specified tasks'.

NFER, Townsend and Brittan (1972) and the Department of Education and Science (1971 Education Survey 10) all stress that work should also be undertaken to improve the reliability and validity of teachers' subjective assessments and, in the words of the latter: 'There is a need to distinguish between standardized tests and methods of assessment which may take a long time to develop and less sophisticated means by which a teacher can check the progress of his pupils and determine their needs. Projects to develop the latter kind of assessment should be given priority.'

C. *The Development of Tests of Attainment in Linguistic Proficiency*

Many of the difficulties for the LEAs and their schools in assessing language needs and teaching standard English, Townsend found, stemmed from the lack of diagnostic instruments which had reliability and validity to measure in such areas as: inter-school proficiency in language; social skills; language proficiency for infant and junior school work; specialized subject language proficiency for secondary school work.

One response was that of Mittler and Ward (1970), which was to devise or adapt existing tests to use as diagnostic instruments to enable teachers to understand the child's level of proficiency in all aspects of language; comprehension, speech, writing and reading.

Mittler and Ward (1970) have administered an expanded edition of the Illinois Test of Psycho-linguistic Abilities (ITPA) on a sample of British four-year-old nursery school children to provide normative data and to see if their performances are comparable to that of the American sample.

This test was designed as a diagnostic instrument to delineate specific psycho-linguistic abilities in children in America. It studies nine different aspects of the child's linguistic functioning, including production and comprehension. They found that the performance of the English sample is comparable with that of the American one. The effect of social class membership was very marked though auditory vocal channels were more affected by social class than visual motor channels.

Once standardized on different groups of British children, whether native or immigrant, it could help teachers and educational psychologists to study different aspects of the child's linguistic development.

The National Foundation for Educational Research has organized a two-stage project in co-operation with Birmingham University based on the research done by Rudd from 1969–70, which provided the specifications for tests which were to be constructed to determine the competence of the immigrant children in the use of English.

The second stage initiated by the Committee on Research and Development in Modern Languages from 1970–73, supervised by C. Burstall, developed diagnostic and proficiency tests to measure the listening, speaking, reading and writing levels of primary school immigrant children whose language or dialect are different from standard English. The individual items and tests have been tested on junior school pupils of all nationalities so that they are reliable and valid. They should enable the teacher to place the immigrant child in appropriate groups or classes (Rudd, 1971a, 1971b). The tests were administered to a nationwide sample by LEAs and teachers from 1973–74. The type of language teaching the children have had was also collated. Ewen and Gipps (1973), who conducted these trials in association with Sumner, have given a detailed description of the tests to be administered.

Such tests should help class teachers and language centre staff to assess more accurately, on an inter-school basis, the actual needs of the pupil in the field of English. The pupil's level of competence in listening, speaking, reading and writing, are tested separately at each level to measure their ability in these skills independently of one another. There are three tests in each field graded for different levels of difficulty to test comprehension of single words, sentences, and longer passages. Most tests have pictures as stimulus material, related to children in multi-racial junior schools—and based on their language and activities. The tests should enable teachers to plan remedial tuition and may be used again to test progress (NFER, 1973).

The DES accepts Professor Vernon's (1968) view that there is no such thing as a culture-fair test: 'Intelligence is a developmental concept and the level of stimulation in the environment has a considerable effect on its development.' He concludes 'that there is no scientific way of finding out a child's potential other than watching how the child progresses as he begins to pick up standard English and settle into school'.

Thus the DES suggest, 'that the best educational arrangement for disadvantaged immigrant children is to expose them to a good rich educational environment and to subject them to a systematic observation of their responses'. Many will need special arrangements to meet their particular needs until they can profit from an ordinary school, as long as regular reassessment of their abilities ensures that transfer will occur. They quote Professor Vernon's statement that, 'the best answer . . . . is that the psychologist should attempt to give quite a wide range of varied tests, verbal and non-verbal, including any that he can get across to the particular pupil and should simultaneously obtain a detailed case study of the pupil's background, education and linguistic history, present situation and behaviour. If the test scores are interpreted in the light of the handicaps that have been ascertained, it should be possible to make a clinical diagnosis of likely progress. . . . In other words, there is no simple mechanical solution to the problem. . . .' (DES, *ibid.*, p. 68).

CHAPTER FIVE

Cultural Factors Affecting the Education of Immigrant Children

I. Cultural Adjustments Faced by the Immigrant Child

Although problems of adaptation and acceptance of immigrants are many, regardless of the country in which they settle, and the literature is fairly large in countries such as the United States of America and Israel, which are composed chiefly of 'immigrants', there were only a few such studies on adaptation problems of immigrants and their families in Britain before the main advent of Commonwealth immigrants. These were by Cunningham (1897) of East Europeans, Tannahill (1958) of European volunteer workers, Zubrzicki (1956) of Polish immigrants and Thompson (1963) on the Irish.

Because of the European background of these immigrants their problems of adaptation and acceptance, though far from easy, were not nevertheless as overwhelming as those faced by the Commonwealth immigrants. Some of these problems were due, particularly in the case of the Asians, to their vastly different cultural, social and religious traditions. The habits and traditions of the West Indians, although based on our own, were also quite different. Their different colour also made them highly conspicuous and easy scapegoats for the insecure. They faced difficulties in adapting to our urban life, to our cultural and social differences and to the climate which, together, often led to physical illness and psychological tension in the family.

The fact also that wives and children may also have been separated from the head of the household for several years, or, in the case of the West Indian children, from both parents, often makes personal relationships in the home less stable. Such adjustment problems in the family inevitably affect the children, and influence their own personal adjustment, as psychologists pointed out in a conference sponsored by the London Council of Social Service in 1964. Typical problems faced by immigrant families and their children in London which stem from inadequate housing or homelessness were examined by a child care officer and psychiatrist at a conference chaired by Professor Titmuss (CRC 1970). The unstimulating environment provided by inadequate child minders may affect the pre-school child's mental and social development as well (Fitzherbert 1967; P.A.C., 1971).

Triseliotis, a contributor to Oakley's (1968) symposium on immigrants' cultural background, mentioned that some of the children's withdrawal or behaviour problems at school may stem from 'cultural shock' involved in adapting suddenly to an alien culture and in some cases to parents not seen for several years. Such behaviour may stem also from the conflict the child faces between behaviour expected at home and that demanded by the school, since, as Williams in Rex and Moore (1966) found from the children's essays, standards of their ethnic culture may clash with those of the school and peer group. The schools in England, as Bowker (1968) and Oakley (1968) point out, in the case of West Indian and Pakistani children for example, are completely different from the schools they have attended, probably for shorter periods in relation to their age than British children. The new teaching methods and techniques, the use of books, the discipline, must all be adapted to. Humphrey and John (1971) present vividly first hand accounts of the experiences of immigrant pupils and their families in Britain, which should help teachers and young people empathize and understand more sensitively some of their reactions. Hashmi's pamphlet on the 'Psychology of Race Relations' is reprinted as an appendix.

Elkin (1971), in her bibliographies for the multi-racial classroom, has a section called Problems, which lists stories and novels depicting adjustment problems faced by immigrant or foreign children in a new country.

Many teachers have been aware of the influence of cultural and social factors on the educational adjustment of immigrant children and realized the need for research. In 1965 the London Head Teachers' Association's memorandum made many recommendations, among which were ones emphasizing that (1) cultural barriers to learning need to be studied; (2) investigations into what constitutes disturbed behaviour for the different ethnic groups should be made; (3) methods of mental and intelligence testing for immigrant children need to be developed.

The young infant child may adapt with less stress than the young teenager. Kitzinger (1972) reports on the problems of West Indian children, as does Burrowes (1972) for all immigrant children. Patterson (1963b) reported that it is the young or second generation immigrant who seems to have the major problem of adaptation and acceptance.

Kitzinger (1972), who is familar with the culture from which the average immigrant West Indian child comes, vividly describes the contrasts the child faces in home, community and church environment, and differences of school life in both countries. In the West Indies, the child shares economic responsibility in the family household in rural areas and has a sense of responsible identity. All this is changed on his arrival in England and many suffer personal deprivation and emotional trauma and may display symptoms alternating between withdrawal and hyperactivity. The West Indian parents' norms of behaviour in the West Indian culture often encourages these symptoms. Because norms of child behaviour are different in English and West Indian society, psychotherapeutic treatment must involve schoolteachers and parents in understanding the child's cultural and psychological stresses.

Milner (1972) points out that even after cultural integration is achieved, colour and caste are determinants of prejudice in American society and appear to be so in British society. Hauser's (1971) study of black American adolescents found that they had very negative self-estimates which in turn 'tended to generate low expectations of educational success in the minds of both pupils and teachers. Self-fulfilling prophecies only continue the process of self-disparagement when they come to fruition.' (Milner, 1972, p. 21). He quotes from his recent British study, which seems to indicate that young immigrant children are giving negative value to their ethnic identity, similar to results in studies for Black Americans (Milner, 1971).

His suggested solution, already commenced here and in the USA, is for black communities to foster their cultural identification and distinctiveness and consider it a resource and not a handicap. Official policy should support cultural pluralism where it does not conflict with British values. There should be greater effort to provide black personnel in all areas of the child's life, successful models who understand his problems and with whom he can identify. Such points will be further discussed in Chapter VI.

II. The Attitudes of the Child's Parents and that of the Immigrant Community

The attitude of the parents towards their children's acculturation to the English culture varies among the different ethnic groups as well as the attitudes of the individual parents within these groups.

Although initially studies on this subject are few, it appears that Asian parents on the whole wish to retain their own separate social and cultural existence. Asian parents, Williams in Rex (1960) found, did not wish their children anglicized even though they encourage them to have high aspirations in educational and vocational fields. They are not always appreciative or understanding of the modern educational methods in English schools and believe the children are not working, or learning. They may be diffident about attending parents' open evenings because their English is inadequate to communicate with the teachers, or their shift work may make it inconvenient. However, in some areas they may visit the school too frequently from the headmaster's point of view to see that their child takes the right courses and appropriate exams for selective entry,[1] or to check on his progress. Taylor (1971) found that 33 per cent of his Asian parents were in favour of their boys staying on at school, compared to 19 per cent of the English parents. Rose (1969), who has drawn on the Survey of Race Relations studies material in his description of Indian and Pakistani ethnic and religious group settlements in Britain, points out the problems the young have to face in adjusting to two cultures, and how social institutions and economic pressures have caused parents to modify some of their attitudes and traditions relevant to the roles of young people and women in the fields of education, work and leisure.

Although the Asian girls initially wear traditional dress in school, many parents are now co-operating on compromise arrangements with the schools. They may still keep them secluded at home after school, but many are permitting their daughters to finish their studies and to work before marriage. Others still arrange marriages for their girls at a very early age. Feeley (1965) found that Asian parents discouraged after-school activities for the boys, unless it was of academic relevance. The tradition for boys in these countries is to spend their leisure with the older men since organized youth activity, other than sport, is not a tradition in their culture.

Many ethnic groups sponsor afternoon and evening schools for their children to offset the influence of English culture and to teach them to read, write and appreciate their parents' language, literature and religious traditions. This may be because only five LEAs reported that language of immigrants' countries of origin were taught in the schools. Languages which were mentioned were Asian languages or Urdu or Punjabi. They were examination subjects but had to be prepared under the pupils' own resources. There is little evidence that LEAs are helping immigrant pupils maintain the learning of their mother-tongue (Townsend, 1971), although some do co-operate with immigrant organizations in allowing the use of their premises for language lessons. However, in his survey of multi-racial schools (Townsend, 1972) found that over half of the sample reported

[1] Personal communication from Glasgow headmaster.

arrangements made by the immigrant communities to teach their own languages.

The Greek Cypriots in London have classes twice a week to teach their children the ideals of the church and nation (George and Millerson, 1967). Authorities such as Bradford and Waltham Forest allow Islamic classes twice a week after school on authority premises. These are taken by trained Muslim teachers (Devlin, 1970). Sikh children frequently attend Punjabi classes.

The West Indian parents, as Fitzherbert (1968) indicates, although ambitious for their children to achieve skilled, white-collar or professional careers, may find it difficult to understand the different educational methods and permissive atmosphere of the English school, which they claim is the cause of their youngsters rejecting the traditional authoritarian discipline wielded by West Indian parents. Many do not always understand or are unable to provide a quiet place for the child to do his homework, which is necessary if he is to realize his academic aspirations. Beetham's (1967) study indicated that his West Indian sample had difficulties which stemmed from living in overcrowded conditions. The occupations they wished to enter were those which were considered desirable in the parents' country of origin, and were not always realistic in terms of opportunities in England. There is also a tradition of respect towards teachers which in the past has led few to question their judgement when their child was classified as ESN. However, as has been pointed out elsewhere, the disproportionate numbers of West Indian children placed in this category has been challenged through their West Indian Associations.

III. **Attitude of the School Staff and Administrators**

The schools staff have been initially so busy coping with language problems, demonstrating the social routines of the school, teaching the children basic safety precautions, that they had little time to help the child or teenager explicitly to come to terms with his new environment, nor to encourage the host children to welcome the newcomers and to learn about their traditions.

There is a paucity of studies on how many schools accept their secondary role as agents of socialization for English children and as agents of acculturation for the immigrant child. Williams (in Rex and Moore, 1968) believed that the success of the school in this latter role is dependent upon:

1. the aims and attitudes of the teachers;
2. the affinity of the parental attitudes with those of the school;
3. the attitudes and aspirations of the immigrant children;

4. the attitudes of the British children (though this cannot be controlled by the school);
5. the attitudes of the wider society.

The heads and teachers in this study showed that the teachers saw their role as one of anglicizing the children and in the sense of teaching them middle-class behaviour patterns and aspirations. 'Integration' is expectated to occur automatically if multi-racial children are educated together.

Dosanjh's (1969) study of Nottingham schools found teachers were fairly equally divided in their attitudes towards Punjabi children—49 per cent believing that they adjusted more easily than English children, 33 per cent that they adjusted less well.

Rose (1969) quotes teachers' reactions to the disturbed and uncontrolled behaviour of some West Indian pupils, due to such factors as long separation from their parents, 'inadequate English' for education, and to the children's difficulties in understanding expected school behaviour, due to differences in school discipline in England.

Feeley (1965), who studied race relations in three northern secondary schools, found staff views ranging from tolerant to severly prejudiced.

Townsend and Brittan, in their (1972) survey of a sample of multi-racial schools, when asked about difficulties in establishing contact with parents from different ethnic groups, found that most of the 119 schools which had difficulties had problems in contacting Asian parents. More than half of the 230 sample schools had problems in establishing home/school links, although one-quarter of the primary schools and one-third of the secondary schools sent information to parents in their own language and some described imaginative means that encouraged parental interest.

The multi-racial schools' Heads were asked whether the attitudes and customs of parents of immigrant children presented any problems in such areas as 'uniform, physical education, school meals, co-education, discipline, extra-curricular activities and employment opportunities'.

About two-thirds of the Heads commented on at least one and generally more than one of the topics. Discipline as an area of difficulty was given by one-third of the primary school heads and one-quarter of the secondary ones.

It was particularly difficult to get parents of immigrant children to allow them to participate in extra-curricular activities and group trips, particularly for Asian girls. Parents were found to encourage the children to stay at school until they could obtain CSE or 'O' levels in the hopes of better employment possibilities, even though their lack of ability in English might make this difficult.

The data on these subjects show the members of schools having some difficulty but does not tell us how severe or how often these occur.

IV. Peer Group Friendship Patterns and Attitudes of Schoolchildren from different Ethnic Groups

A number of studies have now been undertaken among school children to establish whether awareness of ethnic differences exists and their attitudes towards such differences if awareness exists.

Two studies, however, are discussed first, since these may put the other ones in perspective.

Marsh (1970) in reviewing the literature, chiefly American, on awareness of racial differences among young children, divides this process into two stages.

1. The child's perception that some people are white and others coloured and that these people are like me or not like me.
2. The cognitive or affective process which involves attaching secondary value statements to observed racial differences such as approval or disapproval, pleasure or discomfort, acceptance or rejection.

For this second stage the child must either receive instruction direct or indirect of the values to be attached to these differences, or he may derive value association independently.

Marsh studied racial awareness of pre-school children in an area and in families where overt racial consciousness and hostility was not a salient feature in everyday life. Half of the children were North African children being fostered in homes of British families who had young children of similar age. It was found that the children knew about racial differences, but did not attach negative value judgements leading to racial stereotypes unless they were exposed to socializing forces characterized by overt racial consciousness or hostility.

Thus Horowitz (1936), an American researcher, found little difference in the amount of prejudice in white boys who had quite differing degrees of personal contact with negroes. He concluded that it was contact with prevalent attitudes towards negroes which was more important than actual contact. Richardson and Green (1971), however, when exploring the attitudes of children to children with dark as compared to light skin colour (using photographs), found that, although children preferred light to dark skinned children, when choices were presented of a dark skinned child without physical handicap and four light skinned children with the first, crutches, the second, an arm amputation, the third, a facial disfigurement and the fourth, in an obese state, the dark skinned child was liked more than those with handicaps.

Several studies of friendship choices among school children in multi-racial schools indicate that children choose more of their own group as friends than can be expected by chance. The in-group preference of the majority—the English in this instance—is markedly stronger than the in-group preference of the other majority ethnic groups, who choose quite a high proportion of English. Kawwa (1965) found the majority of seven- to eight-year-olds in primary schools were aware of country, nationality and colour, although awareness of differences was confused until about 10 or 11 years. Ethnic prejudices were found in children as young as seven years of age.

Durojaiye (1969) found that, in a junior school, the children's own ethnic group significantly influenced their choice of friends in every form. The ethnic self-preference of the whites and children of mixed parentage was stronger than that of dark children. Interestingly enough, leadership choices were not influenced by ethnic group.

In a study of friendship choices among school children Kawwa (1963) found more prejudices in a comprehensive school in Islington, which contained a minority of coloured and Cypriot children, than in Lowestoft, a town which had few immigrant inhabitants. He found that members of the three ethnic groups chose more of their members than would be expected by chance. Prejudice was much more intense against the Cypriots than against the coloured immigrants, probably due to the fact that they were the largest ethnic group both in the school and in the area.

Saint (1963a) found a strong social cleavage between the majority English and the minority Punjabi groups in the classes studied. The in-group preference of the majority group was markedly stronger than the in-group preference of the minority group. The almost complete lack of English boys' choice of any Punjabis as friends may be an indication of prejudice.

Later Kawwa (1965) studied 750 children, mainly English, with almost equal numbers of such minority groups as Cypriot, West Indian and Asian, in one primary and one secondary school. In secondary schools ethnic cleavage appears to be significant in choice of friendship patterns and rejection patterns, and awareness of colour, national origin and religion is universal. All non-English European children seemed to achieve assimilation rapidly. In contrast, coloured children had a difficult time and probably will have so long as colour is an important sign of alienation. Prejudice among children came out in Kawwa's study, in their stereotyped opinions about different ethnic groups: 'They take our jobs, our homes'; these seem to be echoes of parental attitudes. The attitudes of the immigrant children generally were that the English were not friendly and did not believe that all men were equal; and 95 per cent of the families had no English friends. Tables from these two studies which present the main types of ethnic choices and rejection patterns are summarized and salient points presented in an article by Kawwa (1968). He believes that the high number of English boys chosen as would-be friends by the ethnic out-groups indicate a desire for social acceptance and integration.

Rowley (1967), who gave sociometric tests of friendship choices in a sample of classes from primary and secondary multi-racial schools, found that the pattern of in-group and out-group choices made it clear that:

1. 90 per cent of British children preferred British friends in all situations;
2. 75 per cent of Indians preferred their own nationality.
3. 68 per cent of the West Indians did likewise.

There was a tendency for in-group choices to increase as children became older.

Robertson and Kawwa (1971) in a girls' comprehensive school in London found that, although in general white girls and coloured girls tended to choose friends from their own ethnic group, exceptions were frequent and variations interesting. The higher streams at all age levels had a greater interaction of ethnic friendships.

Ledermann (1969) found that factors on which children in their study rated as important for popularity were intelligibility and scholastic attainment. Behaviour and social standards acceptable to authority were least influential in their choice.

Bhatanagar (1969, 1970) compared the social-personal adjustment of West Indian and Cypriot children with a control group of English children in the same school. He found that there was little mixing of the children of different ages and that the West Indian children were the least adjusted. Hill (1968) on the other hand, although chiefly interested in attitudes of West Indian and English adolescents towards home, school and community, found that West Indians had a higher self-assessment than their English counterparts, as well as more favourable attitudes to education; though both groups expressed in-group preferences, there was evidence of inter-racial tolerance in spite of aspects of colour prejudice which were evident.

Social relationships, though not included as an area of study in the survey of multi-racial schools by Townsend and Brittan (1972), is to be studied in depth in 20 schools in Phase III of the study by Townsend. However, about 26 Heads believed that it was an area which should be studied. Sometimes certain ethnic groups did not always mix happily with one another, nor with English children, though inter-group relations varied considerably.

Hartley (1972) in a review of his report on his three-year-project with coloured teenagers says that, since in his experience friendship patterns do not cut across racial barriers, he advocates that DES should give grants to coloured organizations for youth clubs for their own adolescents to enable them to have adequate leisure facilities.

Few studies are as yet available as to whether the coloured child in Britain is aware of racial prejudice and at what age this becomes apparent to him whether consciously or unconsciously. Milner's (1971) study indicates that infant school children are aware of derogatory attitudes towards colour in British society. A study was carried out of 500 children of Asian, English and West Indian origin between the ages of five and eight years. Questions were asked about coloured and white dolls and it was found that both immigrant groups preferred white dolls, attributing good characteristics to the former and bad characteristics to the latter. Almost 50 per cent of the West Indian children said that white dolls resembled them more than coloured dolls and 72 per cent indicated that they would rather be a white doll. The numbers were lower for the Asians. It is not, as he makes clear, that immigrant children think they are white but rather that they would prefer to be so and don't like to think of themselves as black.

Laishley (1971), who studied children from three nursery schools, two in areas which had few immigrants and one which has a high proportion of immigrants, found that awareness of colour was not a salient feature in these children's interactions nor was it negatively evaluated. There were very small minorities of coloured children in these nursery schools.

Milner's children have reactions similar to the children in the American study by Goodman (1952). The negative effects of such attitudes on motivation and educational achievement have also been studied and described in the previous chapter. In Britain there appears to be some evidence from general descriptive surveys in Liverpool and Cardiff and from other studies in progress that loss of motivation may exist in the same ethnic group when the higher expectations of these youngsters in occupational fields is disappointed (Liverpool Youth Organization, 1968; Bloom, 1968; and Bloom in Rose, 1969, p. 487).

V. Attitudes of the Wider Host Society

As previous studies have indicated, both immigrant parents and children have high educational and vocational aspirations and often the motivation to achieve the former, yet, if the adolescent cannot obtain a job in keeping with his qualifications and knows that in spite of these, opportunities are limited for him in skilled, clerical and other similar fields, this will affect his school adjustment and his attitudes towards society. He will be occupationally frustrated by being identified through colour by the host society, with the older immigrant generations and with the stereotype, however unjustified, as an unskilled newcomer.

In the study of Tapper and Stoppes (1963) the latter claims that many of the West Indian boys constantly meet with discrimination in job seeking. The CIAC (1964) Immigrant School Leavers Report believed that their evidence indicated that there was cause for concern about job prospects for adolescents with above average ability. The Youth Employment Service, DEP (1968) and Beetham (1967), studying young immigrant school leavers in Birmingham, found that the Youth Employment Office had to spend a much greater amount of time placing coloured school-leavers, partly due to what he called 'unrealistic aspirations' and to discrimination.

Figueroa's (1969) study, details of which were abstracted in The Select Committee on Immigration and Race, was of London West Indian school-leavers, who were matched with English school-leavers of similar attainment, and found that the former were less successful in attaining the jobs they wished and had a narrower range of choice. Because many of them came from deprived backgrounds, he is testing further hypotheses to see whether they are disadvantaged because they come from a deprived environment[1] or because there is colour discrimination.

Social contacts among schoolchildren and adolescents after school appear to be few, as indicated from previous studies cited on school friendship choices and that of the Hunt Committee Report (1967) which found little contact between immigrant boys and English peers after school or in youth clubs. Their use of the youth service was related to their acceptance in the local community. The girls from Asian and West Indian backgrounds are often discouraged from making such social contacts.

The Milsom (1966) survey of Birmingham teenagers found that West Indians were likely to belong to multi-racial youth clubs and readier to integrate than the Asian youth. In Manchester, very few immigrants spent their leisure with English friends and few attended youth clubs (Youth Development Trust, 1967). Negative attitudes of the outside community may not affect the children from the Asian

1 He found that only half of the West Indians lived at home and that they all came from large families who lived in over-crowded conditions.

and Cypriot community since their parents seem more successful in enabling them to retain their cultural identity. Those who feel most this rejection are the West Indian young people, since they are used to clubs in their countries of origin and wish to join in such activities here. The Select Committee Report (1969) on *Coloured School Leavers* gives evidence from many areas throughout the country of problems of integration and acceptance faced by these young people both in the youth service and the wider society.

Studies in areas which have had older third generation coloured immigrants indicate that integration has not occurred and that discrimination exists. Bloom's study in Bute Town, Cardiff, Rose (1969) and Bloom (1971) find that few moved out of their area, fearing rebuffs and accepting the narrow occupational roles and social roles assigned to them.[1] Liverpool Youth Organizations Committee (1968) found a similar situation here, particularly for the second or third generation of coloured young people. It is difficult for them to obtain jobs involving contact with the public. Most were conscious of prejudice and discrimination around the age of 10 years, and consciously hesitated to expose themselves to situations or areas where they would encounter these attitudes. Few attended youth clubs. All studies mentioned that immigrant children share the stigma of the socially deprived if they live in the same area.

These latter two studies, though very limited, and relevant mainly to children of African and West Indian descent, and children of mixed marriages, as to the effect of community attitudes of prejudice and discrimination, on educational and vocational aspirations of our earlier first and second generation coloured British citizens, suggests that the present immigrant children may lower their aspirations and remain, as Rose (1969) says, 'encapsulated in their enclave and local culture', unless much more positive action is taken to alter this situation. They may alternatively rebel against this discrimination by political activism, as a study by MacIntyre and Brannan (1971) of black Cardiff-born adolescents indicates. With fewer jobs available in their neighbourhood area and unemployment, many black school-leavers and adults believe they are facing discrimination as they search unsuccessfully for jobs inland and in the city.

Attitudes of the host society, as indicated by surveys, of racial prejudice, political debate and legislation are described in Chapter I.

[1] The results of several surveys among whites and non-whites found first to third generation informants of the latter highly ambivalent about colour—pride in being black but feeling acute dissatisfaction about what being black entails, even though they had lived in Bute town many years. Differences in opportunity and education were stressed. All had suffered discrimination.

How young immigrants interpret the attitudes of the wider society is perhaps more relevant.

Marplan, in a survey of young immigrants aged 16 to 24 commissioned and published by *The Times* (February, 1971) in three reports, set out to find out the attitudes of a sample of West Indians, Pakistanis and Indians, only one per cent of whom (the Asians) had been born in the UK. Evans (1972) has further analysed these data and presented comparatively their reactions to experience in Britain. He points out that 'the future of race relations in Britain may be largely dependent upon the experience and response of young immigrants in three main fields—education, jobs and housing'. The majority in all groups thought they were to blame for doing less well in school than expected.

Though Asians were fairly happy with their jobs, 42 per cent of West Indians thought their jobs below expectations and the same proportion in all groups who felt this, put it down to their colour.

Nevertheless, most young immigrants were optimistic about the future (better neighbourhood, income and job) than working class men in a similar survey done earlier by Marplan. Asked if police dealt unfairly with their ethnic group, 31 per cent of the Indians, 64 per cent of the West Indians and 23 per cent of the Pakistanis felt that this was the case.

Those who believed race relations were worsening were 28 per cent of Indians, 42 per cent of West Indians and 48 per cent of the Pakistanis, who believed that Mr Powell's speeches were the main cause, though only the West Indians thought the main reason was that 'whites don't like us or understand us'. Those who thought the situation was the same were 45 per cent of Indians, 24 per cent of West Indians and 19 per cent of the Pakistanis.

Although a majority in each ethnic group—69 per cent West Indians, 74 per cent Pakistanis and 78 per cent Indians—believed that they should adapt to the customs of English society, an equally high proportion agreed that they should be prepared to fight for their rights.

Recent official reports suggest that the situation of young black people is now giving cause for concern. Runnymede's Race Relations Bulletin (July 1972) gives us extracts from several police authorities representing the national picture,[1] the metropolis[2] and the Working Party on Police Training in Race Relations. All recognize that the police bear the brunt for inadequacies of housing, education, job opportunities, leisure facilities, and of racial discrimination in areas where immigrants settle. These are political and social situations

1 Report of HM Chief Inspector of the Constabulary.

2 Report of the Commissioner of Police for the Metropolis.

which they cannot remedy but all make recommendations on ways to improve understanding in their forces by further training, education in cultures and language of ethnic groups and the positive stimulation of relationships with immigrant communities.

The recommendations of the Select Committee Report on Police and Immigrant Relations, summarized in Runnymede's Race Relations Bulletin (October 1972) makes many positive recommendations, among which is the recommendation that the relevant government department should jointly sponsor a special inquiry to measure and make recommendations for the problem of homeless black youths.

VI. The Attitudes of the Immigrant Child and Adolescent

The attitudes of the school, the peer group, the family and the community towards the aspirations appropriate for the immigrant child or adolescent are often different and contradictory. How does the young immigrant reconcile and adjust to these differing attitudes and expectations, in order to determine his own aspirations? He may find it difficult to come to a 'modus vivendi' between the two cultures and sub-cultures. Do social institutions help him to come to terms with the conflicting roles which are presented to him?

Kaushal (1965) at a conference on 'Racial Tensions among Youth' pointed out that there is an urgent necessity for some agency to help them with these problems. At a conference at Leeds University, Asian teenagers said that, although some parents were adjusting to conditions over here, there were still clashes between their desire to behave as their contemporaries without betraying the beliefs of their parents. A social development officer, Miss Unnisa, with the Community Relations Commission, believes that the problems must be settled by the parents and children themselves and that no outside agency could intervene (*Guardian*, 1970). In *Multi-racial School* (1973) and Hill (1972) describing the adjustments faced by Asian girls, the former vividly describes one girl's approach to solving how to adapt to the conflicting roles of the two cultures.

Taylor (1972b) describes how neither Asian young men nor women reject their parents' traditional approach to marriage.

Lewis (1970) believes that British schools should help the immigrant child explicitly to adapt to the two cultures and two languages. Awareness of the differences[1] may be intense among bilingual immigrants and may produce one of the following results:

1. the immigrant is conscious of his ethnic origin and considers himself distinctly differentiated and may develop hostility;

[1] If differences are not adapted to, emotional instability may develop and this may inhibit the development of intellectual and scholastic competence.

2. he may feel uncertainty in ethnic identity patterns and live on the margins of his own and the dominant culture—a marginal man;

3. he may avoid commitment with either community and try to be non-allied;

4. he may succeed in preserving a stable relationship between the two cultures—keeping delimited areas in which each is meaningful.

Though Evans (1972) found differences between the different immigrant groups in their difficulties and aspirations, each ethnic group was proud of their racial and cultural background and accepted many of its traditions, particularly Indians and Pakistanis. However, because they had been educated in Britain . . . 'Many of these young people are here not only to stay, they are also anxious to fulfill themselves as themselves, and this can only be to the benefit of a society which recognizes and realizes their potential.'

Brandon and Watson (1973) discuss the limited evidence as to whether there is increasing disaffection among young immigrants towards our society as indicated by such conditions as increasing homelessness, unemployment, poor police/immigrant relations and, though they come to different conclusions, both agree on the need for research in this field.

The Home Secretary has asked the Community Relations Commission to have an inquiry into the incidence, causes and consequences of both adolescent unemployment and homelessness amongst ethnic minorities in Britain, and to report on policy implications (Runnymede Bulletin, Feb, 1973).

In other words, the opportunities for the young school-leaver in employment and in social leisure activities are likely to have a strong influence on his attitudes and motivation in school.

Research shows that many have higher educational and vocational aspirations than English children in their schools. Taylor (1971) in his study of Asian boys in secondary schools in Newcastle found that higher proportions of Asians

1. stayed on at school beyond the age of 15;
2. had a higher number of certificates on leaving school;
3. remained in full time education longer;
4. had professional career aspirations;
5. Fewer were chosen for selective schools or places.

Beetham (1967) found his sample of fourth-year pupils that over 10 per cent of immigrant pupils, compared to one per cent of the English, intended to stay longer at school and had higher vocational aspirations than their English contemporaries and a greater number did not anticipate problems in fulfilling their ambitions. He found a high proportion are influenced by their parents in choice of careers.

Triseliotis describes some of the pressures faced by immigrant children who attend a Health Centre (at Oakley) in North London (1968). Feeley (1965) investigated social integration of coloured immigrant pupils in Liverpool Northern Secondary Schools, finding more children in 'A' streams where the child is fluent in English.

There are research studies in progress on comparisons of aspirations and adjustments of young people from different ethnic groups, and of English and coloured people at school and at work which are listed in Sivanandan (1969, *ibid.*) the most comprehensive being that of the Department of Employment and Productivity, which is following the progress of groups in four areas over a five-year period. As Bowker (1968, p. 81) points out, 'the child whose own aspirations coincide with those of the home and the policy of the school is most likely to make a smooth social and economic adjustment to life in this country', assuming he has equal opportunities.

However, although there is a paucity of research studies in this area, in Britain it seems clear from the experience of young immigrants in other countries that:

'all immigrant children and second generation immigrants whatever their relationship with home or peer group, will inevitably find themselves in a marginal situation where they are no longer fully accepted by either the family because of their English education, or by the native community because of their colour or cultural origins. For the individual there is likely to be a crisis of cultural identity. Is he English . . . or Indian . . . or Pakistani . . . or West Indian? The extent to which this becomes an acute problem of identity may depend on the extent of the recognizable prejudice and discrimination in the individual's immediate occupational and social environment.' (Bowker, p. 82)

However, as has been indicated, the approach for a harmonious integration must involve the whole school population. This fact is recognized by the Schools Council Project, who are not only producing materials for the learning of standard English language, but have also set themselves the task of educating the whole school population for life in a multi-racial society.

The importance of social education for a multi-racial society is increasingly realized and work in this field will be discussed in the next chapter.

CHAPTER SIX

Compensatory and Social Education for Children in a Multi-cultural, Multi-racial Society

I. Introduction

The review of existing studies indicates several main needs, in which children growing up in deprived areas in Britain, whether native or immigrant, may need positive help[1] in order to realize their potential, to become accepted and participant members of their society.

1. Parental involvement, co-operation and support in the schools' aims for the child.
2. Compensatory education for language deprivation and, where relevant, social education.
3. Education in the history, culture and traditions of the various ethnic groups in our society.
4. Re-assessment and withdrawal of textbooks which ignore or give negative evaluations of ethnic groups and their contributions to world culture.
6. Opportunities for creative participation in community projects.
7. Knowledge of citizenship processes, rights and obligations.

Programmes and projects to meet some of these needs are being developed and tried by the Educational Priority Area Research Projects, Schools Council's Curriculum Development Projects, Community and Summer Programmes, Urban Aid Projects and in some individual schools, as shall be indicated.

[1] Such policies obviously would be useless unless implemented in conjunction with political and social action to improve the material environment and economic status of the citizens in such areas.

II. Compensatory Programmes for Social and Linguistic Deprivation

A. *Educational Priority Area Projects*

The overall aim of the Educational Priority Area Research Programmes under Halsey (1972), 'to find ways of improving the quality of education provided for children in their area through action research in compensatory techniques and to improve and develop cognitive skills', has been described in Chapter III. However, Plowden's national survey and other studies indicated that, since the child's achievement is chiefly influenced by parental attitudes and that neither he nor his family can be isolated from the community, the programmes also sought to develop community schools where teachers, children and parents might share mutually satisfying enriching activities during school time, evenings and weekends and might learn from one another (Betty, 1969).

As Halsey (1972) states: 'Projects looked for ways to explain schools' aims and methods, and to encourage parents to recognize our role in the educational process and so to develop understanding, skill and enthusiasm in the children's homes, which would help them to get the maximum benefit from their schools.

But not only must parents understand schools, schools must also understand the families and environments in which the children live.' (p. 117).

He describes and evaluates where possible the strategies used by each of the projects to establish closer links and two-way communication between the community and the school:

(1) community Education Centre;
(2) home/school liaison teacher;
(3) home visiting;
(4) the use of an Art Centre;
(5) school visiting by parents; school magazines, exhibitions in local shops and department stores;
(6) education stores;
(7) adult education.

Such links are even more important and require more effort in schools with many pupils of multi-cultural origin. They are described in greater detail in Volumes II–V of EPA Publications (1973).

The Liverpool project under Midwinter (1970) has employed a stimulating range of strategies, which have spawned a continuous flow of literature before and after the final report. All are described in 11 occasional papers, progress reports and in its magazine *Projectile* issues 1, 2, 3 published by the Liverpool EPA Project (1969 and 1971), and now published in several books by Midwinter (1972 a, b, c). The first, *Projections* describes the work of the project and the experiments used to improve educational standards. *Social Environment and the Urban School* is mainly a handbook of suggestions for teachers who wish to link their curriculum work more closely with the pupils' own experiences, and describes methods of encouraging parents to participate in school processes. A third book (Midwinter, 1972c) combines these two titles in one volume.

In the first year of the project the team concentrated on developing curriculum, and home/school links for the primary and nursery schools in the scheme, and encouraging the extension of pre-school education. A double-decker bus was converted into a mobile playgroup which allowed embryonic groups of mothers to form and operate until premises and equipment were found (Pelham, 1969 and 1970).

Community support has been built up in one centre (Salisbury) from a pre-school playgroup, when parents meet informally to identify and consider how best to meet community needs. From this beginning more formal adult educational courses are gaining acceptance.

Of the 12 project school departments, seven have specific parent involvement schemes during schooltime. Teaching kits, schedules, advisory wallets and workbooks with details of project action which have proved useful have been devised to help teachers and children in other EPA schools in Liverpool who are not involved in the project. Some are for teachers, others are for the children. These 'Projectors' include a teachers' advisory wallet on social environmental studies, a locality workbook for junior children, a social-problems game for juniors, etc.

Deptford's (London) strategy in relation to the overall philosophy of all the projects is described in detail by its Director, Betty (1969, 1970 and EPA Barnes, 1974).

The nub of all the projects' activities, Halsey (1972a, p. 191) concludes, is 'to encourage parents to join in the educational process. To foster partnership between home and school it is necessary to move in both directions—to take education into the home and to bring parents into the school.' His recommendations to the government for a continuing programme for EPA areas, '*A New Landmark*', is published with the first issue of the quarterly magazine of *Priority*, the new centre for urban community education, which has been established in Liverpool (Halsey, 1972b). Volumes II–V are to be published in 1974 (EPA Publications, 1974).

The *Priority* centre under Midwinter will co-ordinate and publicize continuing projects in EPA areas and press for a national policy for urban education. Midwinter's (1972d) *Priority Education* for Penguin Education outlines the philosophy of community schools and projects developed by action research teams, colleges, schools and parents in the EPAs to achieve their aims based on the Liverpool project.

B. *Schools Council Compensatory Education Projects*

The Schools Council Compensatory Education Project at the University of Swansea is concerned to develop identification techniques for children of five to eight who need compensatory programmes. Chazan and Williams (1969) describe research plans: (1) to develop indices of disadvantage; (2) to study problems of the project schools in relation to curriculum area and develop materials to overcome these; (3) to study pupils' social development and response to schooling; and finally (4) to develop programmes with a variety of media with special emphasis in language.

Chazan and Laing (1968) have compiled an excellent introduction to sources both here and in the USA on compensatory education for disadvantaged children. *Children at Risk*, by Williams *et al.* (1969) gives a progress report on the work of the four units of the Project. It questions 'the idea of designating an area or school as designated by Plowden as the fairest way of diverting help where it is most needed'. It quotes previous research which indicates that help should be given to children at risk on the basis of individual needs, if they can be identified. A survey of American compensatory education programmes showed that a high proportion used individual child-centred assessment procedures to identify children who most needed help. Two papers by members of the team describe the development and testing of two diagnostic instruments to identify children's reading and phonic skills to see whether such projects are feasible.

Cox and Waite (1970) have edited a report of a conference in compensatory education for infant teachers sponsored by the project which discusses new approaches for teaching language, reading and mathematical skills.

The teams' Identification Techniques Unit has developed an experimental infant evaluation manual[1] whose assessment procedures are designed to identify the child in need of compensatory education on the basis of home and medical background history and the extent of his learning and cognitive development (Evans *et al.*, 1970). It is hoped it will indicate to the school staff in which of the four aspects of development the child is weak—emotional, perceptual, linguistic and intellectual. An infant school amenities index has also been developed (Laing, 1971).

[1] This manual is made widely available so teachers can use it and give their reactions to the project team.

The Project is exploring the potential of media such as television, film, film strip and tape recording in compensatory education. Chazan and Downes (1971) review existing television programmes for pre-school children and find that, though they provide enrichment and exposition of ideas, they are seldom intellectually challenging and in no sense are these programmes based on a developmental conceptual framework. They discuss the possibility of producing a structured television with specific aims for schools. Another chapter discusses tape-recorded projects which help the disadvantaged child learn to read. The first research report of the project was published early in 1972 (Chazan and Laing, 1972; Jackson, 1972).

Cross'd with Adversity (Schools Council WP 27, 1970) surveys the problems of young people of secondary school age who are suffering from social handicaps. The information was derived from the headmasters of a sample of secondary schools in areas of social deprivation. It mentions that the presence of immigrant children in these schools has often stimulated conflict where there is distrust of foreigners and fear for job competition. These young immigrants are finding great difficulty locating desirable jobs, at a time when they are facing tensions within their own families.

It describes the best practices of schools which attempt to give compensatory help to their pupils but it recognizes in its recommendations that there is a need for research and development into curriculum development and for an expansion of courses for teachers of disadvantaged children, some of whom may be immigrant children.

The team, under Laybourn of the University of Manchester, predicts that a new floating generation of adolescent discontent is likely to emerge, particularly in areas where immigrants are concentrated.

C. *Summer Programmes*

Many authorities recognized that during the summer it was important to provide planned activities for children in deprived areas as well as to organize opportunities for immigrant children to improve and practise their English.

In the late 1960s many communities expanded these objectives into imaginative summer programmes. These programmes were organized by the Community Relations Officers, often in co-operation with voluntary organizations with the help of volunteers, students and teachers from England and overseas recruited through IVS, universities, schools and colleges. Initially they were financed by trusts, local authority grants and by the Community Relations Commission for multi-racial projects. With the inception of the Government's

Urban Aid Programme, more grants were obtained from this source in 1970 to increase experimental summer language schools. These programmes are described in greater detail by the CRC (1971), Hawkins (1971), and Townsend (1971). Most of the earlier projects concentrated on providing imaginative play activities and broadening the children's social horizons through visits to places of interest, although a few were providing language practice for immigrants.

1. *Language schemes.* The pioneers in this field appear to be the Language Teaching Centre (LTC) at the University of York, where student volunteers, after a short introduction to language teaching methods, taught English to immigrant children at their school and later at Huddersfield and York for a fortnight during the holidays from 1965–68.

In 1969 the LTC planned much larger programmes, one in Huddersfield and one in York with the co-operation of other University Departments and the school authorities. It used a standard form to obtain information from the teachers on the pupils' levels of ability in English comprehension, speaking, reading and writing, in order to know at which level the child should be approached. Training for tutors expanded from a three-day crash programme at Easter to six weekly two-hour sessions during the summer term. Materials were assembled throughout the year by some teaching teams who could meet for seminars or workshop sessions. They obtained reports on the pupils in their schools.

The programme of the school in Huddersfield alternated between formal language learning, dialogue reading, group activity (projects), games, singing sessions, excursions and film shows. The novel feature of this and similar summer schools is the small tutor-teacher/pupil ratio of 1:2 ranging from 1:1 to 1:5, which appears to be successful in stimulating language learning. The use of student and pupil volunteers to teach children makes this possible. Many more of the projects reported by the CRC (1971) had language teaching and language enrichment aims, although social aims were normally included in the programmes. Only one scheme appears to have attempted to evaluate language gains since standardized instruments for this purpose have not as yet been devised.

However, the LTC Halifax Project (York/Halifax Programme CRC Report, 1971) constructed and used a measure to assess competence in oral expression, and found that the 64 children tested appeared to have made an overall gain of over 16 per cent.[1] Other schemes have relied on subjective assessments by tutors and teachers to evaluate children's linguistic and social gains.

[1] The results at the time of writing had not been statistically treated.

2. *Evaluation of summer programmes.* At a conference sponsored and reported by the Community Relations Commission (1970c), representatives of the projects which had taken place in summer 1970 met to compare their reports[1] in terms of aims, organization, home and school links, staffing and training.

(a) *Aims.* It was believed that these should be clearly stated for each project, e.g. language teaching, social integration, compensatory education, and that they should relate to the needs of the area and availability of staff to achieve them, so that evaluation could take place. Townsend (1971) lists 10 aims given by summer projects studied.

(b) *Organization.* A formal structure was considered most appropriate for language teaching with a 1:1 tutor:pupil ratio, and a more loosely structured one for a socially orientated project with a 1:4 ratio. Three to four weeks was felt to be an ideal period for a project, preferably with staff continuity.

(c) *Home and school links.* These were important in that the parents should be brought to realize that their children's development in language would be helped by the social aspects of the projects as well as the formal language teaching. Indigenous children in EPA areas, as well as immigrant children, need help at many levels of language proficiency.

(d) *Staffing and training.* It was felt that trained teachers were necessary for linguistic projects and that tutors should have training and be given a clearer definition of their role.

The conference was most valuable in that it enabled participants to benefit from one another's experiences and practices. Important issues were raised and discussed. 1. Whether projects should be seen as aspects of community service or as part of the LEA provision to which volunteers could make an urgent contribution was debated by Gordon Burrows of Bedford. 2. Professor Hawkins thought that language competence for secondary education could best be learned on a dialogue basis between child and tutor. He praised summer programmes, but believed this could best be achieved naturally in schools with the help of teacher aides.

Professor Hawkins (1971) has since produced a handbook on summer programmes.

[1] Each participating authority submitted a mimeographed report of their project, and these, together with their abstracts structured by the CRC, were given to the delegates so that comparisons could readily be made.

III. Social Policies to Promote Understanding of Ethnic Cultures and Reduction of Ethnic and Racial Prejudice

There are many uncoordinated approaches being used to achieve the above policies in Britain, but little concrete research is available to evaluate their efficiency.

A. *Educational Approach*

There are two aspects covered by the educational approach.

1. One believes that educational programmes to teach the history, culture and traditions of the major ethnic groups are important not only for children from these groups but for the indigenous children. For the former it will reinforce the immigrant child's pride and respect for his parents' ethnic and cultural traditions. American research has shown that one of the individual's most important needs for school achievement is a positive self-image. It is assumed that, for the indigenous child, it will provide knowledge of the immigrants' traditions[1] which are as valid as our own in fulfilling human needs in his country of origin.

2. The second aspect attempts to promote tolerance of cultural and racial diversity. It is believed that prejudice will be reduced by these programmes.

B. *Community Approach*

Social psychologists believe that the government and educationists should incorporate behavioural procedures as well as cognitive/intellectual ones to achieve social policies of understanding and tolerance. Thus, they stress:

1. that a positive self-image for the ethnic child and the host-child's perception of this is more effective at the behavioural/action level than the intellectual reiteration of such principles;

2. that procedures for the promotion of tolerance (namely attitude change) must be related to the motivating patterns of individuals' behaviour (Kelman, 1970).

To be effective these programmes must be reinforced in other areas of life and in social institutions, and must be designed to take account of the prejudiced individuals' motivational pattern (Sarnoff, *et al.*, 1970).

Brown (1970) makes the distinction between prejudice derived from norm-conforming attitudes (going along with prevalent views) and ego-defensive attitudes which may be derived from repressed or unconscious feelings such as by feelings of hostility, frustration or inferiority.

[1] They may need modification to adapt to conditions in Britain.

Kelman's (1970) concepts[1] on three processes of social influence, in norm-conforming attitudes, are relevant to attitude change. Thus for many individuals, when it becomes illegal to discriminate and the climate of opinion alters, they have greater opportunity to interact with different ethnic groups at work or elsewhere and their attitudes may alter.

Bettelheim and Janowitz (1970) in a study of prejudiced personalities found that men who felt that their social experiences were frustrating and could not integrate them, were most outspoken in ethnic hostility.

Such ego-defensive attitudes are difficult to change by rational argument or new information. Sarnoff, *et al.*, (1970) presents some interesting experimental findings on the use of different attitude-change procedures on the basis of whether they are based on a rational model, reward and punishment model or ego-defence model, and their effectiveness on different personality types.

These findings have important implications for educators and community relations workers in devising programmes for reduction of prejudice. Social psychologists have also pointed out that instead of manipulating prejudiced attitudes in order to alter discriminatory behaviour, it may be easier to do the reverse—to enforce non-discriminatory behaviour. This has sometimes led to spontaneous changes in behaviour and attitudes. Brown (1970) cites studies such as Deutsch and Collins (1951) and Stouffer (1949) showing that, where it is possible to put people in situations where they have to mix with those towards whom they are prejudiced, it has often led to both friendly behavioural changes and also, more slowly, to changes in attitude.

Festinger's (1957) theory of cognitive dissonance postulates that where inconsistencies exist between a person's actions and beliefs, there is a drive for a consonance and balance. Jahoda (1960) nevertheless points out that some people can compartmentalize their actions and values which interfere with ready transfer of norms from one situation to another. Transfer may, however, occur, as Cook (1957) concludes from the results of a nationwide survey in the United States indicated in the following table.

[1] 'Compliance' occurs when the individual accepts the views of others by whom he wishes to be accepted. 'Identification' occurs when an individual adopts the behaviour and attitudes of another because it is associated with a satisfying role relationship. 'Internalization' occurs when an individual accepts influence because the behaviour is congruent with his own value system.

Table 6.1: *Racial segregation preferences according to contact experience with negroes*

Population	*Proportion of sample who prefer negro/white housing segregation*
1. A nationwide poll	4/5
2. People who had had experience of negroes as fellow workers *or* neighbours	2/3
3. People who had had both experiences	1/2

The four principles which seem to be associated with a reduction in prejudice, on the basis of a survey of relevant research by Allport (1958), were found to be:

1. equal status;
2. common goals;
3. dependence on each other;
4. support from laws, customs or authority.

I shall now turn to a description of the educational approach to promote these social policies, and subsequently that of organizations and/or groups which are promoting or embodying the social psychologist's or community approach.

IV. Educational Programmes to Promote Understanding of Ethnic Cultures and Tolerance of Ethnic Minorities

A. *General Background Literature*

1. *Culture and history.* Initially teachers had little information on the cultural background of their immigrant pupils and their school backgrounds. There are now an increasing number of books on the cultural background of the main immigrant groups in Britain, some of which have been already cited. Oakley's (1968) book is a series of articles on the backgrounds of West Indian, Asian and Cypriot children in Britain and some of their common problems of adjustment to school. Bowker (1968) introduces his discussion on education and integration in multi-racial schools by a good introduction to cultural backgrounds of Asian and West Indian children. Butterworth and Kennisbrugh (1970) have written a very informative book on the social background of Asian and Cypriot children designed to support the Schools Council Scope materials. They bring out the differences and contrasts between the values of British culture and those of the Asian ethnic groups. They deal with the influence of Asian religious beliefs in patterns of behaviour, which will enable

teachers to be understanding of the adjustments which the children and parents face in coming to our country. Morrish's (1971) book on the historical, religious, social and educational background of the West Indian, Indian and Pakistani immigrants, is one of the most thorough and informative with excellent extensive bibliographies. He believes that the absorption of immigrants can only be achieved by a total policy which will include a total programme for inter-cultural education for all children in our society.

The Community Relations Commission (1972) have published separate booklets as well as information on teaching English, and on the family, cultural and religious backgrounds of the different ethnic groups. They publish several bibliographies, an annotated one for teachers (CRC, 1972), one of audio-visual material (CRC, 1972) and a more comprehensive, short but excellent annotated select bibliography on race relations in Britain, according to subject area (CRC, 1973). Its Educational Panel now issues a free monthly news sheet, *Education and Community Relations*, to schools, colleges of education and other interested organizations, or individuals, which reviews the latest publications and courses and conferences in the field.

Janet Hill (1971) has edited for a librarians' working party an annotated survey of all children's books (age range seven to 12) published in England about countries from which people have come here to settle. There are sections on Africa, Cyprus, Asia, Ireland, Italy, Poland, Turkey and the West Indies. These are graded into A, B or C, the latter mark being those not recommended. An example quoted in *Education and Community Relations* (1971) is a review: 'Mitchison, N. (1968) *African Heroes*. The author writes from a deep personal involvement with Southern Africa . . . aim has been to restore to Africans the heroes who were taken from them by White Invaders and to serve as a reminder that Africans can seek inspiration from their heroic past.'

Alison Day (1971), writing about the need for the school library to have books mirroring the background of social and ethnic groups in the school, includes an annotated Caribbean booklist covering fiction, history, poetry, folk songs, biography, etc.

Buchanan (1972) for Lambeth Libraries has compiled an excellent annotated bibliography of the literature of Black Britons, which also contains some books from Africa and the United States. Background studies on race relations and current periodicals are included. He has also produced two short bibliographies with fuller reviews of Caribbean and African novels in English.

2. *Surveys of bias in textbooks.* The contribution of members of different ethnic groups, often ignored or distorted in history books, should be made explicit. Hatch's (1962) study of some history and

geography textbooks in two London comprehensive schools found that most authors when discussing African and Asian countries, dealt more with the activities of the European colonisers rather than those of the countries' leaders. Few describe the cultural history of the countries before the Europeans arrived and give undue emphasis to primitive aspects of Africa rather than their modern achievements and racial problems. This conclusion is also echoed by the Ministry of Education (1963) pamphlet which pointed out that there was a lack of teaching about Commonwealth countries. These presentations of coloured people as those without culture or civilization until the European came are myths which should be dispelled. Stewart (1970) in a survey of the reading schemes used in one authority's infant schools, analysed readers in three schemes which were used by the great majority of the schools for their attitudes to minority groups. The main characters were white and middle-class. Foreigners were pictured in stereotyped terms—American Indians as savages, Far Easterners as exotic or in subordinate relationships. Good people are white, bad ones are brown or black.

Of the six other schemes currently in use the early Janet and John scheme contained the most objectionable racial references. ITA had no bias. Only one reading scheme, New Ginns, had multi-racial children in ordinary classroom and playground scenes (Oberist and Bissett, 1968).

Glendenning (1971) believes that history texts may create judgemental attitudes about race, and that many negative texts are still in widespread use. 'Many of these may have helped create a climate of opinion which can develop into racial strength and hostility.'

There are nevertheless a number of recent history and general studies books for secondary school children which he has examined qualitatively for their treatment of race, colonialism and world problems. Most of these 12 books are favourably reviewed and they may help change attitudes of the British to race and imperialism.

A later survey of history books published in 1971 which attempts to rethink history for British schoolchildren is also reviewed critically to see if presentation gives full justice to contributions of other ethnic groups to world culture, and whether they give a full picture of the Western involvement in Asia and the Slave Trade (Glendenning, 1972). A Canadian study, McDiarmid and Pratt (1971), which describes its methods of content analysis of social studies textbooks for 'evaluative assertions', pictorial stereotypes, and the discussion of 'critical issues', recognizes, as he points out, that it sees prejudice as not only 'contemporary, but springing from the presentation of history in the past'.

Another historian, who writes on world history, believes that new school books and syllabuses are needed, but that 'without changes in attitudes and cooperation on the part of history staff in universities, colleges and schools, this cannot be achieved' (*see page 175).

Liverpool Community Relations Councils' (1973) members have surveyed racial bias in children's books and in some textbooks used in Liverpool schools and printed detailed reviews and astonishing quotes from many of these books. There is a report on their findings, which notes that

(1) 'Many books did not reflect the nature and form of the various minority groups in society.

(2) Many textbooks fail to provide balanced information concerning coloured people and are far from accurately mirroring contemporary life in developing countries.'

The reviews are on mimegraphed sheets in a *Jackdaw*-type folder, and the reader may receive, on request, subsequent reviews to add to the collection. There are three recommended booklists.

A checklist (prepared by the National Union of Students) of points to be noted when reviewing books, used by workshop members, is included for groups wishing to survey books in their areas.

It is most disturbing to think that books are still in use in our schools, which perpetuate false stereotypes about other races and present such one-sided accounts of history.

Parker (1972) suggests a pre-publication monitoring system of a committee of experts to whom publishers might voluntarily submit manuscripts of books in subject fields susceptible to racial prejudice. It would be hoped that publishers would voluntarily submit their manuscripts. Alternatively, a post-publication monitoring system could alert teachers to the weaknesses of books which might have bias.

Education panels of local community relations councils, aided by LEAs library and education services, have been mounting mobile multi-cultural book displays for schools, books which a panel of teachers have recommended. Birmingham CRC (1973) has assembled books, audio-visual material, kits, packs, produced by media and other organizations, and project boxes, on teaching in multi-racial and multi-cultural classrooms and urban environments, for loan by teachers in their area. (Education and Community Relations, September, 1973).

Oxfam Education (1972) and the Voluntary Committee on Overseas Aid and Development (1972) are producing balanced educational booklets, project wallets, slides and films for children about life in developing countries to counteract stereotypes that fund-raising drives may have given to the English. Their study of this process includes a survey of British school textbooks for a racial bias. (White (Ed.) 1971).

The results of the activities of the all-party pressure group, the Working Group in Education for the Eradication of Colour Prejudice, to suggest to local education authorities that it be made easier to replace material out-of-date or prejudiced, is described by Corbett (1971).

Although some Directors of Education recognized that many schools are probably using outdated books, others felt there was no problem at all or that all headteachers had the resources to cope should these arise. Not all those with large immigrant populations replied. It is, of course, up to the schools to choose their teaching materials as the LEAs pointed out. However, some authorities encourage or plan to encourage teachers to think about and act on curricula and books suitable for a multi-racial society through various means.

The group also wrote to publishers. This initiative in itself may encourage teachers and authorities to examine their materials more critically.

The Select Committee on Race Relations (1973) recommends that all LEAs draw the attention of Headteachers to the need to choose books that are up-to-date in our multi-racial society. Indeed, one might suggest that this is a need in our international society.

B. *Books and Studies on Race Relations and Attitude Change*

The main British and Unesco works which discuss the teaching tolerance and prejudice are Bibby (1959), which covers the facts about race and the ways in which it can be taught, Leach (1964), who describes useful techniques for use in school and has a comprehensive bibliography for those who wish to obtain more detailed information. Lewis and Rea (1969) leader's/teacher's book suggesting ways of promoting insight into other cultures, and how problems of race relations may be presented in the classroom, is based on 15 Penguin books on various aspects of Race for 14- to 17-year-olds. Stafford-Clark's (1970) and Hashmi's (1971) works deal with prejudice in the communities and the psychology of prejudice respectively. Babun's (1969) work is an introduction to human races written for young people.

Unesco (1956) has edited a symposium on *The Race Question In Modern Science.* Its distinguished contributors discuss the concept of race and racial differences, history, myths, psychology, culture, biology and society. Many of the contributors have also published their articles as individual books, listed in the bibliography under Unesco (1956).

Montague (1972) publishes four statements made by a committee of social and physical scientists on race and prejudice under Unesco's sponsorship. The fourth statement contains an elaborated and annotated exposition of its points. The book has an excellent annotated book list.

Davis (1963) presents a review and bibliography of selected research on attitude-change, as well as a list of 400 relevant books. Williams (1961) discusses changes in pupils' attitudes towards West African Negroes, following the use of different teaching methods. Polack (1957) deals with the promotion of teaching of race questions in primary and secondary schools in Britain. Two recent works by Field and Haikin, (Eds. 1971) and Burnham (1971) are suitable for secondary schools or general studies use. Burnham introduces concepts of race, attitudes, scapegoats, and deals with the history of racism, as well as dealing fully with racism in the modern world. Field and Haikin has produced a book of readings which includes such background data as case histories, work of Community Relations Commission, Race Relations Board, legislation, and discussions of policies in education, social services, etc. The Race Relations Board (1973) has produced a free wallet of sheets with information on the history of immigration and race relations in Britain, discussion of key concepts and the role of law against discrimination. The material is succinct and clear. Two bibliographies on background and literature accompany the wallet.

Himmelstrand (1964), discussing methods of educating against racial discrimination, states that no single method can be used to eradicate racial prejudice since it may have different sources and mean different things to different people. Domnitz (1965) also reports on an international meeting at the Unesco Institute for Education which discussed educational techniques for combating prejudice and discrimination and for promoting better inter-group understanding. The Unesco Associated Schools Project 'Education for International Understanding and Co-operation' has stimulated and aided many interesting programmes. Unesco (1965) describes some of these, which cover information on other cultures, on human rights, and about the United Nations, in English schools, colleges and in similar institutions throughout the world. A Unesco (1959) book describes some of the programmes in teacher training institutions and secondary schools, with examples and suggestions for classroom use. Many projects attempted to evaluate changes in pupils' attitudes (using either their own or Unesco circulated tests) with control groups of pupils, and it appears that new attitudes had been developed in the course of the work. Unesco seminars in this field are reported by Lawson (1969). Different countries deal with topics and factors on which education for international understanding can depend.

The media have produced several programmes for schoolchildren on the ethnic cultures (Granada TV, 1972) or religious faiths (ILEA Television, 1972) of ethnic groups settling in England, as well as programmes for schools which already have courses on Black Studies (BBC Radio London, 1972, and Berrigan, 1973).

Granada's series, *Our Neighbours*, was presented for 10- to 13-year-olds, and introduces the cultures of immigrants from the West Indies, India, Pakistan, Cyprus, Poland and China.

During a year's investigation for ITA to devise a formula for evaluating a selection of the schools' broadcast output by the Independent Programme companies, an evaluation of the 'Our Neighbours from Pakistan' programme of children's reactions was undertaken. Kemelfield (1972), the Research Officer who worked with the Centre for Television Research, University of Leeds, investigated such factors as:

(a) pupils' types of attitudes towards TV as a learning medium and to the presentation of the programme;

(b) the extent to which pupils gained factual knowledge;

(c) the extent to which pupils' prior opinions about Pakistanis were subject to change;

(d) to compare the responses of pupils from high and low density immigrant areas in these respects.

The sample (106 pupils from four schools) was small and discussion of the results is based mainly on a detailed qualitative analysis. It was found that reactions of the children from one school with a high number of immigrants differed from the other three schools. In this school it was found that, though their initial impressions were more favourable towards Pakistanis after viewing the programme, the percentage of favourable impressions fell, and though not becoming more negative, became more uncertain in their reactions. In the other schools, the initial impression progressed from less favourable to more favourable after the programme. The emphasizing of differences, without always providing explanations for those which were contrary to English customs and habits, tended to make them less acceptable to children in the high density school.

Obviously, as the author says, it would be important to replicate this study in a larger number of similar schools, particularly in the light of his conclusion:

'The amount of change and variation in the response from pupils . . . . indicates that the programme is likely to arouse conflicting feelings and opinions in any one class on this subject. There is every indication that we are dealing here with an area of human response, involving fundamental value systems, where the child's desire to conform to the customs of his own culture may result in a natural resistance to ideas that threaten his sense of security and belonging. In the end the greatest benefit from a study of this kind may be in the ability of a producer or Education Officer to use its findings to help teachers to be better informed about and prepared for their difficult task.' p. 56.

This study indicates the fact that attitude change is related to the pupil's total situation and that education material to alter attitudes must be carefully structured.

The 10 television programmes on world faiths for upper secondary school pupils has an adherent discussing the beliefs and practices and their impact on their way of life in this country. A Sikh, Hindu, Buddhist, Jew and Muslim are among the speakers (ILEA Educational Television, 1972).

C. *Initiatives and Syllabuses in Some Multi-racial Schools*

Although I should like to discuss educational programmes under two categories—(1) those which study the history and culture of the ethnic groups and (2) those which are intended to promote tolerance of racial and cultural diversity—there is little published material available on the former and many categories will be discussed together.

Some of the evidence of work being carried out in these fields of improving tolerance has been derived from an unpublished survey of syllabuses and institutions carried out by Crick and Jenkinson (1970) for the Morrell studies in Toleration.

1. *Social studies and Religious studies syllabuses.* Multi-racial schools have been immediately faced with providing information and material about their 'immigrant' pupils' cultural and religious backgrounds. Many teachers are bringing into their classroom, work on the geographical, cultural and religious backgrounds of their immigrant pupils, but until Townsend's third survey of a sample of local authority schools is completed on classroom practices in this curriculum area, one can only describe the work of those who have published their approaches.

The development of course material and the methods, problems and experiences encountered in developing a social studies course for a multi-racial society by a team of teachers in two Leicestershire multi-racial comprehensive schools is described by Margaret Nandy in McNeal and Rogers (1971). She points out 'that although most schools and teachers are not faced with the urgency to create a curriculum which will have some impact on their pupils' thinking on race relations, the reasons for doing this apply in every school, since every child is going to be an adult in a multi-racial society'. The inadequacies of current social studies courses are delineated and their shortcomings as guides to enlarge childrens' perception of the social environment.

In developing the course, her team aims (1) to teach the children the process of inquiry—training them to use the library, media, use of tape recorder, projectors, field work, participation in discussion groups followed by discussion, evaluation and conclusions and to encourage criticism of unsubstantiated statements; (2) to provide comparative material which is the essential perspective necessary to the study of contemporary society and to provide the essential background to an intelligent study of race—to forestall prejudice.

The course was commenced in the first year of secondary school. In the first years the children make a thoroughgoing study of another society's culture. In one test Nandy found that the childrens' essays revealed 'that they had implicitly accepted the notion that no human culture . . . can be regarded as . . . demonstrating a right or wrong way of doing things, and they had seen that another society quite different from their own could work for its members and provide physical and emotional security and provide a code of right and wrong'.

Cunningham in the same volume describes the methods used by a multi-racial modern school to meet the language and integrational problems of children from different ethnic groups and to anticipate and prevent the growth of prejudice and tensions among children from the host community. In retrospect he also discusses mistaken attitudes which may have vitiated some of the work in the school and about which other teachers in multi-racial schools should think.

Dufour, in Advisory Centre for Education Forum (1970) describes how race is taught in the social science curriculum of a secondary school during the first five years, ending with a CSE Mode 3 examination. Its aim is to lead to a limited understanding of other people and cultures. *Education and Community Relations* (March, 1973) describes an imaginative integrated studies programme in an Ealing multi-racial comprehensive school for first-year pupils. The outline scheme of the three terms introduces pupils to the school and their home backgrounds, the contrasting cultures of minority groups and Britons in that particular area.

Bennett (1971) reviews his lesson approach, developing material to help his mainly immigrant pupils develop a positive self concept through awareness of their cultural and historical social roots—through lessons which will also lead to a CSE Mode 3 examination.

Fyson (1973) not only provides a useful detailed model for teachers who wish to teach about people and problems in Asia, Africa and Latin America, but first ensures that they plan explicitly how best to achieve real understanding.

Accordingly, she points out that teachers should be aware of their: (1) motives in presenting these issues in school; (2) objectives in terms of attitudes, knowledge and action to be fostered; (3) predispositions of him/herself and the children towards third world development; (4) process—what specific techniques and materials can be used in the classroom. She has also written a source book for teachers of Third World Studies.

Crick and Jenkinson (1969) have reported on some formal syllabuses dealing with the teaching of race relations in British schools. They found that in the CSE syllabuses Religious Studies was the subject under which racial, class and religious prejudice and problems were studied and which explicitly aimed to promote inter-group harmony. Social Studies appears as a subject option in only half of the schools and their syllabuses treat race relations as one of many contemporary topics. Few GCE syllabuses offer the same contact with race relations topics, although such issues often form part of current affairs discussions. An almost unique exception is a Scottish Certificate of Education syllabus for Modern Studies which covers such topics as race and colour, prejudice and problems of multi-racial societies, with excellent background information, useful bibliographies and film titles and organizations (Glasgow Education Dept., 1969).

Most religious denominations have and are providing bulletins, bibliographies, project kits, literature and materials for different age groups, dealing with race relations, multi-cultural tolerance and other social and personal problems. *Probe* 14 on 'Community Relations' discusses religion and traditions of Asian groups, Black Christian churches, the Jewish Community and some multi-racial communities in Britain (Christian Education Movement, 1971). The British Council of Churches (1973) edits a six-monthly bulletin on 'Church, Community and Race', and the Catholic Institute (1973) for International Relations has produced a kit for sixth-formers on Race Relations. The Council of the Society of Friends (1973) have bulletins of available audio-visual material, as well as an account of their multi-racial community centre.

The Community Relations Commission has published a revised edition of the Shap Working Party (1973) World Religions Aid for Teachers, which contains details of books, periodicals, audio-visual aids, and a calendar of religious festivals, as well as a handbook on teaching techniques for comparative religion. Cole (1973) has edited a collection of information for teachers in multi-faith primary and middle schools. It describes in Part One the religious background of different faiths and its effect on children's behaviour at home and school. In Part Two, suggestions for teaching different faiths are given with resources and book lists, and data about festivals. The last section contains stories of great heroes from the different faiths and stories about traits admired in these cultures.

2. *Black studies*. Courses in Black-Anglo history should be provided in schools attended by children of black ancestry. There are many difficulties in devising such a curriculum, which may best be developed by a project team. Two of these difficulties are:

(1) to see that translations are available of books concerned with the religious and cultural traditions of the Asians and other ethnic groups;

(2) to find appropriate material which will mirror the fluid unsettled situation of the black Afro-Anglo-American West Indian minorities who are searching for their own identities in their African heritage, in their history and in their subsequent countries of settlement.

'They took away our history and without it we was a walking dead man,'—Mohammad Ali, quoted by Dummet (1972), who taught young people whose parents came from the new Commonwealth, and found they had little historical knowledge, either of their own country of ethnic origin or of England. All expressed a desire to know about the history of their ethnic or racial group with whom they could identify. One youngster put it powerfully: 'For a human, he must know about his background, if he don't know anything he can't go on living.'

Lynch (1971) has recently edited a first book on Blyden in a new series of African Heritage Books aimed to republish the works of educators, writers and philosophers of African descent of the mid-19th century who were interested in the problems of Afro-American identity. He points out, however, that 'the multi-cultural reality of British life and history should be part of every school's curriculum regardless of its ethnic composition'. To implement these and other recommendations, Wein (1970) points out that schools would need staff which had received special training about black and working class culture, history and some training in cross-cultural studies.

Walvin (1973) has recently written a history of negro and English society between 1555–1945, though his previous book (Walvin 1971) on the history of the Black people in England from 1555–1860 is more detailed.

There are an increasing number of books now available on African and West Indian history and bibliographies of history and literature of ethnic minority groups in Britain for different age groups reviewed by journals interested in education for a multi-racial society. *Education and Community Relations* (May 1973 and Feb 1973 respectively) reviews books about the Caribbean and history books on Africa. Penguin now has an African Library series.

Owing to the general lack of courses for children from the new Commonwealth which will give them pride in their culture and historical background, some teachers have commenced courses in Black Studies in their schools.

Two approaches are described by 'Teachers against Racism Journal' (Feb. 1972). One introduces the material on a piecemeal basis into various subjects—history, geography, literature. The other is to introduce it as an examination subject, which gives it equal status with other subjects in the school.

At Tulse Hill, Black Studies is offered as an optional choice for 'O' Level GCE in General Studies and is described by *Education and Community Relations* (Dec. 1971). It covers the history, political and social systems of new Commonwealth countries and their settlement in England.

At William Penn School, the course leads to a CSE Mode 3 Social Studies examination and Pollack (1972) outlines a suggested syllabus. These courses are open to both black and white children in the school.

Several members of TAR have found that where children were being exposed to such background courses, 'it not only greatly improved their learning capacity in the general school system, but reduced race tensions in those schools' (p. 2 TAR, Feb. 1972), although no research evidence is offered to reinforce this claim.

Morris (1973) has produced a useful booklet on Black Studies in which he first states the need for such studies both for pride in ethnic and racial identity of the minority group and for appreciation of their culture by the majority group in the community. The second half, a model syllabus for teenagers, is divided into historical periods, with 12 lessons on each. There is a brief outline of the points to be covered in each lesson, the titles of one or two books covering the period, and two important personalities to be studied. The point of origin is African. Other countries are studied as they impinge by exploring or colonizing the country, and conquering and exporting the people away from their homelands. The original inhabitants of the New World are studied also. In contemporary times, the role of the great powers in Africa, EEC and Pan-African-Asia are also to be studied.

D. *Schools Council Curriculum Development Projects*

The Schools Council pamphlet (1972) 'Race relations and the curriculum' states that teachers have to face two major groups of problems:

(1) the need to help *all* the children in all schools to understand that Britain is now more a multi-racial and multi-cultural society than ever before and to give some insight into the challenges which this situation presents;

(2) the problem within classrooms which are themselves multi-racial (p. 9).

Schools should, they say, 'give their pupils a clear understanding of what is involved in race relations—the clash of cultures, beliefs about physical differences and the differences between ethnic groups'. There are disagreements as to how these should be presented.

Several Schools Council curriculum development projects have prepared and tested teaching materials which deal with intergroup relationships, most of which also include the problems of living in a multi-cultural society for children and young people of different age groups.

The *Moral Education Project* under McPhail (1972) is attempting to help children in secondary schools take other people's needs, interests and feelings into account by using material or situations (suggested by adolescents in a pilot survey) which are suitable for discussion and analysis (Ungoed-Thomas, 1970). Its teaching technique is to build on situations in which it is known that the children show consideration for the needs and feelings of others and to extend the material to strange groups and then to totally alien groups. The project uses discussion, writing, art and role-playing in a variety of conflict situations which involve the children emotionally as well as rationally and which they are asked to resolve (Dialogue, 1972; Schools Council Index, 1972).

The *Humanities Curriculum Project* under Stenhouse (1971) attempts to promote understanding and judgement in the human field by providing archive kits of approximately 250 items (as well as relevant recommended films). The teacher's handbook contains an abstract of each item, for discussions of each topic such as The Family, Relations between the Sexes, Poverty and Race. The pack on 'The Family' provides discussion material on the nature and changes in the family, the role of men and women not only in Britain but in other cultures, thus indicating their common functions, though structures and patterns may differ.

The 'Race' pack by Hipkin (1972)[1] has approximately 200 items—poems, stories, extracts from studies and textbooks in many disciplines, etc., as well as audiotapes with interviews and speeches from involved individuals—a priest ejected from South Africa, a self-confessed 'prejudiced' woman, etc.

[1] Publishers' Communication from P. Richardson, Social Science Director, Heinemann Educational Books.

Among key topics of inquiry are apartheid, race and identity and culture, the immigrants' experience, the intelligence issue, Black Power and integration, etc.

The Teachers' Handbook gives the fullest information and guidance on how the topic may be handled in the classroom. It also describes how the materials affected pupils in the trial schools, chosen for their multi-racial character—their impact in pupils' attitudes, relationships and 'understanding'.

The Project on Religious Education in the Secondary Schools adapts its techniques for the different age groups in developing units on the family, racial awareness and social problems (Horder, 1971). It aims to promote understanding and goodwill between people of different religious groups, by enabling pupils to know and experience the teaching and practices of different faiths, particularly those of minority groups in our own culture as well as their own (Schools Council Working Paper 36, 1972). The final units use a variety of media in presentation—discovery by doing, drama and visual aids (SPC Religious Education, 1973).

The General Studies Project is devising courses in general and liberal studies for pupils over 15 built around sets of resource material for individual study and guided discussion and will include material on race relations. (Schools Council Index 1971); (Dialogue Newsletter, 11, 1972). The Schools Council Project on Integrated Studies is based on the theme 'Exploration Man', the title of Unit 1 which describes the organization of such studies. Unit 2 deals with communicating with others and Unit 3, with three alien societies, the Dyaks, the Chinese, islanders from Tristan da Cunha—their family life, leisure, work, religion and other structures (Education and Community News, April 1972). Brooksbank (1972) describes the project's aims.

Thus it is evident that the early 1970s will see much more material available for teachers in this field. Many curriculum projects sponsor inservice training sessions for teachers who intend using their units.

Lecturers in General and Liberal Studies in Colleges of Further Education and Technical Colleges find it best to link discussion about race relations with a general approach to problems in contemporary society. Because many of their students appear to be prejudiced towards immigrants whom they fear are competing for their jobs, there are greater difficulties in teaching tolerance. The difficulties of a rational approach and the importance of personal contacts through multi-racial community projects are discussed in a CRC (1967) reprint of a conference on race in the curriculum in Further Education Institutions.

E. *Conclusions on Education for Cultural Pluralism*

1. *British approach.* As this survey of the literature and of some of the educational programmes indicates, there is as yet too little published evidence to say how many of the latter attempt to, and are successful in fulfilling two necessary objectives:

1. the understanding of ethnic cultures both to bolster the self-image of the immigrant child and to enable the host child to have respect for cultures other than his own;

2. the promotion of tolerance and reduction of prejudice towards ethnic, racial and culturally different groups.

The first objective is achieved by some schools and individual teachers, as our limited evidence suggests, though until the Townsend Survey is completed we shall not know how widespread are such programmes. Berg (1968) suggests that this objective was being achieved in some measure at Rising Hill Comprehensive School. There are some teachers and schools who try to bolster the self-image of children by teaching them about their cultures, but this leaves the onus of integrating the two cultures to the child. The Free University of Black Studies (Bulgin, 1970) is an institution in London for Afro-, Anglo-American blacks and West Indians, which is attempting to make available literature and historical background material for brown and black people to make them aware of their peoples' achievements and to have pride and self esteem for their racial group.[1] The recently formed group 'Teachers against Racism' is collecting and disseminating literature and booklists on the history and culture of the West Indians and other ethnic groups, and is fostering Black Studies courses in secondary schools. (TAR Journal, Feb. 1972). The New Beacon Press is making available in this country, books about African, Caribbean and Afro-American history and literature and background books about race studies. Such material must also be incorporated into the school programmes of the host community. There are special Caribbean booklists for teachers and parents and teenagers as well as more comprehensive ones for adults (New Beacon Press, 1971, 1973). As Wein (1970a) says: 'The Anglo-black working class cultural heritage, whenever brought into the school, should be treated as an integral part of our common legacy.'

The second objective (the promotion of tolerance towards 'different groups in our society'), as Crick and Jenkinson (1970) point out, makes two implicit assumptions:

(a) that racial prejudice exists and can be eradicated through educational programmes;

[1] A National Institute of Black Studies, with similar aims, has recently been formed. (Runnymede Trust, April 1973).

(b) that prejudice against cultural and religious diversity exists, and tolerance can be taught.

Three different approaches which are used in the syllabuses and programmes are:

(1) The 'moral/logical' approach shows pupils how their attitudes may be inappropriate to their views and real life situations. This is used in Certificate of Secondary Education Religious syllabuses and is being evolved by several Schools Council Curriculum projects, the Moral Education Project at the University of Oxford (Ungoed-Thomas, 1972) and the Schools Council Religious Education in Secondary Schools Project (Horder, February 1971) at the University of Lancaster (Schools Council, 1971).

(2) The 'factual/empirical' approach gives the pupil up-to-date information about race, culture and religions to reduce prejudice and promote understanding of diversity. This is used in the Glasgow Syllabuses, Glasgow Education Department (1969) and in the Schools Council Curriculum Projects in the Humanities and General Studies Curriculum Projects.

(3) 'The indirect approach' used by some teachers and Colleges of Education attempt to educate for positive race relations indirectly through all subjects. The efficiency of such an approach is difficult to assess.

Crick and Jenkinson (1970) rightly conclude that there is a need for teachers to examine their aims and assumptions in teaching children, both those from immigrant and host backgrounds, and to prove the effectiveness of different types of teaching programmes.

The Schools Council Humanities Curriculum Project has attempted to assess the effects on attitudes on groups of children in multi-racial schools who have been exposed to the trial material from the Race Kit by Hipkin, to have been published (1971/72) in their Humanities Course. Verma and MacDonald (1971) (*see page 175) mention that, although this project has been advising and testing the problems of teaching other controversial social and ethical issues to adolescents, it was felt that before the one on Race was published, a pilot study on its use in multi-racial schools and others would give them guidance on its presentation problems and also on its positive or negative effects. Their report stemmed from a six- to eight-week race relations programme in particular groups, and was based on five evaluation measurements which were tested both before and after exposure to the programme. 'The effects of the programme, although not generally statistically significant, tended to suggest a shift in the direction of inter-ethnic tolerance.' (Verma and MacDonald, 1971). However, there is no evidence to suggest that the students became generally less sensitive or tolerant of members of other racial groups, although there was not general tendency towards intolerance, as Miller's (1967) study had found after a course on race relations in a college of further education.

Miller's study of his course and methods which were used to teach craft apprentices about the colour problem appeared to show that there was an increase in racial prejudice after exposure to the course. This seemed to support the view of some that direct teaching in this field is bound to increase group hostility or 'provides a forum for its expression' and should thus be avoided. (SC Pamphlet 9, 1972, p. 10).

However, as it continues, this study is not conclusive and it suggests 'at this stage of our experience . . . . we need to have more experimentation with both direct and indirect teaching of race relations before we can be at all dogmatic about what will achieve the aims of understanding, tolerance and a reduction of group hostility' (*ibid*, p. 11).

The Schools Council asked the CRC Advisory Committee on Education to consider the Race pack materials, and they advised against publication in that form. They also 'doubted the wisdom of beginning to teach children about race relations so late in their careers' (CRC, 1972, Annual Report). As a result, the Schools Council decided not to publish the materials at all but to devote resources to a new project on race in the curriculum.

Dummett (1972a) criticizes the aim of the Race project for the teacher which is to see 'that the mode of inquiry in controversial areas like race should have discussion rather than instruction as its core' and that 'discussion should be protection of divergence of view rather than consensus'. She also believes that the wide selection of materials is too bitty and that it cannot be seen in its true context since there is no material on the historical, political and social background from which it rises. Teachers cannot have full background on all this material and she believes that children must have the full facts which can be checked about the roots of racism.

One opinion is 'that it is quite wrong to try to teach race relations as a subject at all'—rather one should destroy the lies told about race in *all* subjects.

Stenhouse and Hipkin (1972) reply that background material is explained, that it is expected that teachers will use these materials as foundation collections to supplement their own presentation.

The debate is not resolved.

However, it has become increasingly evident to those working in the field of education that education for a multi-racial society should take place in all schools. As a result of a joint resolution by the National Federation of ATEPO and the National Union of

Teachers, the Schools Council has commissioned a major research project from NFER (April 1973—December 1976) under Townsend to provide material to prepare all pupils for life in a multi-racial society and for the specific needs of multi-racial classes. This project will follow the third Townsend (1973) survey, *Need and Innovation in Multi-racial Education,* which surveys teachers' techniques and methods of teaching race relations topics and multi-cultural studies in a sample of schools (primary and secondary) in non-immigrant and immigrant areas and in schools with or without immigrants or black/brown British.

Teachers' ideas about needs for curriculum change and development in these fields will also be collected (*Ed. Research News*, Sept. 1972).

The Schools Council Social Education Project under Davis and Rennie at the University of Nottingham is one which uses the community relations approach discussed in the next section. Its aim is to promote active involvement of young people in the community through their recognition of the needs of the community and the development of a sense of identification with it.

The teachers in the first years of secondary school help the children develop skills of observation, communication and presentation, using media such as recording, photography, maps, graphs, discussion, written work, actively to examine structures, attitudes and duties in their class, peer group, school, the community or area. Profiles are drawn up of these groups and children may develop further a particular aspect which they find interesting, should they identify with their communities' needs.

This project has stimulated several classes to social action (Rennie, 1970). An evaluation exercise hopes to measure whether the projects' aims are being achieved in terms of behavioural objectives and has led to a Social Education Newsletter run by the project schools. The full report will be published in 1974 (Schools Council WP 51, Schools Council Index, 1973).

2. *Select Committee Report on Education.* The House of Commons Select Committee on Race Relations and Immigration which reported on education during the 1972–73 session visited a limited number of LEAs which, however, had a representative cross section of the main ethnic and racial minority children in Britain. It also heard evidence from organizations and associations whose members are involved in research and teaching of such minority children, as well as the Department of Education and Science, the Community Relations Commission, the Institute of Race Relations and other bodies.

The report's findings and recommendations reinforce many points already made in other studies in this survey.

(1) The importance of facility in standard English to pupils from ethnic minority backgrounds to enable them to compete on equal terms with the indigenous child. It is suggested that the best teaching practices be brought to the attention of all LEAs. Since there is a shortage of teachers able to teach English as a second language, DES should examine how best this situation can be remedied.

(2) The value of nursery education for linguistic and social reasons for deprived children, among whom there may be children from ethnic minority backgrounds, is made explicit. Structured language learning exists in all nursery classes in Leicester and appears to help children learn English quickly. Nursery provision, including day nurseries, should be expanded in areas of deprivation.

(3) Courses in race and community relations should be given in some areas in colleges of education, and awareness that Britain is a multi-cultural society should be promoted in colleges of education for all students, and in-service courses in this field for teachers should be expanded.

(4) Greater use should be made through the curricula and examinations to broaden horizons by drawing on the background of the multi-racial commonwealth.

(5) The collection of statistics of immigrant children under the present Department formula should cease since they are misleading and are not used for grant purposes; nor do they indicate language deficiencies (*see page 175).

(6) There should be established an immigrant advisory unit in the Department of Education and Science and a central fund to which LEAs could apply for resources to meet educational needs of ethnic minority groups, both children and adults. As a condition of their use of such services, Local Education Authorities should report to DES on the situation in their area and what they are doing about it.

This is a brief summary of some of the recommendations in the first volume of the report—sensible and in some cases long overdue proposals. However, it may be wise for such proposals to be carried out under existing programmes or policies for socially and linguistically disadvantaged indigenous children and adults, as is the case in some measure in Educational Priority Areas and under Urban Aid programmes. A total approach to disadvantage, whether social and linguistic or economic, must be approached in a multi-cultural context. Education for tolerance in a culturally plural society at public and school level is equally essential throughout the country.

3. *International approaches.* The recent publication Eppel (Ed.), 1972, resulting from an international conference held in 1970 on Education for Cultural Pluralism has as its theme 'the recognition

of the view that the appropriate approach to the problem of minorities no longer lies in an attempt to bring about the assimilation and virtual disappearance of their cultures but rather to foster their health and development and assist them to exist in fruitful relationships with other cultures, both majority and minority in any complex society'.

One basic assumption of all the speakers was that it was not enough to seek to understand conflict and tension between groups, but that they should attempt to inculcate and extend sympathetic interest in the cultures of other groups.

A first group of papers deals with the theoretical implications of the conference theme and principles of group interaction; the second group comprises studies of problems and practices in different countries with different ideologies, such as the USA, Israel and Yugoslavia. Many valuable lessons can be learned and practices adapted by reading how these societies are attempting to meet the challenge of their culturally diverse ethno-racial populations.

Professor MacRae sees societies of the past, and most contemporary ones, as culturally plural. Societies of the future will be even more so due to the development of physical and symbolic communication characteristics of the modern world. It is the great fact of our time. He sees no easy answers as to how institutionalized education can help to inculcate positive attitudes and feelings for cultural diversity, but believes it must be attempted (MacRae, in Eppel, 1972).

V. The Community Relations Approach

A. *Principles*

The community relations approach stresses the promotion of participant action and the instigation of legislation for positive intergroup interaction in order to promote positive attitudes. The proponents of this approach believe, in Banton's (1967) words, that 'British behaviour is a rational response to the customary meaning of colour and that custom can be changed by conscious policy.' He quotes, from Dean and Rosen's (1955) principles manual of intergroup relations, relevant principles which, assuming the continuation of favourable political and economic tendancies, can help promote intergroup harmony. These are:

1. The more frequently members of two groups meet in everyday situations, the more friendly will relations be. Misconceptions are often abandoned. Relations are most effective when working together in pursuit of common objectives.
2. Understanding between groups is impeded by ignoring indi-

vidual and group differences and treating all people as though they were alike.

3. People tend to accept and perpetuate customary ways of behaving towards minority members irrespective of personal inclinations. If new customary practices of a more valuable character appear to be accepted by most people then individuals will accept them themselves and newcomers will conform to practices prevailing.

4. Determined leaders can establish practices that would be resisted were they introduced in a halting fashion.

5. Objectionable behaviour should be publicly challenged with an explanation of why it is not acceptable; the person challenged should be helped to understand that the criticism is of the behaviour and not of himself.

6. Attempts to modify discriminatory behaviour are unlikely to be successful unless they counter the social pressures that give rise to such practices.

Organizations such as the Community Relations Commission, the Race Relations Board, the local Community Relations Council and their panels, Community Projects, the Educational Priority Area Projects and voluntary and religious associations embody some of these approaches in their work.

B. *Fields of Action*

These bodies attempt to promote intergroup activity and to combat racial, ethnic and religious discrimination in our society which does not legally permit such behaviour even though our recent immigration bills are not free from racial and ethnic discrimination. A review of their work may be read in the annual reports of those organizations who publish such reviews, as the Race Relations Board (1968+), Community Relations Commission (1969, 1971, 1972) and those of the local CRCs and other organizations and associations. Such reports are listed in Runnymede Trust Bulletins.

The Community Relations Commission has been active in the following fields.

1. *Housing*. The Select Committee on Race Relations and Immigration Report on Housing (1971) stresses the effect of housing on race relations. 'Improvements in housing both of indigenous people and immigrants will improve race relations because they remove some deep causes of friction and resentment. Failure to cope with bad housing has the reverse effect.'

CRC has received funds from the Gulbenkian Foundation to complement its own special fund for the support and evaluation of Fair Housing Groups and other community projects. It has given support to housing advice trusts (CRC Annual Report, 1972). Perry (1973) for PEP has studied these projects and brought out the difficulties of CRC in helping minority groups with local authority housing while being dependent on the LA for financial support, and the fact that it is in the private housing market that there is most need of action to promote fair dealing. The CRC is to establish a post in London to deal with housing (CRC, 1973).

2. *Work in employment and industrial relations* has been emphasized by the Commission and local Councils' panels. All maintain contact with groups of employers and trade unions, in order to encourage equal opportunity policies. Visits and conferences on the facilities of the employment exchanges have been brought to the attention of immigrants. The Runnymede Trust has published Meth's (1970) survey of successful techniques and practices pioneered by firms to ensure the integration of coloured and white workers on the shopfloor and elsewhere.

The Commission points out that the proportion of unemployment among young minority members, particularly among West Indian youths of 16–20, is disturbingly higher than the national average (CRC, Annual Report, 1973). It is preparing a report on the whole question of unemployment and homelessness among this group and has also made positive recommendations for both preventative and curative measures to the National Youth Employment Council Working Party, on how to help young people from ethnic minority groups (CRC Journal, Sept. 1973).

It is granting policy aid for projects to prepare young minority groups for entry into the job market, and the provision of greater opportunities for more extended consultations with career teachers and the Youth Employment Service as well as with counsellors (CRC Education Dept., 1973 and CRC Journal, May 1973).

3. *Health and welfare activities* are actively promoted. There has been encouragement for immigrant mothers to allow their pre-school children to attend playgroups, both for their own and the children's benefit. It has supported and given advice to organizations pressing for comprehensive provision of nursery classes, centres, pre-school playgroups and day nurseries. It has also stimulated institutions which have professional social workers to include community relations courses in their courses—both basic and inservice (CRC Annual Report, 1972). Local community relations councils have been running social clubs for immigrant women. The Commission itself attempts to provide as much information as possible on acquainting the immigrant women of their rights and benefits, through the distribution of leaflets in their own languages, conferences and broadcasts by their social development officer. Policy aid is being

given for projects with parents to help bridge the cultural gap between minority group parents and their children (CRC Education Report, 1973).

4. *Youth and community.* The Commission is aware that the Youth Service has difficulties in meeting the needs of coloured adolescents. It is aware of the problems involved and in conferences, training sessions and discussions with voluntary and statutory organizations dealing with youth. Many local community relations councils are taking an active interest in activities with young people in conjunction with local statutory and voluntary services. They have suggested that the local Youth Service experiment with schemes of self-determination for young people to run their own type of clubs, and that more appointments be made of unattached workers to help the large numbers who do not identify with existing institutions. They have instigated research into problems of homeless young immigrants, and suggested statutory residential provisions, while aiding several voluntary hostels (CRC Annual Report, 1972; Birmingham CRC, 1973). The majority of young people do not attend clubs.

Birmingham Community Relations Council (1973) in a report on young people (mainly black) in the Handsworth area also recommends that youth work should be diversified to cope with the needs of alientated youth and that money should be made available for informal groups.

The Home Secretary has asked the CRC 'to inquire into the incidence, causes and consequences of both adolescent unemployment and adolescent homelessness amongst ethnic minorities in this country and also . . . report on the policy implications of their findings.' (Runnymede Trust, February 1973). This study has encountered opposition among ethnic communities, who assert that such facts are known and that policies to remedy the situation are needed. The Commission is engaged in an interchange of views on this inquiry, (CRC Journal, April 1973).

5. *Education.* The CRC Annual Reports (1971, 1972) mention that 'the value of integrating educational theory with practical community relations work in a coherent programme is coming to be more widely appreciated.'

It has had consultations and conferences with LEAs and Colleges of Education on the educational implications of a multi-racial society. It has stimulated such activities as the development of home/school links, suggested provisions for cultural and religious requirements of minority groups, represented parental and minority interests on particular issues. It has initiated a register in which Colleges of Education indicate whether they have courses for a multi-racial society and multi-racial teaching practice for students, so that Colleges who wish to exchange students for such experiences can do so with Colleges who wish to take advantage of the specialized courses, e.g. Rural Environment studies, etc., which they may offer in return (CRC Education Officer, 1971a). Another register lists forthcoming summer programmes for Immigrant/Indigenous children by Local Authorities, who would like colleges of education and university students' help. These registers are circulated to the appropriate institutions (CRC, 1971b).

They have worked with the local community relations councils on meeting parents concerned with West Indian children's attainment, helping organizers to train voluntary language tutors for Asian women and it has prepared some teaching materials for tutors (CRC, 1972). The Commission gave evidence to the James Committee suggesting that teachers in training be given a broader world view of history, geography and arts, and that all teachers should be given training for life in a multi-cultural society (CRC AR, 1972), as well as specialist training in teaching English as a second language and the cultural backgrounds of ethnic minorities.

The CRC newsletter for Colleges and Departments of Education, 'Teacher-Training and Community Relations' (1973), has developed from such needs also expressed by members of teaching staff in these institutions for a publication to facilitate the exchange of information on material and courses about English as a second language and ethnic, racial and community relations by lecturers and others for teachers in initial or inservice training. The first issue surveys such teaching in the colleges and education departments, describes some syllabuses, and reviews a recently published resource pack for English language teaching. It should be a useful forum for institutions of education to enable them to meet the needs of teachers in our own multi-cultural society and our responsibilities in an international world whose increasingly rapid communication systems are making us all responsible neighbours.

Most local CRCs have active educational panels who may act as 'developers' (Butterworth, 1972) to help ethnic communities meet such needs as Saturday schools for children requiring additional tuition and ethnic studies, day nurseries, and adventure playgrounds, theatre productions which portray their cultural heritage or current life situation, mobile book displays of multi-cultural literature for schools, as described by annual reports of Southampton CRC, 1973, Liverpool, 1973 and others.

The Dark and Light Theatre, Britain's first professional multi-racial theatre, with financial support from the Arts Council of Great Britain performs in multi-racial communities. The Director Frank

Cousins aims to tour twice a year with plays which explore the culture or which reflect the lives of the many groups in the community. These plays both entertain and may promote understanding between indigenous and ethnic communities alike. These are often more effective than lectures. Performances are sponsored by community relations councils, regional arts councils and LEAs.

In addition, it has recently been announced that the Association which represents lecturers in Colleges and Departments of Education has set up a Joint Working Party with the Commission to produce guidelines for teacher education (CRC Journal, April 1973). An annual conference with the Association is sponsored by CRC and deals with new developments in community relations, experimental work, research and college courses for the education of ethnic and indigenous children in language and cultural understanding (CRC Journal, 1973).

6. *Community projects.* Professor Hawkins points out that over half of the summer projects had social aims as well as that of improving the young people's English. These community projects have accepted children from different racial and cultural backgrounds, who, while sharing holiday activities, are taught to know more about one another in the hope that they will understand one another better (CRC, 1971).

Others have aimed to involve the young immigrant in serving their own communities and in acting as tutors. Such activities enabled them to identify with the community, and to have confidence in their ability to help others. A multi-racial project avoids the criticism that only one section of the community is being catered for, since a project for immigrants alone may create even greater resentment in the host community towards the minority. As yet it has been found difficult to measure changes of attitude which may occur as a result of such programmes.

The Community Service Volunteers Programmes have a variety of approaches to suit local circumstances which enable young immigrants and indigenous children to work together in helping others. Their initial efforts have been so successful that, as Green and Anderson (1970) have pointed out, their future projects will emphasize social and cultural enrichment.

They have produced School and Community Kits (SACK) for the use of secondary schools wishing to sponsor community work. These kits contain different types of material, also a reference section with information on voluntary service organizations and descriptions of community service projects, one of which is run by a multi-racial school (CSV, 1972). The first 1973 number of its 'School and Community' magazine, contains a leaflet 'Outline for Action', compiled by Cooper, which gives ideas and projects for teachers and pupils in the field of Race Relations. They are imaginative suggestions on schemes involving groups and the class to learn about racial backgrounds and help integration. 'Resettlement' is a game they have devised which gives players some idea of the problems faced by Ugandan Asians in England (Community Service Volunteers, 1973).

International Voluntary Service and Voluntary Overseas Service (1971) have produced a booklet of suggestions and information for voluntary work in community relations, which also contains addresses of relevant organizations in the field.

Conclusion

As Ungerson (1971) says, 'Community action in the widest sense—action for, or rather through, a broad spectrum of groups defined according to need and not simply by colour—is the only basis on which Community Relations Councils will be able to gain legitimacy for the exercise of their other, equally vital role—the exposure of injustice and the undertaking of civil rights work. Programmes which help to drive home the wide degree of identity of black and white interests in the inner city are a step towards politicisation, towards making people examine the structures which distort, and cramp their lives, instead of simply looking for scapegoats. . . . Community Relations Councils (and officers) (*see page 175) can never be more than initiators, both stimulating other agencies to act and helping people to recognise the power that lies within their own (organized) hands. Encouragingly the point seems to have won acknowledgement in the 1972 Community Relations Commission Annual Report.'

However, in surveying the events of 1973 which have influenced community relations during the year and public opinion and attitudes towards them, the Community Relations Commission stresses that work at local level requires support and backing by more positive national policies and public education to overcome attitudes and fears. It calls for 'bold co-ordinated policies aimed at meeting strategic social needs—in education, employment, housing, and the social services—which must be pitched not at some minimum acceptable level, but towards a positive optimum standard. Training is needed by all professional groups. Information must be assembled about the scale of need among ethnic minorities, and its relationship with disadvantage among the majority. Parallel with this, objectives in Race Relations policy must be clarified, and existing means of achieving frequently unstated objectives examined' (CRC, 1973, Annual Report).

CHAPTER SEVEN

Conclusions

I. A Multi-dimensional Problem

It is evident from this survey that Britain has become a culturally and ethnically plural society during the last two centuries, as well as a multi-racial one in the last three decades.

This is more evident in the large cities and industrial areas of Britain than in the rural areas, although through political pressures and debate over immigration policy the whole country is aware of the fact.

The influx of these visibly different immigrants has highlighted and exacerbated conditions which have been inadequate in these central areas for many years—in housing, educational and recreational facilities and health conditions. Such conditions are shared by the children of both immigrant and indigenous socially disadvantaged families in slum and problem areas with the added dimensions of language difficulties and ethnic and racial prejudice to overcome for the former.

The the educational problems of both immigrant and indigenous socially disadvantaged children are based on a multi-dimensional situation has been increasingly accepted by successive governments. Funds and programmes to improve physical conditions—better schools, housing and leisure facilities for pre-school children and adolescents—are slowly being implemented.

The social problems of attitudes of prejudice and intolerance, and practices of discrimination or indifference to needs by certain sections of the public towards immigrants or citizens of different ethnic, racial and/or social backgrounds have not always been dealt with so directly or positively. Marsh (1972; 1973) briefly reviews research studies which attempt to measure the changing attitudes of the British towards new Commonwealth immigrants, although there has not been agreement among social scientists as to the validity of indices used to measure prejudice in the different studies. He points out that 'problems of comparison in trend analysis stem not only from differing methodologies in the studies included but also from differences in the criteria used and the interpretations imposed upon measures of tolerance or prejudice' (Marsh, 1973 p. 284). He discusses the variations of those showing moderate to consistent hostility to blacks in the five boroughs by different researchers, ranging from 10 per cent by Abrams to 46 per cent by Bagley, and more recently Schaeffer's 25 per cent, which he considers definitive.

However, comparing answers in a national sample survey conducted in 1968 and 1973, it appears that feeling between black and whites is improving, although it has still a long way to go (Kohler, 1973c). Thus, when asked whether feeling between white and coloured people is getting better or worse, respondents' answers were as in Table 7.1.

Table 7.1

Respondents answering	*April* 1968	*July* 1973
a. 'getting better'	6%	24%
b. 'getting worse'	55%	33%

Such attitudes and discriminatory practices negate against equal opportunities in many areas of life and, in relation to immigrant education, appear specifically to influence children's motivation, aspiration for school achievement and subsequent career level, and also to encourage a negative self-image.

It has taken successive governments a considerable time to realize that we shall not, as in the case of previous immigrants, such as the Irish, East European Jews, Poles and Hungarians and post-war refugees, integrate our latest immigrants unless many more positive measures are taken, since their colour identity makes them easy scapegoats for those dissatisfied with their own social conditions or those in their town or country.

Marsh, in his discussion of studies comparing factors which contribute to expressed prejudice in areas with similar proportions of immigrants, found that these tended to support the hypothesis that such negative prejudice was higher in areas where there had been rapid social change and where individuals had little sense of civic, corporate community identification, or any feeling of social control over their conditions. Thus 'a community uncertain of its geographical reality will be especially sensitive towards any new element which threatens further erosion of the few corporate and integrative characteristics it possesses. . . . Stable, well defined towns like Nottingham and Bradford can take quite large numbers of migrant dilution before any but the paranoid feel the town is being taken over' (Marsh, 1973, p. 408).

Positive measures such as the establishment of the Community Relations Commission, legislation against discrimination and the establishment of the Race Relations Board, Urban Aid for projects in urban areas, and more recently the support for a survey of, and research into techniques and educational programmes to teach tolerance and respect for cultural ethnic and racial diversity—all these are steps in the right direction. Action research in the field of intergroup relations—racial, ethnic, political, social class, community relations—are also relevant and necessary, though a discussion of these is not within the scope of this book.

Negative measures have been increasingly severe, such as legislation controlling and drastically limiting entry of new Commonwealth immigrants, while allowing entry to more white Commonwealth immigrants, EEC members and aliens.

This survey, like the one in 1966, highlights the fact that the educational problems which have arisen and the measures taken to overcome them cannot be isolated from larger social and political issues. We are faced with a multi-dimensional situation, not with a narrowly-based school problem. It cannot be separated from questions of immigration policy, housing, occupational opportunities, leisure facilities, youth employment and many other factors that have been mentioned.

Recommendations which follow are those relevant to educational policy, which, if supported and encouraged by the government and accepted by educational institutions, research organizations and local education authorities, may be implemented.

These relate to language programmes, infant and pre-school education, the training of teachers, and students, assessment of academic development, and education for a multi-cultural, multi-racial society.

It is clear that a central clearing house of information about methods and curriculum programmes in use in teaching minority and indigenous children in our society should be available in a Data Bank or in an Immigrant Education Advisory Unit under DES, as suggested by the Select Committee, for more efficient diffusion of experience and techniques.

The government in addition to promoting these recommendations in the educational field must also promote positive policies in the social, political and environmental aspects of urban society.

II. Language Programmes

The work of Bernstein and others during the late 1950s and 1960s on the importance of acquisition of an adequate language for cognitive developments for the indigenous child has equal relevance for immigrant children whose partial mastery of English is a barrier to achieving their potential.

Although the linguistic problems of the non-English-speaking immigrant children have been first recognized and catered for by schools on an ad hoc basis and more recently by the curriculum development research projects of the Schools Council, on the basis of different age groupings, the language problems of the West Indian children speaking a dialect English has been much slower to be diagnosed. Townsend's recent (1971) survey of local authority provision provides evidence that this group, though the largest of 'immigrant' schoolchildren, has had less help linguistically than other groups.

Naturally enough, this belated recognition of the linguistic handicaps faced by West Indian children (who may in addition have cultural problems of adjustment to conflicting home, school and peer group expectations) has contributed to incorrect assessment of their academic potential and a disproportionate percentage being assigned to ESN schools. Townsend's (1971) research workers also believe that these younger West Indian children should not necessarily be taught in classes with retarded non-immigrant children whose needs are not necessarily linguistic.

Surely now that it has been demonstrated both by the DES and by the NFER that such a high proportion of English children of West Indian origin have not had an opportunity to learn an adequate English, the following recommendations are in order.

1. That the language problems of the West Indian children be tackled with the same urgency with which many LEAs are tackling the question of teaching English to Asian, Italian or Cypriot children. The Schools Council West Indian Curriculum Course for Juniors, Scope 7–9, for use in multi-racial classes should be provided for all teachers of children in this age range, in such classes if they so wish.

2. That a programme of language courses should be made available at Further Education Colleges or in youth centres to help adolescents who have not had an adequate help in schools, and that this should be related to vocational training, as is being done in some Further Education Colleges. Inservice courses and material should be made available for teachers of such courses.

3. That a review should be made of all West Indian and other ethnic minority children who have been classified as ESN and, if children have been incorrectly placed, that other educational arrangements be made.

4. For second stage English language learners, many studies indicate that not enough help is given by LEAs to schools to enable

them to give continuing help to second stage immigrants who find it difficult to cope with the language of specialized subjects, even though their basic English may be adequate. Such help must be made available.

III. Infant and Pre-School Education

Initially, most schemes of English language teaching concentrated on the junior age group. However, as a result of surveys and studies of infant classrooms, it has been found that few children in this age group pick up language automatically as had been assumed, and that structured language teaching is necessary. To do this effectively the infant teachers concerned need assistance with methods, audio-visual materials and ancillary help. Teachers with extra help in multi-racial infant classes have found, as Eavis points out, that it is only in small groups that it is possible to give children the chance to talk and to be listened to by an adult.

The Schools Council Project on Teaching of English to Immigrant Children at the University of Leeds is to produce a bulletin for infant teachers.

A number of projects are now in progress developing and testing materials to help the infant teacher with structured language work using a variety of media, ranging from Schools Council Projects in teaching English to Immigrants, Compensatory Education Project at Swansea, EPA Action Research Projects, National Foundation for Educational Research, and others. The problem will be to make this information and experience in its use available to the teachers who require it.

However, there are many educationists who believe that it is too late to commence structured language teaching in infant classes.

There is mounting evidence that the pre-school period is the most advantageous time to help socially and linguistically deprived children, an increasing number of whom may be cared for by unregistered child minders.

There are a limited number of pre-school research projects to encourage language development, many of which have yet to be assessed. The Schools Council Pre-School Language Project is testing the effectiveness of their teachers' guides in improving language deficiencies. These techniques may be as effective for immigrant children if they have an equal competence of English as the indigenous child, however inadequate.

Information about the experiences of authorities such as Leicester, who have structured language learning in all their nursery classes, and who have places for 36 per cent of the relevant age-group, should be more widely available (Select Committee Report on Education, 1973).

There is also a division of opinion as to whether it is educationally and emotionally sound to teach pre-school or indeed infant school children another language and culture before their own is firmly established, or alternatively to teach them bi-lingually simultaneously. Research studies or an analysis of existing educational programmes where this occurs and subsequent research studies would be a sound way to assess this point of view.

IV. Diffusion of New Techniques and Training of Teachers

How techniques and new material in this experimental field of English as a second language teaching can be made available to teachers, both those in the classroom and to student teachers, must be carefully considered, since the resources and the time of those developing such programmes are limited; as well as that of the teachers in the field. Inservice English language teaching courses for those already in or about to enter English as a Second Language teaching may be the most economical and efficient in terms of resources. These could also be attended by College of Education lecturers who are in LEA areas where there is a high concentration of immigrant children.

Townsend's (1971) study of LEA provision for immigrant education found that where authorities had a centralized rather than an entirely school-based system for English teaching, more opportunities were created in other aspects of the field. Thus in most of these LEAs there were 'additional payments for teachers, to encourage the demand and opportunity for inservice training, the establishment of working parties and language centres where specialist teachers can meet'.

The Commission suggests that these courses may come from DES, the LEAs and Colleges of Education and 'must not only deal with appropriate teaching material and strategies, but equally important be helped to understand and deal with the identity problems of minority group children' (*Education and Community Relations*, March, 1973).

Even though the entry of non-English-speaking Commonwealth immigrants has been curtailed, specialized and compensatory language education will be required urgently for:

1. West Indian children or children from other ethnic groups who have not had specialist English language teaching in their schools;
2. children whose parents do not speak English at home;

3. children of EEC or alien non-English speaking parents;
4. linguistically deprived children in our own sub-cultures;
5. dependent new commonwealth children, who will continue to enter annually in large proportions for some time in the future.

The Community Relations Commission, in giving evidence to the Select Committee on Race Relations and Immigration on education, recommends that the DES should establish a national policy for deprived Urban Areas—'With DES help local education authorities should set up advisory teams in multi-racial education to develop curricula, train teachers and organize language teaching for children at all stages of competence in English' (*Education and Community News*, June 1973). The Select Committee Education Report suggests that the DES should set up an Immigrant Education Advisory Unit (Select Committee, 1973).

V. Assessment of Academic Development

On the basis of the survey of research into problems of assessing academic potential of children from immigrant backgrounds or minority groups with tests designed for children from the dominant host culture, it is clear that most psychologists would accept that this is rarely possible with any degree of validity.

It is recognized that no test is culture-free and that many factors, such as language ability, length of exposure to the host culture, membership of ethnic group, attitudes of parents and host community, influence test scores. It has also been found that, although non-linguistic tests may be thought to be more suitable for children from non-technical cultures, such tests are not culture free, and that verbal tests in English or the children's own language are preferable.

The experience of some psychologists in using different techniques to administer intelligence or achievement tests to children from developing countries, is that certain techniques are more successful than others in helping them to understand the tests. Certain variables have more influence on test scores than would be the case among European groups. These experiences should be taken into account by educational psychologists assessing educational potential of immigrant children in this country.

Thus, although few psychologists and the DES now believe in the ability of current intelligence tests to assess educational potential, they nevertheless believe that tests may be devised which are useful as diagnostic instruments. These might measure operating capacity at a particular time in particular skills—linguistic, oral and written skills, aural understanding, numeracy, and social development, for example.

In the field of linguistics several measures have been devised to provide teachers with indications of the current skills of immigrant children. Mittler and Ward have adapted and tested the Illinois Test of Psycholinguistic Abilities, which studies nine different aspects of linguistic functioning; this is one attempt at providing a useful instrument. Tests, based on specifications drawn up by Rudd and developed by Burstall, to measure the speaking and listening and linguistic and writing skills of primary school immigrant children are to be administered on a nationwide sample in 1973 and 1974 and will provide teachers with welcome valid instruments to assess accurately the competence and needs of pupils whose English is not adequate.

The Schools Council Compensatory Education Project is developing and testing diagnostic instruments to identify reading and phonic skills and areas of development in which the child is weak. These should be made available to all teachers of children whose language is not adequate.

Culture-free instruments to assess children's learning ability, in spite of linguistic handicaps, have been developed by Haynes (1971) on a group of Indian children, and research is now in progress to validate the tests for use with children from other ethnic groups. These have been found to be superior to traditional intelligence tests in predicting children's attainment.

These are most valuable breakthroughs but until they are available for teachers there is a need for the development of other methods of assessment, perhaps less scientific, which will help teachers to determine the needs of their pupils. Such research projects should be encouraged, and the results of those in progress publicized.

It is likely that by the mid 1970s teachers will have a choice of diagnostic instruments to help them in assessing immigrant and indigenous children's strengths and weaknesses.

VI. The Task of Education and Community Relations

The importance of parental interest, attitudes and expectations for indigenous children's motivation and academic achievements has been brought out by many recent studies, both here (Peaker, 1971) and in the United States (Coleman, 1966).

The few studies which are now available on immigrant parental aspirations for their children's achievement, show that these are often higher than those of indigenous parents of similar social and economic status.

There is some indication that negative attitudes and discrimination by others in social and occupational fields may negatively affect the coloured adolescent's self-image, academic motivation, performance and job aspirations.

Legislation against discrimination in the wider society and the greater use by the Race Relations Board of Section 7 to initiate inquiries where discrimination in employment is suspected, should help to decrease the number of instances where such discrimination occurs. Many young coloured people believe that they are more unfairly treated than white adolescents by the police when situations appear compromising or are disturbed. These and other complaints must be dealt with immediately by an impartial outsider (CRC, 1971).

Educationally, however, schools must take some initiative to promote understanding for ethnic and racial minorities and their British children in our increasingly multi-cultural, multi-racial society. Although there are many multi-racial schools, we do not know how many have the types of social studies curricula outlined by McNeal and Rogers (1971): courses which should be in the curricula of all schools in our multi-cultural society and the world. Many of these initiatives are reported in CRC *Education and Community Relations* monthly bulletin. There are also more books and bibliographies, such as Hill (1971), Day (1971), Elkin (1971), New Beacon Press (1971, 1973), Buchanan (1973), and those compiled by the Community Relations Commission (1971, 1973) now available to enable teachers to develop such courses, many of which, although certainly not all, have been mentioned.

There are now a number of syllabuses available which aim to provide the essential background to an intelligent study of racial, religious and cultural differences and underlying similarities. Some have been devised by teachers in multi-racial schools in the course of their Social Studies teaching, and others are part of CSE Religious Studies syllabuses, whereas the excellent Scottish Modern Studies syllabus is devoted wholly to multi-racial societies. Unesco programmes are designed to promote international understanding. Townsend's (1973) third study provides us with further details of successful practices. Schools Council Curriculum Projects on Religious Education, General Studies, Moral Education and the Humanities include the topic of race and multi-cultural relations in their syllabuses.

Unfortunately the publication of the most recent Humanities Curriculum Project, the 'Race Pack', directed by John Hipkin, to have been published early in 1972, has been postponed since the Council's Curriculum Programme Committee feel that, 'Some of the material in the pack is too disturbing or shocking—in terms of being "disturbing" rather than "sensational"—to be suitable material for teachers to give out to 14- to 16-year-olds'. (*Guardian*, Windsor, J., 20 January 1972). This statement is rather extraordinary at a time when the evidence of disturbing racial, religious and other political conflict situations are readily available when and as they occur on television screens, radio broadcasts and in the newspapers: apartheid in South Africa, the Ugandan Asian crisis, sectarian conflict in Northern Ireland. Surely it is healthier for events which are disturbing to the self-image of the ethnic, sectarian or racially different child should be discussed openly in a sympathetic atmosphere rather than repressed, or channelled into violence.

One does not dispute the removal of individual items considered 'disturbing' if it is thought to be difficult for teachers to handle these tactfully in a discussion group. It is a pity that modifications could not have been agreed upon since this topic is one already discussed in many schools, with material which has not been so carefully tried out and where possible problems of presentation have not been pointed out to the teacher. Although one welcomes the project commissioned by the Schools Council to provide material for life in a multi-racial society, this will not be available until 1976 and time is running out.

There are an increasing number of Black Studies courses for black and white young people who wish to follow such a course with the emphasis on the history of the particular groups they choose. Tulse Hill Comprehensive School in South London is offering Black Studies courses as one of three options for 'O' Level GCE in General Studies. An outline of some of the topics covered by such courses is described in *Education and Community Relations* (1971; and by Pollack, 1972) and ranges widely through the social and cultural patterns of the West Indians, Africans, South Americans, Afro-Americans and Asians. There is a detailed section on the West Indies.

It is hoped that such courses and action may bolster the self-image of the minority child and promote respect for other cultures in the indigenous child. This is essential for the children from all communities in Britain, whether or not minorities live in the children's own community.

Nevertheless, educational programmes are not sufficient in themselves to create a climate of tolerance for cultural diversity nor eradicate discrimination on racial grounds.

Principles of inter-group relations are relevant, and programmes based on those principles are being applied, rather intuitively in the community relations field, by Community Relations Councils, statutory and voluntary community workers and, increasingly, minority group organizations themselves, often supported by Urban Aid and CRC grants. The aims of projects and programmes have not always been made explicit and thus evaluation is not always possible. These aims must necessarily be short- and long-term in terms of their success in achieving their goals. Summer school programmes and international camps for minority and indigenous children, which involve students and secondary school pupils as tutors or camp leaders, operate on the principles that better understanding is achieved in the more relaxed atmosphere of summer school and camp.

The Community Service Volunteers, some Youth and Community Projects and the Schools Council Social Education Project involve the young people in serving the community and in the belief that they are working together for common aims that mutual respect may be achieved. These groups embody the principles that Allport and Dean and Rosen found to be important in reducing prejudice—equal status, common goals, dependence on each other and support from laws, customs or authority.

Community projects in the field of ethnic and race relations should be monitored, and processes published as monographs to be available in a data bank or advisory unit for use by other communities, groups and schools wishing to instigate similar projects. Many future projects might start as action research programmes in order that assessment procedures could be built into the project. These projects are as important as formal education in improving tolerance for cultural, social, and racial differences in our society. In both fields—educational and community relations—more controlled research is necessary to assess the efficacy of different methods and programmes.

There has been only limited space to mention a few of the studies indicating that the reduction of prejudice is a very complex exercise, dependent as it may be on a number of needs or situational attitudes in the individual, his reference group, and on the many sociological factors in his culture. These alone make clear the complexity in planning a programme to achieve such an aim.

Bloom (1971) deals much more fully with such points and describes evidence, both positive and negative, on the effects of programmes of integration in different situations on changing attitudes. He mentions Cole's (1963) study in the United States which indicated that desegregation at school and further education institutions encouraged mild optimism. He found that there were marked changes in attitudes even by the most segregation-supporting adolescents.

These are not, however, inevitable as Bloom points out, since a decrease or increase in prejudiced attitudes is influenced by, for example, the attitudes of school and education officials, the social atmosphere, attitudes of parents, neighbourhood and, I would add, the policies of the government. Dispersal of school children in areas of heavy immigrant settlement or catchment area reorganization to ensure diversity might be justified on the basis of promoting the cultural education for both indigenous and immigrant child, as long as the teachers take advantage of this diversity in their social studies programmes. It should enable the newcomers 'to learn about their new environment from their non-immigrant contemporaries'. (DES, 1971). This would probably be a contravention of the Race Relations Act, and might not be so efficient in teaching English with the scarce resources available. The Select Committee Education Report has recommended that dispersal should be phased out except where there are enough parents who prefer their children to be dispersed—in a sense the choice permitted to indigenous parents. Nevertheless, this approach should be evaluated empirically, although in this instance one would also wish to assess the effect of integrated schools and multi-cultural programmes on attitudes, as well as on academic achievement, if this were possible.

Psychological, sociological and educational approaches, and not least political approaches, are all needed to solve the problems of race relations which will influence educational progress of immigrant children, since as Bloom states:

'A psychologist can reasonably demand that in the interest of social and individual health and stability—no less than in the interests of justice—no person nor group should be an outcast; nor should any person or group be made to forego his sense of identity' (Bloom, 1971, p. 17).

It is evident that, in facing the education of coloured ethnic minority children in our society, we are involved, not only with the techniques of language teaching and difficulties in assessment of learning potential, but in the field of multi-cultural education.

Learning itself is bound up with the growth of self concepts and levels of aspiration are bound up with group identification. Thus, an important field for inquiry is, as Goldman and Taylor (1966a) pointed out, not only how the varied incoming groups perceive or misperceive the host community but also how the host community perceives the incoming groups and how these perceptions can improve or deteriorate, and influence the structure of intergroup relations. Although one would agree with the comment of the Home Office White Paper on Police/Immigrant Relations (1973) that one source of difficulty for the newcomers is unfamiliarity with the ways and institutions of this country, equally one might say that it is also the ignorance of the indigenous community which is at fault.

There are also an increasing number of publications by individuals and organizations, which provide educational material for understanding and tolerance. The Community Relations Commission and Urban Aid are also encouraging projects such as Saturday schools and independent youth groups with programmes for minority groups, particularly West Indians. Such projects may have talks on the cultural heritage, which is more important for West Indians whose background has been neglected in conventional history books in the past and where youngsters have not had such teaching in schools. Best (1973) describes Acton Community Relations Council's after school and Saturday school projects.

Education for tolerance for such diversity is necessary not only in the schools but in our society as a whole, since the school is only a part of this society, and its members are influenced by the attitudes of the wider society. To summarize how society's attitudes may be influenced:

1. The mass media could take greater initiative in providing television, radio programmes and articles for adults on such topics as the cultural and historical heritage of the different ethnic groups as well as British colonialism's responsibility towards the destruction of some of these group's cultural traditions. A good example of the latter is a recent programme on British responsibility for slavery on West Indian sugar plantations, part two of a 13-part television series on the British Empire (*Radio Times*, 18/1/72). Plays and serials which include ordinary members of different ethnic groups with whose problems the average person might identify could make cultural differences seem less important.

2. Greater resources could be diverted to improve our long-standing inadequate housing and social services in inner urban areas for which the newcomers have become scapegoats.

3. Greater resources could be allocated to enable Urban Aid projects to simulate and structure more rigorous programmes in Youth and Community Development projects, and Compensatory pre-school education, although much valuable work is now in progress in the latter field.

4. Support for the community relations approach should be more wholehearted. Community Relations Councils need support from an independent CRC mission which can help them resist the inevitable pressures they must face in their task. The councils exist to articulate immigrant needs and interpret them to the host society; to make known the customs of that society to the immigrants.

In helping to counter social pressures which contribute towards discriminatory behaviour they are inevitably subject to pressures. Bonham Carter in CRC (1971) Report says, 'What we are attempting is to see whether under contemporary conditions a statutory body can stimulate voluntary activity, can come to terms with dissent, can mobilize good will and direct it to those areas where it is required, that is not to say that our task is to help people, it is rather to help people help themselves.'

In our shrinking world with the increasing migration of workers into highly industrialized countries and the growing demands of the third world for a more equal distribution of world resources and educational opportunities, it is incumbent upon us to learn to respect one another's cultural and racial differences and to help develop both the human resources of all children wherever they make their homes.

Educational needs for ethnic and racial minority children in Britain are not so different from those necessary for all children, namely:

1. Education for an adequate language for cognitive development.
2. Education in the culture, history, and traditions of the country of settlement and of their own and other ethnic or cultural groups.
3. The promotion of tolerance for cultural diversity in the tradition of education for world citizenship, which is already established in many schools in the country and some teaching on the nature of prejudice.

Specifically, however, we feel that education for ethnic minority children, whether coloured or white, should have as a minimum aim 'integration', which, sociologically defined, means that the incoming group adapts itself to permanent membership of our society as a group conforming to our systems of education, employment, legal and political structures, and is accepted by the host community as an entity differing in religion, culture and family patterns. A term now increasingly used by sociologists as a substitute for 'social integration' is 'cultural pluralism'. Halevy (in Eppel, 1972) points out that it was first used in America by sociologists who expounded the doctrine of active preservation of difference in ethnicity and culture which Americanization policies were attempting to obliterate.

Cross (1972) defines types of pluralism as political, legalistic, societal and commonsense pluralism. The latter becomes a condition of cultural, ethnic (and possibly racial and social) diversity and heterogenity. He and other authors in the issue of *New Community* (Summer, 1972) devoted to exploring concepts of community and pluralism, claim that studies indicate that in Britain and the USA there is no consensus on values or cultural standards. We are not a homogeneous society but a heterogeneous one.

Accordingly, to speak, as many have, of assimilation or even accommodation as 'stages of integration it implies that we have a notion of what a particular group is being assimilated into . . . '

'But if that entity does not have any consistency or homogenity, then this begs the crucial question' (Cross, 1972, p. 244).

There is no consensus as to the importance of race and ethnicity and their relationship to other variables of social differentiation in theories of heterogeneous and plural societies. However, it is recognized that ethnic and racial minorities are distinctive groups in our society who require legal support to obtain 'formal equality before the law and full citizenship rights' (Cross, 1972, p. 246).

Some groups in our society and some of the ethnic groups' organizations are exploring how best we can help one another to understand our respective cultures, religions and ethnic and racial identities as enriching contributions within the whole British social structure.

Many past and most contemporary societies are culturally plural and will become increasingly more so, largely due to the development of worldwide rapid physical and symbolic communication, as well as to the emigration of people for political, social and technological reasons. In this global society, through the media of mass communication, we are presented with many diverse perspectives.

All individuals must have the opportunity of deciding which to choose and *his* reference group, to decide Who am I? and not have a limited identity imposed upon him.

We shall not have a socially just society unless *all* children, whether minority or indigenous children, have equal opportunity to develop their potential in educational institutions and to attain economic wealth, respect and political power in our society, as adults. A socially just, multi-racial, multi-cultural society will not evolve automatically but must be developed through positive explicit action by all citizens who accept the inherent dignity of men and women of all creeds, colours or cultures.

Additional Notes to the Text

Page 137.* History 'O' and 'A' Level syllabuses designed for Commonwealth students overseas could be studied by ethnic minority students in Britain. The Associated Examining Board (1974) History 031, 11, options include the history of South Africa, the West Indies, India and South-East Asia.

Page 149.* Parkinson and MacDonald (1972) describe some of the experiences and dynamics met in one discussion group from an all boys school which was participating in the trial of Race Pack materials. It should help teachers to anticipate problems with which they may have to cope. The authors agreed that more experience of this nature is needed to gain knowledge of what is involved.

Page 152.* The then Secretary of State for Education and Science, Mrs Thatcher, announced in a written Commons reply on 27th November 1973, that the DES was to cease publication of statistics about immigrant children in schools as a result of the Select Committee's report.

Page 159.* Ann Dummett (1973), a former community relations officer and teacher believes that community relations activity cannot alleviate the racist nature of English social structure without committment on the part of the government to provide equal opportunity in all spheres of life. She describes concrete examples from her experiences as a CRO to illustrate her thesis and also gives examples of racism from the media, comics, fiction and history texts.

Select list of Periodicals and Journals

British Journal of Educational Psychology
3 issues per annum. British Psychological Society/Association of Teachers in Colleges and Departments of Education.

Community Relations Commission Journal
Monthly. Community Relations Commission.

Dialogue: Schools Council Newsletter
3 per annum.

Education and Community Relations
Monthly. Education Department, Community Relations Commission.

Educational Research News
3 per annum. National Foundation for Educational Research.

Educational Research
3 per annum. National Foundation for Educational Research

English Language Teaching Journal
3 per annum. O.U.P: British Council.

Language Teaching Abstracts
Quarterly. Cambridge University Press.

Language Teaching and Community Relations
Quarterly. Education Dept., Community Relations Commission. This is a new publication dealing with Home Language schemes, courses, problems.

Multi-racial School (formerly *English for Immigrants*)
3 per annum. National Association for Multi-racial Education.

New Community
Quarterly. Community Relations Commission.

Race
Quarterly. Institute of Race Relations.

Race Today
Monthly. Towards Racial Justice.

Runnymede Trust Bulletin (formerly *Race Relations Bulletin*)
Monthly. Runnymede Trust.

Teacher Education and Community Relations
2–3 per annum. Community Relations Commission.

Trends in Education
Quarterly. Department of Education and Science.

Bibliography

Although this book attempts to provide a comprehensive bibliography of relevant work on this topic, it is inevitable that some references may have been overlooked and that some works were published too late for review and inclusion. The literature on race relations is so large that it has only been possible to include a relatively small proportion of the total.

ABBOTT, S. (ed.) (1971). *The Prevention of Racial Discrimination in Britain.* London: OUP.

ADVISORY CENTRE FOR EDUCATION (1970). *Education in Multi-Racial Schools. Forum* 6. Cambridge: ACE.

ALLEN, S. (1971). *New Minorities, Old Conflicts.* New York: Random House.

ALLEYNE, M. H. (1962). 'The teaching of bi-lingual children. Intelligence and attainment of children in London, Wales and Trinidad whose mother tongue is not English'. Unpublished MA dissertation, University of London.

ALLEYNE, M. H. (1965). 'Research on the effects of bi-lingualism on education', see JONES J., (ed). (1965), p. 60.

ALLPORT, G. (1958). *The Nature of Prejudice.* London: W. H. Allen.

ANDAR, E. (1966). *Abilities of the African in Sub-Saharan Africa,* 1784–1963. Johannesburg: NIPR.

ASSOCIATION OF MULTI-RACIAL PLAYGROUPS (1970). *Priority.* Cambridge: AMP.

ASSOCIATION OF TEACHERS OF ENGLISH TO PUPILS FROM OVERSEAS* (1966). (ATEPO) Journal title *English for Immigrants.* Until Summer 1971. *Multi-Racial School.* Autumn 1971. (*Now National Association for Multi-Racial Education). Other publications, see: HANSEN, HESTER, LEVINE, LEICESTERSHIRE TEACHERS, WILLES.

ATEPO (1970). 'Editorial', *English for Immigrants,* 33.

ASSOCIATION OF TEACHERS OF ENGLISH AS A FOREIGN LANGUAGE (1967). (ATEFL) *English Language Teaching.* London: OUP Subscriptions Dept.

ASSOCIATION OF TEACHERS OF ENGLISH AS A FOREIGN LANGUAGE (1970). 'Editorial', *English for Immigrants,* 3, 3.

AURORA, G. (1968). *The New Frontiersman.* Bombay: P. Prakashan.

BABUN, E. (1969). *The Varieties of Man.* London: Crowell Collier.

BAGLEY, C. (1968a). PhD dissertation, University of London.

BAGLEY, C. (1968b). 'Educational performance of immigrant children', *Race,* July.

BAGLEY, C. (1970). *Social Structure and Prejudice in Five Boroughs.* London: IRR.

BAKER, G. (1965). 'The language problem of immigrant children in junior school'. Unpublished study for Dip Ed, University of Nottingham.

BARNES, J. (1973). see EPA Publications.

BANTON, M. (1957). *White and Coloured.* London: Jonathan Cape.

BANTON, M. (1967). *Race Relations.* London: Tavistock Ltd.

BANTON, M. (1972). *Racial Minorities.* London: Fontana.

BARATZ, S. (1967). 'Race of the examiner and effect on pupils' performance', *J. Pers. & Soc. Psych.,* 7.

BARROW, J. (1971). 'Greater London Meeting', *Education Bulletin.* London: CRC

BEETHAM, D. (1967). *Immigrant School-leavers and the Youth Employment Service in Birmingham.* London: IRR.

BELL, R. (1966). 'The grammar of the English spoken by Indian immigrants in Smethwick', Unpublished MA dissertation, University of Birmingham.

BENNETT, R. (1972). 'Teaching materials for social education', *Multi-Racial School,* Autumn 1971 and Spring 1972.

BEREITER, C. *et al.* (1966). *Teaching Disadvantaged Children in the Pre-school.* New York: Prentice Hall.

BERG, Leila (1968). *Risinghill: Death of a Comprehensive School.* Harmondsworth: Penguin Books.

BERNSTEIN, B. (1958). 'Some sociological determinants of perception', *Brit. J. Sociol.,* 9, 2.

BERNSTEIN, B. (1960). 'Social Structure, Language and Learning', *Educ. Res.,* V. III, No. 1.

BERNSTEIN, B. (1961). 'Social Class and Linguistic Development' in HALSEY, A. *et al. Education, Economy and Society.* New York: Free Press.

BERNSTEIN, B. (1971). *Class Codes and Control: Theoretical Studies Towards a Sociology of Language,* 1. London: Routledge & Kegan Paul.

BERNSTEIN, B. (1972). *Applied Studies Towards a Sociology of Language,* 2. London: Routledge & Kegan Paul.

BERRIGAN, F. (1973). 'Black studies: educational organization and Radio London', *Multi-Racial School,* Summer.

BEST, W. (1973). 'School on Saturday', *School and Community,* 1.

BETTELHEIM, B. and JANOWITZ, M. (1970). 'Ethnic tolerance: a function of social and personal control', in OPEN UNIVERSITY: *Understanding Society.* London: Macmillan.

BETTY, C. (1969). 'Race, community and schools', *Race Today,* June.

BETTY, C. (1970). 'Deptford spearheads fight for viable policy', *Education,* November 20th., p. 511.

BHATNAGAR, J. (1970). *Immigrants at School.* London: Cornmarket Press.

BHOGAL, D. (1972). *Sikhism.* Birmingham: John Plummer.

BIBBY, C. (1959). *Race, Prejudice and Education.* London: Heinemann.

BIESHEUVEL, S. (1949). *Psychological Tests and their Application to Non-European Pupils.* London: Evans Brothers.

BINYON, M. (1969). 'Inner London Education Authority Report', *Times Educ. Suppl.,* 26th December.

BIRMINGHAM COMMUNITY RELATIONS COUNCIL (1973). 'Alienated Youth in Birmingham'. Birm.: BCRC.

BIRMINGHAM COMMUNITY RELATIONS COUNCIL (1973). *Aids for Teachers Collection.* Birm.: BCRC.

BLOOM, B. (1964). *Stability and Change in Human Characteristics.* New York: Wiley.

BLOOM, L. (1970). 'Study of Bute Town, Cardiff'. In ROSE, (1969).

BLOOM, L. (1971). *The Social Psychology of Race Relations.* London: Allen & Unwin.

BLYDEN, E. (ed.) (1967). *Christianity, Islam and the Negro Race,* (African Heritage Books) Edinburgh: EUP.

BOLTON, F. and LAISHLEY, J. (1972). *Education for a Multi-Racial Britain.* London: Fabian Society.

BOULTER, H. (1971). *The Work of ATEPO.* Leeds: ATEPO.

BOWKER, G. (1968). *The Education of Coloured Immigrant Children.* London: Longman.

BOYLE, Sir E. (1963). Speech in House of Commons. *Hansard,* 27th November, vol. 685, col. 433.

BOYLE, Sir E. (1968). 'Race relations and the limits of voluntary action', *Race*, 3.

BRANDON, D. (1973). *Not Proven*. London: Runnymede Trust. (Watson, James. *A Dissenting Note*.)

BRAZIER, D., COOKE, E. and JONES, E. (1965). *Living Together*. Books 1–10. Oxford: Pergamon Press.

BRITISH BROADCASTING CORPORATION (1965). Edited by R. Hooper. *Colour in Britain*. London: BBC.

BRITISH BROADCASTING CORPORATION (1972). 'Black Studies'. London: Radio London ILEA Media Resources Centre.

BRITISH BROADCASTING CORPORATION (1972). 'English by Radio'. see Huggins *et al.*

BRITISH COUNCIL (1967). *Audio-visual Material for English Language Teaching*. London: Longmans.

BRITISH COUNCIL OF CHURCHES (1973). 'Church, Community and Race'. London: BCC.

BRITISH COUNCIL OF CHURCHES, CRRU and IRR (1972). *Facts and Figures*. London: IRR.

BROWN, J. (1970a). 'Why immigrant statistics are unreliable', *The Times*, 24th March.

BROWN, J. (1970b). *The Unmelting Pot*. London: Macmillan.

BROWN, H. (1970). 'Attitudes and Prejudice'. In OPEN UNIVERSITY: *Understanding Society*. London: Oxley Press.

BUCKBY, M. (1968). 'The role of games in language teaching', *Audio Visual Language*. 5, 3.

BULGIN, S. (1970). 'Free University of Black Studies', *Race Today*, June.

BURGIN, T. and PICKUP, K. (1964). 'Problems of Testing the IQ of Non-English speaking children'. Unpublished study of work at the Spring Grove School, Huddersfield.

BURGIN, T. and EDSON, P. (1966). *Spring Grove: An Experiment in the Education of Immigrant Children*. London: The Institute of Race Relations/Oxford University Press.

BURNHAM, C. (1971). *Race*. London: Batsford.

BURNEY, E. (1967). *Housing on Trial*. London: IRR.

BURROWES, H. (1972). 'Common emotional problems in immigrant children', *Therapeutic Education*, Spring.

BURROWS, L. (1969). 'Research on Testing'. In: SELECT COMMITTEE ON RACE RELATIONS, (1969) Vol. IV., App. 14.

BUTCHER, H. J. (1969). *Human Intelligence*. London: Methuen.

BUTCHER, H. J. (1972). See Jensen (1971).

BUTTERWORTH, E. (1967). 'The presence of immigrant school children: a study of Leeds', *Race*, January.

BUTTERWORTH, E. (ed.) (1967). *Immigrants in West Yorkshire: Social Conditions and Lives of Pakistanis and West Indians*. London: IRR.

BUTTERWORTH, E. (1972). 'Dilemmas of community relations, 1', *New Community*, 1, 3.

BUTTERWORTH, E. and KENNISBRUGH, (1970). *The Social Background of Non-English Speaking Immigrant Children*. Scope Handbook 1. Harlow: Longmans.

CANDLIN, C. (1969). 'Pronunciation problems of Asian immigrants', *English for Immigrants*, 2, 2.

CANDLIN, C. and DERRICK, June (1972). *Education for a Multi-cultural Society*. Monograph 2: *Language*. London: CRC.

CASSIDY, F. (1961). *Jamaica Talk*. New York: Macmillan.

CASSIDY, F. and LE PAGE, R. B. (1966). *Dictionary of Jamaican English.* New York: Cambridge University Press.

CATHOLIC INSTITUTE FOR INTERNATIONAL RELATIONS (1973). *Race Relations Kit for Sixth-Formers.* London: Catholic Institute.

CAVAGE, P. (1965). 'An experiment in sampling the spoken language of immigrant children'. Dissertation for Post-graduate Diploma in English as a Second Language, University of Leeds.

CENTRE FOR INFORMATION ON LANGUAGE TEACHING (CILT) (1968). See under Bibliographies section.

CILT (1969). *English for the Children of Immigrants: Guide to Sources of Information.* London: CILT.

CILT REPORTS AND PAPERS 3 (1970). *Aspects of Preparation of Language Teachers.* London: CILT.

CILT (1972a). See under Bibliographies section.

CILT (1972b). See under Bibliographies section.

CHAZAN, M. and DOWNES, G. (1971). See Schools Council Compensatory Education Project.

CHAZAN, M. and WILLIAMS, P. (1968). See Schools Council Compensatory Education Project.

CHAZAN, M. and LAING, A. (1971). See Schools Council Compensatory Education Project.

CHAZAN, M. and WILLIAMS, P. (1971). See Schools Council Compensatory Education Project.

CHILD LANGUAGE SURVEY (1969). *List of Papers on Language Transcripts of Year Groups* 8–16. York: University of York. Schools Council Modern Language Project.

CHRISTIAN EDUCATION MOVEMENT (1971). '*Probe*' 14: *Community Relations.* London: CEM.

CLARK, K. and CLARK, M. (1947). 'Racial identification and preference in Negro children'. In NEWCOMB, F. and HARTLEY, E. (eds.) *Readings in Social Psychology.* (1950c). 'Emotional factors in racial identification and preference in Negro children', *J. Negro Educ.* 19.

COARD, B. (1971). *How the West Indian Child is made Educationally Sub-Normal in the British School System.* London: New Beacon Books.

COLE, W. O. (ed.) (1973). *The Multi-Faith School.* Bradford: BESC and YCCR.

COLEMAN, J. (1966). *Equality of Educational Opportunity.* Washington DC: US Dept. of Health, Education and Welfare.

COLES, R. (1963). *The Segregation of Southern Schools.* New York: APL.

COLLINS, S. (1957). *Coloured Minorities in Britain.* London: Butterworth.

COMMITTEE FOR RESEARCH & DEVELOPMENT IN MODERN LANGUAGES (1968). *Child Language Survey.* (First Report) York: Schools Councils Modern Language Project, University of York.

COMMONWEALTH IMMIGRANTS ADVISORY COUNCIL (1964). (Second Report.) *Education of Commonwealth Immigrants in British Schools.* Cmd. 2266. London: HMSO. (Third Report.) *Immigrant School Leavers.* Cmd. 2796. London: HMSO.

COMMUNITY RELATIONS COMMISSION (1967). *Race in the Curriculum.* Reprinted from World Studies Education Service Quarterly Bulletin No. 4. London: CRC.

COMMUNITY RELATIONS COMMISSION (1968). *Practical Suggestions for the Teachers of Immigrant Children.* London: CRC.

COMMUNITY RELATIONS COMMISSION (1969). *Religious Education in a Multi-Religious Society.* Report of a joint consultation with the British Council of Churches and CRC, July. London: CRC.

COMMUNITY RELATIONS COMMISSION (1970). *Education for a Multi-Cultural Society:* 1. *Syllabuses.* Technical Monograph Series. London: CRC.

COMMUNITY RELATIONS COMMISSION (1970). *Annual Report.* (Also 1971, 1972, 1973.) London: CRC.

COMMUNITY RELATIONS COMMISSION (1970). *Social Change and the Immigrant Child.* Report of a Conference. London: CRC.

COMMUNITY RELATIONS COMMISSION (1971). *Seminar on Summer Programmes* 1970*: Retrospect and Prospect.* London: CRC.

COMMUNITY RELATIONS COMMISSION, EDUCATION OFFICER (1971a). 'Student Exchange in Colleges in England and Wales', mimeographed. London: CRC.

COMMUNITY RELATIONS COMMISSION, EDUCATION OFFICER (1971b). 'Some Projected Programmes for Summer using College of Education Volunteers', mimeographed. London: CRC.

COMMUNITY RELATIONS COMMISSION, EDUCATION OFFICER (1971c). *Education and Community Relations* (Monthly).

COMMUNITY RELATIONS COMMISSION, EDUCATION OFFICER (1973a). *Teacher Training and Community Relations* (quarterly).

COMMUNITY RELATIONS COMMISSION, EDUCATION OFFICER (1973b). *Policy Aid* 1973–75. London: CRC.

COMMUNITY RELATIONS COMMISSION publishes many booklets, among them:

The Background to the Educational Problems of some West Indian Children.

HASHMI, F. (1968). *The Pakistani Family in Britain.*

HIRO, D. (1967). *The Indian Family in Britain.*

HALL, S. (1968). *The Young Englanders.*

YUDKIN, S. (1965). *The Health and Welfare of the Immigrant Child.*

COMMUNITY RELATIONS COMMISSION (1973). 'Ugandan Asian Survey', conducted by Opinion Research Centre. London: CRC, reviewed in *Runnymede Trust Bulletin* (April, 1973).

CRC Journal (1973). 'Greater London Census'. London: CRC, April.

CRC Journal (1973). 'Projects eligible for policy aid'. London: CRC, May.

COMMUNITY SERVICE VOLUNTEERS (1973). *School and Community Kits.* London: CSV.

COMMUNITY SERVICE VOLUNTEERS (1973). *Race Relations: An Outline for Action.* London: CSV.

COMMUNITY SERVICE VOLUNTEERS (1973). *Resettlement: A Simulation Game.* London: CSV.

CONTE, J. (1971). 'Bilingual, bicultural education', *Race Today.* July.

COOK, S. (1957). 'Desgregation: a psychological analysis', *Amer. Psychol.,* 12.

CORBETT, A. (1968). 'Priority schools', *New Society,* 30th May.

CORBETT, A. (1968). 'Immigrant education', *New Society,* 12th September.

CORBETT, A. (1971). 'Coloured textbooks', *New Society,* 28th October.

COUCH, M. (1963). 'A select list on intelligence and other tests as used with non-western peoples', *Education Libraries Bulletin,* 18.

COUNCIL OF THE SOCIETY OF FRIENDS (1972). 'Friends and Neighbours in Islington' and bulletins of audio-visual and other aids. London: Friends House.

COX, T. and WAITE, C. (ed.) (1970). See Schools Council Compensatory Education Publications.

CRAIG, D. (1963). 'A comparative study of the written English of some fourteen-year-old Jamaicans and English children'. Unpublished MA thesis, University of London Institute of Education.

CRAVEN, A. (1969). *West Africans in London.* London: IRR.

CREED, T. (1967). 'English for immigrant teachers', *English for Immigrants,* 1.
CRICK, B. and JENKINSON, S. (1970). *Memorandum on the Teaching of Race Relations in Schools and Colleges in Great Britain.* London.
CROSS, M. (1972). 'Pluralism, equality and social justice', *New Community,* 1, 4.
CUNNINGHAM, H. (1971). 'Race in the Curriculum'. In: McNeal & Rogers, (1971).
CUNNINGHAM, W. (1897). *Alien Immigrants to England.* London: Swann Sonnenskhein.

DAKIN, J. (1971). *A Survey of English Courses for Immigrant Teachers.* London: Centre for Information on Language Teaching.
DALRYMPLE, A. H. (1966). 'Preparing immigrants for the master's desk', *Times Educ. Suppl.,* 4th February.
DANIEL W. (1968). *Racial Discrimination in Britain.* Harmondsworth: Penguin.
DAVIES, H. (1971). 'Social education project'. *Schools Councils Index.* London: Schools Council.
DAVIES, M. (1971). 'Different approaches to teaching about race relations in schools and colleges in Manchester and Stretford'. *Education.* London: CRC.
DAVIS, E. E. (1963). *Attitude Change: A Review and Bibliography of Selected Research.* Reports and Papers in Social Sciences. Paris: Unesco.
DAVISON, R. B. (1964). *Commonwealth Immigrants.* London: OUP.
DAY, Alison (1971). 'The library in the multi-racial secondary school: a Caribbean book list', *School Librarian,* 19, 3.
DEAKIN, N. (1965). *Colour and the British Electorate.* London: Pall Mall Press.
DEAKIN, N. with COHEN, B. and McNEAL, J. (1970). *Colour, Citizenship, and British Society.* London: Panther.
DEAN, J. and ROSEN, A. (1955). *A Manual of Intergroup Relations.* Chicago: University of Chicago Press.
DEPARTMENT OF EDUCATION & SCIENCE (DES) (1965a). *The Education of Immigrants.* C7/65. London: HMSO.
DES (1965b). *Bi-lingualism in Education.* London: HMSO.
DES (1970). *Statistics of Education* 1969. Vol. 1. London: HMSO.
DES (1972). *Statistics of Education* 1971. London: HMSO.
DES (1972a). Teachers' course list No. 1. *Programme of One-year and One-term Courses for Qualified Teachers.* London: HMSO.
DES (1972b/1973). *Programme of Short Courses for Teachers and Others.* London: HMSO.
DES (1972). *Potential and Progress in a Second Culture.* A Survey of the Assessment of Pupils from Overseas. Education Survey 10. London: HMSO.
DES (1972). *The Education of Immigrants.* Education Survey 13. London: HMSO.
DES (1972). *The Continuing Needs of Immigrants.* Education Survey 14. London: HMSO.
DES (1972). *Slow Learners in Secondary Schools.* Education Survey 15. London: HMSO.
DES (1972). *Educational Priority Area Publications.*
DES (1973). *Statistics of Education—1972. Schools.* Vol. 1. London: HMSO.
DERRICK, J. (1966). *Teaching English to Immigrants.* London: Longmans.
DERRICK, J. (1968). 'The work of the Schools Council project in English for immigrant children', *Times Educ. Suppl.,* 25th October.
DERRICK, J. (1968). 'The education of immigrant children', *Special Education,* April.
DERRICK, J. (1973). See National Book League (1973).

DEUTSCH, M. and GOLDSTEIN, L. (1965–1968). *An Evaluation of the Effectiveness of an Enriched Curriculum in Overcoming the Consequences of Environmental Deprivation.* Washington DC, NY Univ. US Office of Educ.

DEUTSCH, M. and COLLINS, M. (1951). 'The Effect of Public Housing Projects upon Inter-racial Attitudes'. In PHOSHANSKY, H. and SEIDENBERG, B. (eds.), *Basic Studies in Social Psychology.* New York: Holt, Rinehart and Winston.

DESAI, R. (1963). *Indian Immigrants in Britain.* London: Oxford University Press.

DEVLIN, T. (1970). 'Charter for Muslims', *Times Educ. Suppl.,* 15th May.

Dialogue 6 (1970). 'Child language survey: progress report', (Schools Council).

Dialogue 11 (1972). 'Schools Council project on general studies', *Dialogue,* 11, Summer.

Dialogue 12 (1972). 'Moral education project', *Dialogue,* 12, Autumn.

DOMNITZ, M. (1965). 'Educational techniques for combatting prejudice and discrimination and for promoting better inter-group understanding'. Report of International Meeting, 30th May 1964. Hamburg: Unesco Institute for Education.

DOMNITZ, M. (1972). *Thinking about Judaism.* London: Butterworth Press.

DOSANJH, J. (1969). *Punjabi Immigrant Children: their Social and Educational Problems.* Educational Papers No. 10. Nottingham University, Institute of Education.

DOUGHTY, P., PEARCE, J. and THORNTON, G. (1972). *Language in Use.* London: Arnold. (Schools Council Programme in Linguistics and English Teaching.)

DOUGLAS, J. W. B. (1966). *The Home and the School.* London: MacGibbon & Kee.

DOUGLAS, J. and ROSS, J. (1964). 'The later educational progress and educational adjustment of children who went to nursery school or classes', *Educ. Res.* 7, 1.

DUFOUR, B. (1970). 'Race relations in the curriculum', *Forum,* 6 (ACE).

DUMMETT, A. (1972). 'Comments on Schools Council race pack', *Race,* XIII, 3, January.

DUMMETT, A. (1972). 'A walking dead man', *Multi-Racial School,* 1, 3, Summer.

DUMMETT, A. (1974). *A Portrait of English Racism.* Harmondsworth: Penguin.

DUROJAIYE, M. (1969a). 'Ethnic choices in friendship in junior school', *Brit. J. Educ. Psychol.,* February.

DUROJAIYE, M. (1969b). 'Race relations among Junior School children', *Educ. Res.,* 11, 3.

DUROJAIYE, M. (1971). 'Social context of immigrant pupils learning English', *Educ. Res.,* 13, 3, June.

DUTHIE, J. H. (1970). *Primary School Survey. A Study of the Teacher's Day.* Edinburgh: HMSO.

EAVIS, J. (1971). 'Deprivation and One Infant School'. In MCNEAL and ROGERS. (1971).

Education Bulletin (1971). 'Greater London Regional Meeting'. London: CRC.

Education and Community Relations (1971). 'Curriculum Change'. London: CRC, Dec.

Education and Community Relations (1972). 'More "Scope" for Teachers'. London: CRC.

Education and Community Relations (1973). 'Integrated studies'. London: CRC, March.

Education and Community Relations (1973). 'Teaching the history of Africa'. London: CRC, Feb.

Education and Community Relations (1973). 'Teaching about the Caribbean'. London: CRC, May.

Education and Community Relations (1973). 'Aids for Teachers in Birmingham'. London: CRC, Sept.

EDUCATIONAL PRIORITY AREA PUBLICATIONS: DES and Social Science Research Council. London: HMSO.

Vol. I *Educational Priority*, ed. by A. H. Halsey (1972).

Vol. II *EPA Surveys and Statistics*, ed. by Joan Payne (1974).

Vol. III *EPA: Evaluated Action in London and Birmingham*, ed. by Jack Barnes (1974).

Vol. IV *EPA: A Case Study in the West Riding*, ed. by G. Smith (1974).

Vol. V *EPA: A Scottish Study*, ed. by C. Morrison in collaboration with Joyce Watts and T. Lee (1974).

Educational Research News (1972). 'Towards a multi-racial society', Sept. (published by NFER).

EELLS, K. *et al.* (1951). *Intelligence and Cultural Differences: A Study of Cultural Learning and Problem-solving*. Chicago & London: University of Chicago Press.

ELKIN, J. (1972). *Books for Multi-Racial Classrooms*. Birmingham: Library Association.

ENGLISH LANGUAGE TEACHING INFORMATION CENTRE (1968). See CILT under Bibliographies Section.

EPPELL, E. (ed.) (1972). *Education for Cultural Pluralism*. Papers from an International Conference in London, December 1970, under auspices of the Cultural Department, World Jewish Congress: London.

EVANS, P. (1971). *Attitudes of Young Immigrants*. London: Runnymede Trust.

EVERSLEY, D. and SUKDEO, F. (1969). *The Dependants of the Coloured Commonwealth Population of England and Wales*. London: IRR Special Series.

EVERTON, A. and FREAKES, H. (1968). 'Immigrants learn by word games', *Education*, 131, 3.

EWEN, E. and GIPPS, C. (1973). 'Tests of English for immigrant children', *Multi-Racial School*, 2, 2. (*Educ. Res. News*, 17, January.)

EYSENCK, H. J. (1971). *Race, Intelligence and Education*. London: Temple Smith.

EYSENCK, H. J. (1971). 'Race, IQ and education', *New Society*, 17th June.

FEELEY, M. (1965). 'An investigation of the social integration of coloured immigrant children in selected secondary schools'. Dissertation Diploma, University of Liverpool.

FERRON, O. (1964). 'A study of certain factors related to the tested intelligence of groups of some West African children'. Unpublished PhD thesis, University of Edinburgh.

FERRON, O. (1965). 'The test performance of "coloured" children', *Educ. Res.*, VIII, 1.

FERRON, O. (1966). 'The effects of early environmental stimulations among Freetown Creoles—a comparative study', *Educ. Res.*, VIII, 3.

FESTINGER, L. (1957). *A Theory of Cognitive Dissonance*. New York: Harper and Row.

FIELD, F. and HAIKIN, P. (eds.) (1971). *Black Britons*. London: OUP.

FIGUEROA, P. (1969). 'School Leavers and the Colour Barrier'. In: SELECT COMMITTEE ON IMMIGRATION AND RACE RELATIONS (1969). *Problems of Coloured School Leavers* Vol. II.

FIGUEROA, P. (1969). 'A Comparative Study of Employment Prospects of West Indian and English School Leavers'. In SELECT COMMITTEE ON IMMIGRATION AND RACE RELATIONS, Vol. II.
FITCHETT, N. (1967). 'Children who don't speak English', *Dialogue,* 1. (Schools Council)
FITZHERBERT, K. (1967). *West Indian Children in London.* London: Bell.
FITZHERBERT, K. (1967). 'West Indian children in London), *Race,* 2, October.
FLOWERS, C. E. (1966). 'Effects of an arbitrary accelerated school placement on the tested academic achievement of educationally disadvantaged students'. Unpublished PhD Dissertation, Teachers College, Columbia University.
FOOT, P. (1965). *Immigration and Race in British Politics.* Harmondsworth: Penguin.
FORBES, J. (1966). *Afro-Americans in the Far West: A Handbook for Educators.* Berkeley, Calif.: Far West Laboratory for Educational Research.
FRASER, E. (1959). *Home, Environment and the School.* London: University of London Press.
FYSON, N. (1973a). 'Third-world needs and multi-racial schools', *Multi-Racial School,* summer.
FYSON, N. (1973b). *Development Puzzle: a Source Book for Teaching.* London: UCOAD.

GAARDER, A. B. (1972). 'Bilingual, bicultural education: the special case of the Mexican American'. In: EPPELL, E. M. ed. (1972).
GEORGE, V. and MILLERSON, G. (1967). 'The Cypriot community in London', *Race,* VIII, 3.
GHAI, D. P. (1965). *Portrait of a Minority: Asians in East Africa.* London: OUP/IRR.
GLASGOW EDUCATIONAL DEPT. & HAMILTON COLLEGE OF EDUCATION SOCIAL STUDIES DEPT. (1969). *Race Relations.* Glasgow: Corporation of Glasgow.
GLENDENNING, F. (1971). 'History and General Studies: some recent books for schools', *Race Today,* September.
GLENDENNING, F. (1972). 'Teaching prejudice and world history', *Race Today,* September.
GLASS, R. and POLLINS, H. (1960). *The Newcomers: The West Indian in London.* London: Allen & Unwin.
GOLDMAN, R. (1968). *Research and the Teaching of Immigrant Children.* London: NCCI (now CRC).
GOLDMAN, R. and TAYLOR, F. (1966). 'Coloured immigrant children: a survey of research studies and literature on their educational problems and potential—in Britain', *Educ. Res.,* VIII, 3.
GOLDMAN, R. and TAYLOR, F. (1966). 'Coloured immigrant children: a survey of research studies and literature on their educational problems and potential—in the USA', *Educ. Res.,* IX, 1.
GOODMAN, M. (1964). *Race Awareness in Young Children.* New York: Collier-Macmillan.
GORER, G. (1955). *Exploring English Character.* London: Cresset Press.
GRANADA TELEVISION (1972). *Our Neighbours.* Six programmes for 10 to 13 year–olds, to introduce them to the culture of immigrants who have settled in Britain. London: Independent Broadcasting Authority.
GRAY, S. and KLAVS, R. (1965). 'An experimental programme for culturally deprived children', *Child Dev.,* 36.
GREEN, J. and ANDERSON, H. (1970). *Youth Tutors Youth.* London: Community Service Volunteers.

GREVE, J., PAGE, D., GREVE, S. (1971). *Homlessness in London*. Edinburgh: Scottish Academic Press.
GRIFFITH, J., HENDERSON, J., OSBORNE, M., WOOD, D. and LONG, H. (1960). *Coloured Immigrants in Britain*. London: Oxford University Press.
Guardian (1970). 'Strain of dual culture', 27th April.
Guardian (1971a). ' "Below par" children—"an error" ', 22nd February, p. 7.
Guardian (1971). 'Social values of children', September. A report of Dr E. Midwinter's talk before Education Section, Br. Ass. Adv. Science.
Guardian (1971). 'Immigrant, alien and EEC quarterly entry', June 9th.
Guardian (1972). WINDSOR, J. 'Another look at lessons on race', 20th February.
GUILDFORD, J. (1967). *The Nature of Human Intelligence*. New York: McGraw-Hill.

HALEVY, J. (1972). Forword in EPPEL, E. (1972).
HALSEY, A. (1972a). *Educational Priority, V. 1: EPA Problems and Policies*. Department of Education and Science and Social Science Research Council. London: HMSO.
HALSEY, A. (1972b). 'A new landmark', *Priority News*, Liverpool: Priority.
HARTMAN, P. and HUSBAND, C. (1972). 'British scale for measuring white attitudes to coloured people', *Race*, October, XIV, 2.
HANSON, C. (1969). 'Language teaching techniques in a secondary school remedial situation', *Remedial Education*.
HANSON, C. (1970). 'Tenses at a second level', *English for Immigrants*, 3, 2.
HANSON, C. (1971). *Teaching Tenses*. Leeds: ATEPO.
HARTLEY, B. (1968). *The Pakistani Family in Britain*. London: CRC.
HARTLEY, B. (1972). 'Report on a three year project', *Race Today*, July (and TES 16/6/72).
HASHMI, F. (1972). *Psychology of Racial Prejudice*. London: CRC.
HATCH, S. (1962). 'Coloured people in school textbooks', *Race*, 4, November.
HAUSER, R. (1971). *Black and White Identity Formation*. New York: Wiley.
HAWKES, N. (1966). *Immigrant Children in British School*. (Institute of Race Relations) London: Pall Mall Press.
HAWKINS, E. (1971). *A Time for Growing*. London: CRC.
HAYNES, J. (1970). 'Immigrant ability', *Race Today*.
HAYNES, J. (1971a). *Educational Assessment of Immigrant Pupils*. Slough: NFER.
HAYNES, J. (1971b). 'Race, intelligence and education', *Multi-Racial School*, 1, 1.
HEPPLE, B. (1968). *Race, Jobs and the Law in Britain*. Harmondsworth: Penguin.
HESTER, H. (1969). 'Stories in language teaching', *English for Immigrants*, 3, 1.
HESTER, H. (1970). *Devloping Oral Skills*. Leeds: ATEPO.
HILL, B. (1972). 'Daughters of the temple', *Times Educ. Suppl.*, 1/9/72.
HILL, C. (1970). *Immigration and Integration*. London: Pergamon.
HILL, D. (1968). 'The attitudes of West Indian and English adolescents in Britain' (Dissertation for the degree of MEd, University of Manchester) *Brit. J. Educ. Psychol.*, (1969), 39, 2.
HILL, J. (ed.) (1971). *Books for Children: The Homelands of Immigrants in Britain*. London: IRR.
HILL, M. and ISSACHAROFF, R. (1971). *Community Action and Race Relations*. London: OUP.
HILLMAN, J. (1971). 'Better homes aid racial harmony', *The Guardian*, September 16th.
HILTON, J. (1972). 'The ambitions of school children', *Race Today*, March.
HINNELLS, J. and SHARPE, E. (eds.) (1972). *Hinduism*. London: Oriel Press.

HIMMELSTRAND, U. (1964). *Content and Methods of Education in Dealing with Racial Discrimination.* London: The International Federation of Workers' Association.

HIPKIN, J. (1972). *The Race Pack.* See Schools Council Nuffield Humanities Project.

HIRO, D. (1970). *The Indian Family in Britain.* London: CRC.

HIRO, D. (1971). *Black British: White British.* London: Eyre & Spottiswoode (paperback published by Penguin).

H.M. GOVERNMENT (1973). *Pakistan Bill,* 1973. London: HMSO.

HOLMAN, R. (1971). 'The urban programme appraised', *Race Today,* 3, 7, July.

HOME OFFICE (1962). *Commonwealth Immigration Act* 1962. London: HMSO.

HOME OFFICE (1965). *Immigration from the Commonwealth.* Cmnd. 2739. London: HMSO.

HOME OFFICE (1965). *Race Relations Act* 1965. London: HMSO.

HOME OFFICE (1968a). *Commonwealth Immigrants Act* 1968. London: HMSO.

HOME OFFICE (1968b). *Race Relations Act* 1968. London: HMSO.

HOME OFFICE. Commonwealth Immigrants Advisory Council (1963–1965). London: HMSO.

First Report (1963). *Housing* (Cmnd 2796).

Second Report (1964). *Education of Commonwealth Immigrants in British Schools* (Cmnd 2266).

Third Report (1964). *Immigrant School Leavers.*

Fourth Report (1965). *Housing* (Cmnd 2796).

HOME OFFICE (1973). *Commonwealth Immigrants Acts* 1962 *and* 1968. *Statistics,* 1972. Cmnd 5285. London: HMSO.

HOME OFFICE (1973). *White Paper on Police—Immigrant Relations.* London: HMSO.

HOOPER, R. (ed.). See BRITISH BROADCASTING CORPORATION.

HOPKINS, J. (1962). 'Bibliographies des recherches psychologiques conduites en Afrique', *Revue de Psychol. Appl.,* 12.

HORDER, D. (1971). 'The fourth R'. *Dialogue,* 7.

HOROWITZ, E. (1936). 'Developing of attitudes towards negroes'. In PROSHANSKY, H. and SEIDENBERG, B. (eds.) *Basic Studies in Social Psychology* (1969). New York: Holt, Rinehart & Winston.

HOUGHTON, V. (1966). 'A report on the scores of West Indian immigrant children and English children on an individually administered test', *Race,* 8, 1.

HOUGHTON, V. (1970) 'White Jamaican hypothesis', *Race,* XI, 3.

HUBBARD, D. (1972). 'The Staveley experiment', *Trends in Education,* October, 28.

HUDSON, L. (1971). 'Intelligence, race and the selection of data', *Race,* XII, 3.

HUDSON, L. (1971). 'Science and popularization', *New Society,* July.

HUGGINS, V., MARRIOTT, L. and WELLS, J. (1972). *The University of Brixton.* BBC English by Radio. London: BBC, Bush House.

HUMPHREY, D. and JOHN, G. (1971). *Because they're Black.* Harmondsworth: Penguin.

HUNT REPORT (Committee of the Youth Service Development Council) (1967). *Immigrants and the Youth Service.* London: HMSO.

HUXLEY, E. (1964). *Back Street: New Worlds.* London: Chatto & Windus.

INNER LONDON EDUCATION AUTHORITY (1967). *Education of Immigrant Pupils in Special Schools for Educationally Subnormal Children.* London: ILEA.

INNER LONDON EDUCATION AUTHORITY (1971). Education Television Service. *Exploring World Faiths.* Ten programmes for Upper Secondary pupils. London: ILEA.

INSTITUTE OF RACE RELATIONS (1966). 'Survey of courses in colleges of education', *Newsletter,* January.
INSTITUTE OF RACE RELATIONS, FACTS PAPER (1969). *Colour and Immigration in the United Kingdom,* 1969. London: IRR. Also: 1970, 1971, 1972, 1973 editions.
INTERNATIONAL SOCIAL SERVICE OF GREAT BRITAIN (1973). *Annual Report for* 1972. London: ISS.
INTERNATIONAL VOLUNTARY SERVICE and VOLUNTARY SERVICE OVERSEAS (1971). *Voluntary Work in Community Relations.* Harlesden, London: IVS.
IRVINE, S. (1966). 'Towards a rationale for testing attainments and abilities in Africa', *Brit. J. Educ. Psychol.,* XXXVI.
IRVINE, S. (1968). 'A five-year follow up of secondary school selection procedures in central Africa, 1962–1967', *Brit. J. Educ. Psychol.,* 38.

JAHODA, G. (1969). 'Crosscultural use of the perceptual maze test', *Brit. J. Educ. Psychol.,* 39, 1.
JAHODA, M. (1960). *Race and Mental Health.* Paris: Unesco.
JENSEN, A. (1969). 'How much can we boost IQ and scholastic achievement?' *Harv. Educ. Rev.,* 39, Winter.
JENSEN, A. (1971). 'Do schools cheat minority children?' *Educ. Res.,* Vol. 14, and *Comments* by Burt, Butcher, Eysenck, and Vernon, on Jensen (1971) article, *Educ. Res.,* 14, 1.
JEPHCOTT, P. (1964). *A Troubled Area.* London: Faber.
JESSEL, D. (1971). 'Intelligence tests on immigrant pupils unfair', *The Times,* 17th March.
JOHN, A. (1972). *Race in an Inner City.* London: Runnymede Trust.
JOHN, Jr., DEWITT (1969). *Indian Workers' Associations in Britain.* London: OUP/IRR.
JONES, J. (ed.) (1965). 'Linguistics, and Language Teaching in a Multilingual Society'. Report of Conference, 6th–9th April 1964. University of West Indies, Kingston, Jamaica. Old Woking, Surrey: Unwin Bros.
JONES, J. (1966). 'English in the Commonwealth: The West Indies', *English Language Teaching,* XX, 2. London: OUP.
JONES, J. (1969). 'English language teaching in a social cultural dialect situation', *Language Teaching,* 2.

KAUSHAL, T. (1965). *Racial Tensions Among Youth.* Birmingham UNA Conference Report. Birmingham: BUNA.
KAWWA, T. (1963). 'The ethnic prejudice and choice of friends among English and non-English adolescents'. Unpublished MA dissertation, University of London Institute of Education.
KAWWA, T. (1965). 'A study of the interaction between native and immigrant children in English schools with special reference to ethnic prejudice'. Unpublished PhD thesis, University of London Institute of Education.
KAWWA, T. (1968). 'Three sociometric studies of ethnic relations in London schools', *Brit. J. Soc. & Clin. Psychol.,* 7.
KEESINGS (1968). *Contemporary Archives:* 1967–1968. London: Keesings.
KELMAN, H. (1970). 'Three processes of social influence'. *Understanding Society.* London: Open University/Macmillan.
KEMELFIELD, G. (1972). *The Evaluation of Schools Broadcasts: Piloting a New Approach.* Leeds: Centre for TV Research, University of Leeds and Independent Television Authority.
KITZINGER, S. (1972). 'West Indian children with problems', *Therapeutic Education,* Spring.

KLEIN, J. (1965). *Samples from English Culture.* Vol. 2. London: Routledge and Kegan Paul.

KLYHN, J. (1969). 'On the integration into school of young immigrant children', *English Language Teaching,* 23.

KNAPP, D. (1969). 'Using structure drill to teach cultural understanding', *English as a Second Language,* 4, 2.

KNOWLES, F. (1969). 'A breakthrough in initial literacy', *Dialogue,* 3, June.

KOHLER, D. (1973). 'The 1971 Census', *CRC Journal,* March.

KOHLER, D. (1972/3). 'Commonwealth coloured immigrants and the 1971 census', *New Community,* 2, 1.

KOHLER, D. (1973). 'Poll finds general public opinion unfavourable to illegal immigrants', *CRC Journal,* Sept.

KRAUSZ, E. (1971). *Ethnic Minorities in Britain.* London: MacGibbon & Kee.

KREAR, S. (1969). 'The role of the mother tongue at home and at school in the development of bilingualism', *English Language Teaching,* 24, 1.

KWEE CHOO, N. (1968). *The Chinese in London.* London: OUP.

LAING, A. (1971). See Schools Council Compensatory Education Project.

LAISHLEY, J. (1971). 'Skin colour awareness and preferences in London nursery school children', *Race,* XIII, 1, July.

LAWRENCE, D. (1969a). 'How prejudiced are we?' *Race Today,* October.

LAWRENCE, D. (1969). Letter to *New Society,* 21/8/69 and 28/8/69.

LAWSON, T. (ed.) (1969). *Education for International Understanding.* Hamburg: Unesco.

LAWTON, D. (1968). *Social Class, Language and Education.* London: Routledge and Kegan Paul.

LEACH, P. (1964). 'Teaching tolerance: the role of the school in furthering constructive inter-group relations', *Internat. Rev. of Educ.,* X, 2.

LEDERMAN, S. (1969). 'Social acceptance of immigrants', *Race Today,* June.

LEE, R. (1965). 'The education of immigrant children in England', *Race,* VII, 2.

LE PAGE, R. B. (1968). 'Inter-comprehensibility between West Indian English and other forms of English', *Remedial Education* (Oxford), 3.

LEICESTER TEACHERS (1970). *Making Audio-Visual Materials.* Leeds: ATEPO.

LEISHAMN, J. (1971). '£4M. aid for 530 welfare projects', *The Guardian,* 19th January.

LEVINE, J. (1970). *Developing Writing Skills.* Leeds: ATEPO.

LEWIS, E. G. (1970). 'Immigrants, their language and development', *Trends in Education,* 19.

LEWIS, I. and REA, N. (1969). *The Race Kit.* Harmondsworth: Penguin Books.

LITTLE, A. *et al.* (1968). 'The education of immigrant pupils in Inner London primary schools', *Race,* IX, 4.

LITTLE, A., MABEY, C. and RUSSELL, J. (1971). 'Do small classes help a pupil?', *New Society,* 21st October.

LITTLE, K. (1972). *Negroes in Britain.* 2nd revised edition. London: Routledge and Kegan Paul.

LIVERPOOL YOUTH ORGANIZATION COMMITTEE (1968). *Special but not Separate.* Liverpool: LYOC.

LIVERPOOL COMMUNITY RELATIONS COUNCIL (1973). *Sowing the Dragon's Teeth.* Liverpool: LCRC.

LIVERPOOL EDUCATIONAL AREA PROJECT, PUBLICATIONS (1969–1971).

(Dr Eric Midwinter, Project Director.)

Occasional Papers 1–11.

1. *Educational Priority Areas: A Philosophic Question.*

2. *Liverpool EPA: A Description.*
3. *Role of School Managers in EPA Schools.*
4. *Home and School Relations in EPA.*
5. *Teachers' Education and the EPA.*

Miss M. Byrne, Projects Secretary for Liverpool EPA for other titles.
Progress Reports I, II, III from Dr E. Midwinter.
'Projectile 1, 2, 3.' *Journal of the Liverpool EPA Project.*
Projectors: 1. *Social Environment and Downtown Schools.*
2. *Down our Way.*
3. *Home-School Horse-sense for Teachers.*
4. *Social Problems Game.*
Liverpool, L7, 3EA: Paddington Comprehensive School.

LLEWELLYN, G. (1968). Project on 'The language needs of immigrants when they first start work.' Birmingham: Dept. of English and Foreign Languages, City of Birmingham, College of Commerce, University of Birmingham.

LONDON COUNCIL OF SOCIAL SERVICES (1964). *The Young Immigrant at Home and at School.* Report of a Day Conference, 19th May.

LONDON HEAD TEACHERS' ASSOCIATION (1965). *Memorandum on Immigrant Children in London Schools.* London: Pegg & Sons.

LUCAS, E. (1972). 'Language in the infants' playground', *Multi-Racial School,* 1, 2 and 2, 1.

LYNCH, H. R. (ed.) (1971). *Black Spokesman: Selected Published Writing of Edward Wilmot Blyden.* London: Frank Cass.

MACINTYRE, D. and BRANNEN, J. (1971). 'Equality or complacency', *Race Today,* October.

MALPAS, C. (1968). 'All by chance', *Remedial Education,* 3, 1.

MANLEY, D. (1971). 'Teaching English to Immigrants at a Secondary Girls' School'. In McNEAL and ROGERS (1971).

MANLEY, D. (1973). See Schools Council English for Immigrants.

MARRIOTT, L. and WELLS, J. (1972). See Huggins *et al.*

MARSH, A. (1970). 'Awareness of racial differences in West African and British children', *Race,* XI, 3.

MARSH, A. (1973). 'Race, community and anxiety', *New Society,* February 22nd.

MASON, P. (1969). 'Race, intelligence, and Professor Jensen', *Race Today,* July.

MASON, P. (1970a). *Race Relations.* London: IRR.

MASON, P. (1970b). *Patterns of Dominance.* London: IRR.

MASON, P. (1971). Letter in *New Society,* 24th June.

McCART, M. (1973). 'Ugandan Asians . . .', *CRC Journal,* Sept.

McDIARMID, G. and PRATT, D. (1971). *Teaching Prejudice.* Penhurst, Kent (Ontario): Ontario Inst. for Studies in Education.

McFIE, J. and THOMPSON, J. (1970). 'Intellectual abilities of immigrant children', *Brit. J. Educ. Psychol.,* 40, 3.

McNEAL, J. and ROGERS, M. (1971) (eds.). *The Multi-Racial School.* Penguin (Education).

McLEOD, W. (1972). *The Sikhs of the Punjab.* Newcastle: Oriel Press.

McPHAIL, P. (1970). 'Education for change', *New University,* February.

McPHAIL, P. *et al.* (1972). See Schools Council Project on Moral Education.

METH, M. (1970). *Here to Stay. A Study of Good Practices in the Employment of Coloured Workers.* London: Runnymede Trust.

MIDWINTER, E. C. (1970). *Education: A Priority Area.* London: NUT.

MIDWINTER, E. C. (1972a). *Projections: An Educational Priority Area at Work.* London: Ward Locke.

MIDWINTER, E. C. (1972b). *Social Environment and the Urban School.* London: Ward Locke.

MIDWINTER, E. C. (1972c). *Projections and the Social Environment and the Urban School.* London: Ward Locke.

MIDWINTER, E. C. (1972d). *Priority Education.* London: Penguin Education.

MILLER, G. (1970). 'Social class link with achievement examined', *J. Educ. Psychol.,* 61, 4.

MILLER, H. J. (1967). 'A study of the effectiveness of a variety of teaching techniques for reducing colour prejudice in a male sample (15–21 years)'. Unpublished MA thesis, London University.

MILLINS, P. (1970). *Education for a Multi-cultural Society: Syllabuses.* London: Teacher Training and Curriculum Development Group. Advisory Committee on Education, CRC.

MILNER, D. (1971). 'Prejudice and the immigrant child', *New Society,* 23rd September.

MILNER, D. (1971). 'Attitudes', *Race Today,* November.

MILNER, D. (1972). 'Identity conflict in immigrant children', *Therapeutic Education,* Spring.

MILSON, F. (1966). *Operation Integration Two.* Birmingham: Westhill College of Education.

MINISTRY OF EDUCATION (1963). *English for Immigrants.* (Pamphlet No. 43). London: HMSO.

MITTLER, P. and WARD, J. (1970). 'The use of the Illinois Test of psycholinguistic abilities on British four-year-old children', *Brit. J. Educ. Psychol.,* 40, 1.

MONTAGUE, A. (1972). *Statements on Race by Unesco.* New York: OUP.

MOORE, R. (1971). *Race Relations in Britain Today.* London: SCM.

MORRIS, S. (1973). *A Treatise on Black Studies.* London: Committee on Black Studies.

MORRISH, I. (1971). *The Background of Immigrant Children.* London: Allen and Unwin.

MORTON, D. and GOLDMAN, R. (1969). *The Formal Institution of Pre-school Education in Britain.* Occ. Paper 1. Manchester: Didsbury College of Education.

Multi-Racial School (1972). 'The University of Brixton'.

Multi-Racial School (1973). 'Problems of a Sikh girl', Spring issue.

MUNDY, J. H. (1970). 'Language teaching and the young immigrant', *Trends,* (London: DES).

NANDY, D. (1969). 'Unrealistic aspirations', *Race Today,* October.

NANDY, D. (1972). 'Britain and the EEC', *Race Relations Bulletin,* January.

NANDY, Margaret (1971). 'Social Studies for a Multi-Racial Society'. In McNeal and Rogers.

NATIONAL ASSOCIATION FOR MULTI-RACIAL EDUCATION (formerly ATEPO) (1971). *Multi-Racial School* (quarterly).

NATIONAL ASSOCIATION OF SCHOOLMASTERS (1968). *The Education of Immigrant Children.* London: NAS.

NATIONAL BOOK LEAGUE (1967). *English for Immigrant Children.* London: NBL.

NATIONAL COMMITTEE FOR COMMONWEALTH IMMIGRANTS (NCCI). London: NCCI.

NCCI (1967). *The First Six Months.*

NCCI (1967). *Report for* 1966.

NCCI (1968). *Report for* 1967.

NCCI (1967). *Practical Suggestions for Teachers of Immigrant Children.*
Towards a Multi-Racial Society.

NATIONAL FOUNDATION FOR EDUCATIONAL RESEARCH (1973). *English Proficiency Tests.* Aylesbury: Ginn.
NATIONAL UNION OF TEACHERS (1967). *Education of Immigrant Children.* London: NUT.
N'DEM, E. (1953). 'Negro immigration in Manchester'. Unpublished MA dissertation in Anthropology, University College London.
NEFF, W. (1938). 'Socio-economic status and intelligence', *Psychol. Bull.*, 35, 727.
NEW BEACON BOOKS (1971). *Special Caribbean Book List for Teachers, Parents and Teenagers.* London: New Beacon Books.
New Community (1972). Vol. 1, No. 4. London: CRC.
NISBET (1972). See Jensen (1971).
NORRIS, R. (1972). 'Helping children understand', *Multi-Racial School,* **1**, **2**, Spring.

OAKLEY, R. (1970). 'The Cypriots in Britain', *Race Today,* April.
OAKLEY, R. (ed.) (1968). *New Backgrounds.* London: OUP.
OBERIST, C. and BISSET, D. (1968). *It's Time for Reading.* London: Ginn.
O'BRIAN, J. (1972). *Brown Britons—The Crisis of the Ugandan Asians.* London: Runnymede Trust.
OKONJI, M. (1970). 'The effects of special training on the classification of behaviour of some Nigerian Ibo children', *Brit. J. Educ. Psychol.*, 40, 1.
OXFAM EDUCATION (1973). *Lists of Educational Materials for Primary and Secondary Schools.*
(1972). *Project Wallet on India.*
(1972). *Story Books about India for Infants.* (9 books). Oxford: Oxfam.
PARKER, J. (1972). 'Textbooks and racial prejudice: a strategy for change', *Multi-Racial School,* 2, 1, Autumn.
PARKINSON, J. and MacDONALD, B. (1972). 'Teaching race neutrality', *Race,* V, 13.
PARRY, M. (1969). 'A bold adventure', *Dialogue,* 3.
PARRY, M. (1971). 'The under fives', *Dialogue,* 8.
PARRY, E. M. (1971). 'Pre-School Education Project'. In SCHOOLS COUNCIL (1971).
PATHWAY FURTHER EDUCATION CENTRE (1970). *Report on Investigation, Materials and Organization of Classes.* Industrial English Language Teaching. Middlesex: PFEC.
PATTERSON, S. (1963a). *Dark Strangers.* London: Tavistock Publications.
PATTERSON, S. (ed.) (1963b). *Immigrants in London.* Report of a Study Group (set up by the London Council of Social Service). London: NCSS.
PATTERSON, S. (1968). *Immigrants in Industry.* London: OUP/IRR.
PATTERSON, S. (1969). *Immigration and Race Relations in Britain* 1960–1967. London: OUP/IRR.
PAYNE, J. F. (November 1969). 'A comparative study of the mental ability of seven- and eight-year-old British and West Indian children in a West Midland town', *Brit. J. Educ. Psychol.*, 39, 3.
PAYNE, J. F. (1969). 'Mental ability: a comparative study', *Race Today,* December.
PEACH, C. (1965). 'Immigrants and the 1961 Census', *Newsletter.* (Institute of Race Relations) 10th October.
PEACH, C. (1968). *West Indian Migration to Britain.* London: IRR.
PEAK SERIES (1963–65). *Textbooks of an Integrated 3-year Course for Asians in English Schools in Kenya.* London: OUP.
PEAKER, G. (1971). *The Plowden Children Four Years Later.* Slough: NFER.
PERRY, J. (1973). *The Fair-Housing Experiment: Community Relations Councils and the Housing of Minority Groups.* London: PEP.

PIDGEON, E. (1969). 'Intelligence, a changed view', *Educ. Res. News,* 6.
PIDGEON, D. (1970). *Expectation and Pupil Performance.* Slough: NFER.
PLOWDEN, Lady B. *et al.* Central Advisory Council for Education (England) (1967). *Children and their Primary Schools.* London: HMSO.
POLACK, A. (1957). 'The promotion of teaching of race questions in primary and secondary schools', *Anglo-Jewish Association Journal,* 3, 2.
POLLACK, M. (1972). 'A suggested black studies syllabus', *Teachers against Racism,* June 2nd.
PEP REPORT (1967). *Racial Discrimination in England.* London: IRR.
PORTEUS, S. (1930). 'Race and social differences in performance tests', *Genel. Psychol. Mono.,* 8, 2.
POWER, J. (1967). *Immigrants in School.* London: Councils and Educational Press.
PRATT, D. and McDIARMID, G. (1972). *Teaching Prejudice.* Penhurst, Kent: Ontario Inst. Studies in Education.
PRIORITY AREA CHILDREN (1971). *The Illegal Childminders.* Cambridge: Advisory Centre for Education.
PULHAM, K. (1970). 'Evaluation in action research', *Projectile* 3, Liverpool: EPA.
PULHAM, K. (1969). 'Liverpool EPA pre-school campaign', *Journal of Liverpool EPA Project,* 1.

QUIGLEY, H. (1972). 'NFER pre-school project', *Multi-Racial School,* 1, 2, Spring.

RACE RELATIONS BOARD (1973). *Information Kit on Race Relations.* London: RRB.
Race Today (1969). 'Ealing: education and race', *Race Today,* October.
Race Today (1970). 'ESN children in ILEA schools', *Race Today,* February.
REDHEAD, P. (1972). 'English lessons at work pay dividends', *Financial Times,* 14th June.
RENNIE, J. (1970). 'Children and their community', *Dialogue,* 6, August.
REX, J. and MOORE, R. (1967). *Race, Community and Conflict: A Study of Sparkbrook.* London: OUP.
REX, J. (1971). Letter, *New Society,* 24th June.
RICHARDSON, K., SPEARS, D. and RICHARDS, M. (1972). *Race, Culture and Intelligence.* Harmondsworth: Penguin.
RICHARDSON, S. and GREEN, A. (1971). 'When is black beautiful? Coloured and white children's reactions to skin colour', *Brit. J. Educ. Psychol.,* 91, 1.
RICHMOND, A. (1954). *Colour Prejudice in Britain: A Study of West Indian Workers in Liverpool* 1942–1951.
RICHMOND, A. (1955). *The Colour Problem: A Study of Race Relations.* Harmondsworth: Penguin.
RICHMOND, A. (ed.) (1972). *Readings in Race and Ethnic Relations.* London: Pergamon.
ROBERTSON, T. and KAWWA, T. (1971). 'Ethnic relations in a girls' comprehensive school', *Educ. Res.,* 13, 3.
ROSE, E. (1968a). 'The Institute's survey of race relations', *Race,* IX, 4.
ROSE, E. *et al.* (1969). *Colour and Citizenship.* London: IRR.
ROSENTHAL, R. and JACOBSON, (1968). 'Teachers' Expectations of the Disadvantaged'. In PIDGEON, D. (1970).
ROWLEY, K. (1967). 'Social relations between British and immigrant children', *Educ. Res.,* 10, 2.
RUCK, S. K. (ed.) (1959). *The West Indian Comes to England.* London: Routledge and Kegan Paul.

RUDD, E. (1970). 'Language for immigrant children', *English Language Teaching*, 24, 3.

RUDD, E. (1971a). 'Immigrant test trials under way', *Educ. Res. News*, January.

RUDD, E. (1971b). 'Language tests for immigrant children', *Multi-Racial School*, 1, 1.

RUDD, E. (1971c). *Pronunciation for Non-English speakers from India, Pakistan, Cyprus and Italy. Scope Handbook* 2. London: Schools Council.

RUNNYMEDE TRUST (1970). 'Annual report: race relations board: special feature', *Race Relations Bulletin*, July.

RUNNYMEDE TRUST (1971). 'Urban programme and community relations', *Race Relations Bulletin*, February.

RUNNYMEDE TRUST (1971). 'Race Relations Board', *Race Relations Bulletin*, January.

RUNNYMEDE TRUST (1971). 'Education', *Race Relations Bulletin*, February.

RUNNYMEDE TRUST (1972). 'Assessing educational needs', *Race Relations Bulletin*, April.

RUNNYMEDE TRUST (1972). *English Lessons at Work Pay Dividends*. Occ. Reprint, 5. London: Runnymede Trust.

RUNNYMEDE TRUST (1972). *Race Relations Bulletin*, July.

RUNNYMEDE TRUST (1972). 'Census 1971. Advance analysis', *Runnymede Trust Bulletin*, Dec.

RUNNYMEDE TRUST (1973). 'Special feature: revised immigration rules', *Runnymede Trust Bulletin*, March. (formerly *Race Relations Bulletin*).

RUNNYMEDE TRUST (1973). 'Repatriation', *Runnymede Trust Bulletin*, May. ('Special feature—1971 Census data on Greater London').

RUNNYMEDE TRUST (1973). 'Pakistan Bill 1973', *Runnymede Trust Bulletin*, July.

RUNNYMEDE TRUST (1973). *Questions and Answers on Race Relations and Immigration*. London: Runnymede Trust.

SAINT, C. K. (1963a). 'Scholastic and sociological adjustment of the Punjabi speaking children in Smethwick'. Unpublished MEd dissertation, University of Birmingham.

SAINT, C. K. (1963b). 'Handling the immigrants: English classes at Smethwick', *Times Educ. Suppl.*, 1st January 1965.

SAMPSON, O. (1963). 'Eleven plus for immigrants', *Times Educ. Suppl.*, 5th April.

SAUNDERS, I. (1969). 'New horizons at school'. *The Scotsman*, February 19th.

SARNOFF, I., KATZ, D. and McCLINTOCK, C. *et al.* (eds.) (1954). 'Attitude Changing Procedure and Motivating Patterns'. In OPEN UNIVERSITY (1970). *Understanding Society*. London: Macmillan.

SCHAEFER, R. (1972). 'The racial attitudes of Englishmen'. Unpublished draft thesis, University of Chicago.

SCHOOLS COUNCIL: COMPENSATORY EDUCATION PROJECT:

CHAZAN, M. and LAING, A. (1968). *Compensatory Education: an Introduction* (annotated reading list).

WILLIAMS, P., FERGUSON, N., FISHER, B. and SIMS, N. (1969). *Children at Risk*.

CHAZAN, M. and DOWNES, G. (ed.) (1971). *Compensatory Education and the New Media*.

COX, T. and WAITE, C. (eds.) (1970). *Teaching Disadvantaged Children in the Infant School*.

EVANS, R., FERGUSON, N., DAVIES, P. and WILLIAMS, P. (1970). *Swansea Infants Evaluation Profile.* (Exp. version.)

LAING, A. (1971). 'The construction of an infant school amenities index', *Brit. J. Educ. Psychol.,* February.

CHAZAN, M., LAING, A. and JACKSON, A. (1971). *Just Before School: First Research Report.* London: Blackwells.

CHAZAN, M. and WILLIAMS, P. (1968). 'The deprived and the disadvantaged', *Dialogue,* 2.

Bulletin No. 3 (1972). Swansea: The University.

SCHOOLS COUNCIL (1969). *Report* 1968/1969.

SCHOOLS COUNCIL WORKING PAPER 13 (1967). *English for the Children of Immigrants.* London: HMSO.

SCHOOLS COUNCIL WORKING PAPER 27 (1970). *Cross'd with Adversity.* London: Evans/Methuen.

SCHOOLS COUNCIL WORKING PAPER 36 (1972). *Religious Education in Secondary Schools.* London: Evans/Methuen.

SCHOOLS COUNCIL (1971). *Project Profiles and Index.*

SCHOOLS COUNCIL: ENGLISH FOR IMMIGRANT CHILDREN CURRICULUM DEVELOPMENT PROJECT:

(1969) *Scope* 1*: An Introductory Course* for pupils 8–13 years.

(1971) *Scope Handbook* 2*: Pronunciation for Non-English Speaking Children from India, Pakistan, Cyprus and Italy.*

(1972) *Scope Senior Course* for non-English speaking students 14 years and over.

(1972) *Scope* 2 for pupils 8–13 years at 2nd Stage of English. Harlow: Longmans.

(1973) *Scope Handbook* 3: Language Work with Infant Immigrant Children.

(1973) TAYLOR, J. and INGLEBY, T. *Scope Storybook* 5–12 years.

(1973) MANLEY, D. *Scope Supplementary Plays and Dialogues.*

SCHOOLS COUNCIL PROJECT ON TEACHING ENGLISH TO WEST INDIAN CHILDREN (1972). *Concept* 7–9. Four units for multi-racial classes.

Unit 1. *Listening with Understanding.*

Unit 2. *Concept Building.*

Unit 3. *Communication.*

Unit 4. *The Dialect Kit.*

SCHOOLS COUNCIL: MORAL EDUCATION PROJECT:

McPHAIL, P., CHAPMAN, H. and UNGOED-THOMAS, J. (1972). *Moral Education in the Secondary School.*

UNGOED-THOMAS, J. (1972). *Our School.*

McPHAIL, P. (1972). *In Other People's Shoes* (series of cards and 1 teacher's book).

CHAPMAN, H. (1972). *Proving the Rule.*

UNGOED-THOMAS, J. (1972). *What Would You Have Done?*

All published by Longmans.

SCHOOLS COUNCIL/NUFFIELD HUMANITIES PROJECT (Director: L. Stenhouse.):
The Family (1970).
Relations between the Sexes (1970).
Poverty (1970).
Race (1972) by J. Hipkin.
(Teacher's handbook and complete pack of materials for each project.)
All published by Heinemann Educational Books.

STENHOUSE, L. (1970). *Humanities Project: an Introduction.* London: Heinemann.
STENHOUSE, L. (1970). 'Pupils into students', *Dialogue,* 5, Feb.
SCHOOLS COUNCIL (1972). *Race Relations and the Curriculum,* 9. London: Schools Council.

SCHOOLS COUNCIL: RELIGIOUS EDUCATION IN SECONDARY SCHOOL PROJECT:

HORDER, D. (1971). 'The fourth R', *Dialogue,* 7.
SCHOOLS COUNCIL (1972). *Religious Education in Secondary Schools.* Working Paper 36. London: Evans/Methuen.

SCHOOLS COUNCIL (WORKING PAPER 29) (1970). *The Teaching of English to West Indian Children.* London: Evans/Methuen. See Schools Council Project of above title.
SELECT COMMITTEE ON RACE RELATIONS AND IMMIGRATION (SCRRI) (1969a). *The Problem of Coloured School-leavers.* No. 413, Vol. I–IV, HC. 2, July. London: HMSO.
SCRRI (1969b). *Department of Education and Science Memorandum on Colleges of Education, ibid.,* Vol. IV, p. 8.
SCRRI (1971). *Housing Report,* V. I, Vols. II, III: Evidence, documents and index. London: HMSO.
SCRRI (1972). *Police-Immigrant Relations.* London: HMSO.
SCRRI (1973). *Education.* Vol. I (Report). London: HMSO.
SHAP WORKING PARTY ON WORLD RELIGIONS (1973). *World Religions: Aids for Teachers.* London: CRC.
SHAP (1972). Second edition. *Supplement to World Religions* (for those who have 1972 edition).
SHARMA, U. (1971). *Rampal and his family.* London: Collins.
SHARMA, R. (1969). 'IQ and environmental effects of organizing degrees of exposure to an English environment on Indian and Pakistan children', *Race Today,* May.
SHARROCK, A. (1968). 'Relations between home and school', *Educ. Res.,* 10, 3.
SOOKHDEO, P. (1972). *The Asian in Britain.* London: British Council of Churches.
SOUTHAMPTON CRC (1973). *Annual Report.* Southampton: SCRC.
STAFFORD-CLARK, D. (1970). *Prejudice in the Community.* London: CRC.
STENHOUSE, L. (1970). 'Pupils into students', *Dialogue,* 5.
STENHOUSE, L. (1971). *Humanities Project: An Introduction.* London: Heinemann.
STENHOUSE, L. and HIPKIN, J. (1972). 'Reply on criticisms of Race Pack', *Race,* 3, January.
STEPHEN, D. (1970a). *Immigration and Race Relations.* London: Fabian. Research Series, 291.
STEPHEN, D. (1970b). 'Immigrant regulations: Commonwealth citizens and aliens', *Race Today,* August.

STEWART, I. (1970). 'Readers as a source of prejudice', *Race Today*, January.

STOKER, D. (1970). *Immigrant Children in Infant Schools*. Leeds: Evans/Methuen.

STOUFFER, S. A. (1949). 'The American Soldier' in *Studies in Social Psychology in World War II*. Vol. 1. Princeton: PUP.

STREET, H. *et al.* (1967). *Report on Anti-discrimination Legislation*. London: PEP (Summary published by NCCI, now Community Relations Commission.)

Sunday Times (1973). 'Transforming the politics of race', (Leading Article).

SWIFT, D. (1965). 'Education, psychology and social environment', *Brit. J. Sociol.*, 16.

TANNAHILL, J. (1958). *European Volunteer Workers*. Manchester: Manchester University Press.

TAPPER, O. and STOPPES, E. (1963). 'Educating the immigrants', *East London Papers*, 6, 2.

TAYLOR, F. (1969). 'Colloquium on problems of migrant workers and their families in Council of Europe countries', *Race*, XI.

TAYLOR, J. H. (1971). 'Achievements in school, job aspirations and acculturation', Unpublished data for PhD thesis, University of Newcastle, Dept. of Social Studies.

TAYLOR, J. (1972a). *Thinking about Islam*. London: Lutterworth Press.

TAYLOR, J. (1972b). 'A tradition of respect', *New Society*, 5th October.

TAYLOR, J. and INGLEBY, T. (1973). See Schools Council (EIC).

TEACHERS AGAINST RACISM (1972). 'The question of black studies', *TAR Jornal*, 1, 1. (London: 9 Huddleston Road, London, N7.)

TEMPEST-WOODS, J. (1970). 'Report from the language department', *English for Immigrants*, 3, 3.

THOMPSON, E. (1963). *The Making of the English Working Class*. London: Gollancz.

TILBE, D. (1972). *The Ugandan Asian Crisis*. London: Community & Race Relations Unit of the British Council of Churches.

The Times (1971). 'Assessment of immigrant pupils', March 16th.

TITMUSS, R. (1970). 'Social change and the immigrant child'. (Conference.) London: CRC.

TOUGH, J. (1971). 'Pre-school language project', *Schools Councils Index*. London: Schools Council.

TOWNSEND, H. E. R. (1970). 'Report on preliminary results on NFER survey on procedures in schools for the education of immigrant pupils', *Education*, 136, 23.

TOWNSEND, H. E. R. (1970). In: *Statistics of Education. Special Series*, No. 2, *Survey of Inservice Training for Teachers*. London: HMSO.

TOWNSEND, H. E. R. (1971). *Immigrant Pupils in England: The LEA Response*. Slough: NFER.

TOWNSEND, H. E. R. (1973). *Multiracial Education: Need and Innovation*. Schools Council Working Paper 50. London: Evans/Methuen Educational.

TOWNSEND, H. E. R. and BRITTAN, E. M. (1972). *Organization in Multi-Racial Schools*. Slough: NFER.

TRISELIOTIS, J. (1969). 'Psycho-social problems of immigrant families'. In: OAKLEY, R. (1969).

TRUMAN, A. (1970). 'Specialized Training for Teachers of Immigrant Children'. *Aspects of the Preparation of Language Teachers*. London: Centre for Information on Language Teaching, Report No. 3.

UNESCO (1959). *Education for International Understanding*. (Examples and suggestions for classroom use.) Paris: Unesco.

UNESCO (1965). *International Understanding at School.* Paris: Unesco.

UNESCO (1956). *The Race Question in Modern Science Series.* Containing chapters by the following authors, some of which have been published as separate books (dated).

COMAS, J. (1965). *Racial Myths.*
DUNN, L. (1965). *Race and Biology.*
KLINEBERG, O., *Race and Psychology.*
LEIRIS, M. (1958). *Race and Culture.*
LEVI-STRAUSS, C. (1958). *Race and History.*
LITTLE, K. *Race and Sociology.*
MORANT, G. *The Significance of Racial Differences.*
ROSE, A. (1951). *The Roots of Prejudice.*
SHAPIRO, H. (1965). *Racial Mixture.*

UNGERSON, C. (1971). 'Community development—what future?' *Race Today,* October.

UNGOED-THOMAS, J. (1970). 'Race relations and moral education', *Race Today,* October.

URE, J. N. (1969). 'Practical Registers A & B', *English Language Teaching,* 23, 1 and 2.

VAN DER EYKEN, W. (1969). *The Pre-School Years.* Harmondsworth: Penguin.

VERMA, G. and MACDONALD, B. (1971). 'Some effects of race teaching on the attitudinal and sociometric patterns of adolescents', *Race,* XIII, 2, October.

VERNON, P. (1961). 'Intellectual Development in Non-Technological Societies'. Proceedings of the 14th International Congress of Appl. Psychol. Vol. III. Copenhagen: Munksgaard.

VERNON, P. (1965a). 'Environmental handicaps and intellectual development', *Brit. J. Educ. Psychol.,* XXX, 1 and 2.

VERNON, P. (1965b). 'Ability factors and environmental influences', *Amer. Psychol.,* 20, 9.

VERNON, P. (1966). 'Educational and intellectual development among Canadian Indians and Eskimos', *Educ. Rev.,* Feb. and June.

VERNON, P. (1967). 'Administration of group intelligence tests to East African pupils', *Brit. J. Educ. Psychol.,* 37, 3.

VERNON, P. (1968). *What is Potential Ability?* Fifth C.S. Meyers Lecture, 1968. London: University of London, Institute of Education.

VERNON, P. (1969). *Intelligence and Culture.* London: Methuen.

VERNON, P. (1971). Letter, *New Society,* July 8th.

VERNON, P. (1972). See JENSEN (1971).

VOLUNTARY COMMITTEE ON OVERSEAS AID AND DEVELOPMENT (1972).
The Development Puzzle—Source book on projects on developing countries.
Everyday Life in India—41 photographs with teachers' notes.
A Family in Jamaica—Slide set and work cards.
Jamaica—Film on economic and development problems.
Free Fact Sheets—on world development issues, menu sheets.
Publications Lists—on developing countries.
London: VCAD.

WALLIS, B. (1963). 'English for Immigrant Children in Batley'. Dissertation for post-graduate Degree in English as a Second Language, University of Leeds.

WALVIN, J. (1971). *The Black Presence: A Documentary History of the Negro in England.* London: Orbach & Chambers.

WALVIN, J. (1973). *Negro and English Society,* 1555–1945. London: Allen Lane.

WANDSWORTH COMMUNITY RELATIONS COUNCIL (1973). *Ugandan Asians in Wandsworth.* Wands.: WCRC.

WANN, K., DRON, M. and LIDDLE, E. (1962). *Fostering Intellectual Development in Young Children.* NY: Teachers College, Columbia University.

WATSON, P. (1971). 'Immigrant children', *New Society,* November 4.

WATSON, P. (1973). 'Stability of IQ of immigrant and non-immigrant slow-learning pupils', *Brit. J. Educ. Psychol.,* 73, February.

WARD, R. (1971). *Coloured Families in Council Houses.* Manchester: Manchester Council for Community Relations.

WEIN, N. (1970a). 'Compensatory education', *Race Today,* March.

WEIN, N. (1970b). 'Education of disadvantaged children', *Educ. Res.,* 13, 1.

WHITE, L. (ed.) (1971). *Impact: World Development in British Education.* London: Voluntary Committee on Overseas Aid and Development.

WHITE PAPER (Cmnd. 2793). *Immigration from the Commonwealth.* The Prime Minister. London: HMSO.

WIGG, D. (1970). 'Wolverhampton: as tolerant as anywhere else?' *Times Educ. Suppl.,* Oct. 7th.

WRIGHT, P. (1968). *The Coloured Worker.* London: IRR.

WIGHT, J. (1970a). 'Questions about the West Indian', *Dialogue,* 5.

WIGHT, J. (1971). *Teaching English to West Indian Children.* Schools Council Working Paper 29. London: Evans/Methuen.

WILES, S. (1968). 'Children from overseas', *Institute of Race Relations Newsletter,* Feb./June 1968.

WILLES M. (1971). *Books About the Education of Immigrants.* Aldridge Staffs: ATEPO.

WILLIAMS, H. (1961). 'Changes in pupils' attitudes towards West African Negroes following the use of different teaching methods', *Brit. J. Educ. Psychol.,* 31.

WILLIAMS, P. *et al.* (1971). *Swansea Test of Phonic Skills.* London: Blackwell.

WILLIAMS, P. and CONGDEN P. *et al.* (1971). See: SCHOOLS COUNCIL (Compensatory Education Project).

WILSON, E. (1971). 'A multi-racial infant school', *Learning for Living,* (London: SCM Press) January.

WILSON, J. (1967). 'Projection training of teachers of English as a foreign language by team teaching'. London: University of London.

WISEMAN, S. (1964). *Education and Environment.* Manchester: Manchester University Press.

WISEMAN, S. (ed.) (1967). *Intelligence and Ability.* Harmondsworth: Penguin.

WISEMAN, S. (1971). 'The shell of holy writ', *Educ. Res. News,* January.

YOUTH DEVELOPMENT TRUST (1967). *Youth and Community in Manchester.* Manchester: YDT.

YOUTH EMPLOYMENT SERVICE (1968). *Survey of Employment Aspirations, Prospects and Problems of Coloured School Leavers.* London: DEP Study 1970–75.

YUDKIN, S. (1965). *The Health and Welfare of the Immigrant Child.* London: NCCI.

YUDKIN, S. (1965). 0–5: *A Report on the Care of Pre-school Children.* London: National Society of Children's Nurseries.

ZUBRZYCKI, J. (1956). *Polish Immigrants in Britain.* The Hague: Nijhoff.

BIBLIOGRAPHIES

BRITISH COUNCIL (1967). *Audio-visual Material for English Language Teaching*. London: Longman.

BUCHANAN, J. (1972). *Black Britons: a Select Bibliography on Race*. London: Lambeth Libraries. Also *Ten African Novels* and *Ten Novels from the Caribbean.*

CENTRE FOR INFORMATION ON LANGUAGE TEACHING (CILT) (1969). *English for the Children of Immigrants*. London: CILT.

CILT (1968). *Language and Language Teaching: Current Research in Britain.* London: CILT.

CILT (1972a). *Language and Language Teaching: Current Research in Britain.* London: Longman.

CILT (1972b), and ENGLISH TEACHING INFORMATION CENTRE. *A Language Teaching Bibliography*. Cambridge: CUP.

COMMUNITY RELATIONS COMMISSION (1972). *A Bibliography of Teaching Materials: Audio-visual Aids*. London: CRC.

COMMUNITY RELATIONS COMMISSION (1972). *A Bibliography for the Teachers of Immigrants*. London: CRC.

COMMUNITY RELATIONS COMMISSION (1973). *Race Relations in Britain.* London: CRC.

COUCH, M. (1963). 'A select list on intelligence and other tests as used with non-western peoples', *Education Libraries Bulletin*, 18.

DAVIS, E. E. (1963). *Attitude Change: A Review and Bibliography of Selected Research*. Reports and Papers in Social Sciences. Paris: Unesco Series.

DAY, A. (1971). 'The library in the multi-racial secondary school: a Caribbean book list', *School Librarian*, 19, 3.

DERRICK, J. (1973). See NATIONAL BOOK LEAGUE (1973).

ELKIN, J. (1972). *Books for Multi-Racial Classrooms*. Birmingham: Library Association.

GOLDMAN, R. and TAYLOR, F. (1966). 'Coloured immigrant children: a survey of research studies and literature on their educational problems and potential—in Britain', *Educ. Res.*, VIII, 3.

GOLDMAN, R. and TAYLOR, F. (1966). 'Coloured immigrant children: a survey of research studies and literature on their educational problems and potential—in USA', *Educ. Res.*, 4, 1.

HILL, J. (ed.) (1971). *Books for Children: the Homelands of Immigrants in Britain.* London: IRR.

HOPKINS, J. (1962). 'Bibliographies des recherches psychologiques conduites en Afrique', *Revue de Psychol. Appl.*, 12.

NATIONAL BOOK LEAGUE (1967). *English for Immigrant Children.* London: NBL.

NEW BEACON PRESS (1971). *Special Caribbean Book List for Teachers, Parents and Teenagers.* London: New Beacon Press. Also: *Specialist Caribbean Booklist* (1973).

SIVANANDAN, A. (1970). *Coloured Immigrants in Britain: A Select Bibliography.* London: IRR.

SIVANANDAN, A. *et al.* (1970). *Register of Research on Commonwealth Immigrants in Britain.* London: IRR.

WILLES, M. (1971). *Books about the Education of Immigrants.* Leeds: ATEPO.